σώζω

Sozo, Survival Guide
For a Remnant Church

σώζω
SOZO

Survival Guide
For A Remnant Church

σώζω, sozo (Strong's No. 4982),
to save, i.e., deliver or protect,
to heal, preserve, save,
do well, make whole.

By Ellis H. Skolfield

FISH HOUSE PUBLISHING

Except where noted, Bible quotations are from
the King James Bible

A very few are from the
New American Standard version
The Lockman Foundation
1960, 1962, 1963, 1968, 1972, 1975, 1975, 1977
and are quoted by permission.
One quotation is from the NIV.

This book, in its entirety,
including graphs and illustrations,
was generated in Word Perfect 6.1.

Page proofs were produced on a
HP DeskJet 320 Portable

ISBN 0-9628139-3-1

FISH HOUSE PUBLISHING
P.O. Box 453
Fort Myers, Florida, 33902

Printed in the United States of America

σώζω

PUBLISHERS NOTE
to the 1st Edition

Much of this book will be familiar to those who have read the *Hidden Beast* series. However, there is also much here that is new. *Hidden Beast 2* needed updating because the Lord, through His holy Word, has again used current events to enlighten us to what lies ahead. This book also includes a few chapters on the time of the Gentiles, Antichrist, bifids, chiasms, day=years, time-times, and so on. Please forgive the repetition, but those not familiar with the prophetic principals explained in *Hidden Beast 2* would be totally lost without that data, so it had to be included.

The *Hidden Beast* series began in 1981, with *The Revelation Chart* and a little book entitled *Daniel is Out of Order* (both now out of print and collectors' items). In those early works Skolfield taught that the final anti-Christian empire to come against the Church and Israel would not be the communist world or some New Age, one-world religion. It would be Iraq, Iran, Syria, and the radical Mohammedan fundamentalists of the Middle East. Truly astonishing insights for 1981. Back then, all notable prophecy teachers thundered that the USSR was THE final satanic end-time empire of all time. The concept that Scripture showed the Mohammedan world to be the final enemy of the Christian world went against the conventional wisdom of major prophetic authorities of the time, and still does to a great degree.

In 1989, the first *Hidden Beast* was published in English and later in Korean. In 1990, *Hidden Beast 2* was released, and in 1991, the much expanded *Hidden Beast 2, Second Edition.* Because of our rapidly changing world, few books on Bible prophecy remain valid for more than a year or so. By the grace of the Lord, the prophetic principles chronicled in the *Hidden Beast* series still ring true.

May the Lord richly bless an anonymous brother, 3000 miles away, who was led to defray the cost of publishing this book. Thanks are also due to a very patient English professor who kept the author from looking like a total illiterate.

v

What is that proverb
that ye have in the land of Israel,
saying,
The days are prolonged,
and every vision faileth?

❧

Tell them therefore,
Thus saith the Lord GOD;
I will make this proverb to cease,
and they shall no more use it
as a proverb in Israel;
but say unto them,
The days are at hand,
and the effect of every vision.

Eze 12:22-23

Contents

List of Illustrations

Dedication

They were stoned,
they were sawn asunder,
were slain with the sword:
they wandered about in sheepskins
and goatskins;
being destitute, afflicted, tormented;
of whom the world was not worthy:
they wandered in deserts,
and in mountains,
and in dens and caves of the earth.

HEB 11:37-38

It began with Stephen, saints dying for the Lord Jesus' sake: stretched on the rack, boiled in oil, thrown to lions, cast in among serpents. Four to twenty million killed by the Roman Empire, and thirty million since: skinned alive, burned at the stake, pregnant women ripped open, babies dashed against walls. Eleven million murdered by Nazis, a half-million Sudanese crucified by Mohammedans. A million Cambodian saints slaughtered, and Nigerian Christians, too. Those brethren, gone before us, now stand beneath the altar and never cease to cry: "How long, O Lord, holy and true, dost thou not judge and avenge our blood on them that dwell on the earth?" (Rev 6:10)

This unworthy work is dedicated to those precious tribulation saints and to the saints who have yet to face their murderers in some dank and rat-infested dungeon. And it is to you, beloved brother or sister in the Lord, for as sure as night follows day, that same fate awaits many who will read this book.

Introduction

For we are his workmanship,
created in Christ Jesus unto good works,
which God hath before ordained
that we should walk in them.

But avoid foolish questions,
and genealogies, and contentions,
and strivings about the law;
for they are unprofitable and vain.

EPH 2:10 & TIT 3:9

Most Protestant denominations were founded by brethren who were used of the Lord in great spiritual revivals. At the time, every one of those earlier evangelists was considered a radical cult by the established church. Those new believers taught fanatically unacceptable doctrinal systems like salvation "by grace through faith," believer baptism, or communion of both bread and cup for all believers. New converts followed those "right wing extremist elder brethren," supporting their "strange" positions, and almost before you knew it, those new church groups became new denominations.

Four hundred years have passed, and we have become those extremists: the Baptists, Presbyterians, Lutherans, Free Methodists . . . the whole Protestant Christian world. We are now the established churches, and, unfortunately, we have become just as set in our ways and just as close-minded as the dogmatists that came before us. We cling to the label of our particular group, and before we can hear anything different from the Bible, someone has to explain away the hallowed traditions upon which we are now standing. We have forgotten that Huss, Van Braght, Luther, Calvin, Zwingli,

Wesley, Scofield, Chafer, Ironside and Gabalein were just men. We have placed these elders of the Protestant church on such lofty pedestals that to question the doctrines they have passed down to us is considered heresy.

To make matters worse, over the years the lines between these various doctrinal schools have blurred with denominations adopting each other's views to the point where some churches now hold positions that are downright counter-scriptural, or contradictory within themselves. So now, we not only bow down to hallowed traditions, but to inconsistent hallowed traditions, as well.

Some of these traditions are obviously wrong, and since it is provable that we are at the end of this age, what if our views on Bible prophecy are among them? If so, we could be using false doctrines to determine how we should live out our last few days before the hour of trial: "that trial which is to come upon the whole inhabited earth" (Rev 3:10).

If ever we should get our doctrine right, now is the time. It is 1995AD, and the world is being shaken by natural disasters, not to mention political, social, moral, and religious upheavals. If we are brutally honest with ourselves, we can see that our traditional end-time scenarios just don't fit what is happening in the world around us. It is apparent to all that we are at the end of the Christian Era, but as yet there is no *visible* one-world government in force, no antichrist yet, and still no Great Tribulation. Why not? Well, maybe the Bible doesn't teach that these events are ever going to take place. Hard as it may be to accept, is it possible that the Lord's plan for these end-times is totally different from the traditions we learned in Sunday school?

When the prophetic doctrines we now hold were first proposed, England was *the* great world power, Europe was thought to be the cultural center of the universe, and the United States was a minor nation. In their wildest dreams, theologians of horse-and-buggy days could not have imagined what today's world would be like. A hundred years have passed, and the political, spiritual, and social fabric of the whole planet has changed. Earth is a terribly different place now, and because it is, maybe we should stand back from our traditions a bit, and take a fresh look at Bible prophecy itself. Maybe the Lord has opened His prophetic Word in a new way through two almost unbelievable fulfillments of prophecy that have taken place in the Holy Land during the last 50 years.

In 1948AD, the new nation of Israel was established, and in 1967, Jerusalem again came under Jewish control for the first time in 2573 years!

Σώζω (sozo) is the Greek word for salvation, or to make whole. Here in the end of time, the Lord is indeed going to save His people and make them whole, but probably not in the way we think. It is apparent from Scripture that a rocky road lies ahead for the brethren before Jesus stands on Mount Zion. Spiritual storm clouds are on the horizon, and there are questions that need to be answered: How soon will a new holocaust come? Can we escape it? Where would the Lord have us be while it is here? How long will it last, and how will this time of trouble come to an end?

To find out, we need to take an honest look at the spiritual conditions in our country and see how these conditions parallel what is going on in the rest of the world. Then we need to see what God's Word has to say about it all.

"God changes not," and since He does not change, He will probably deal with the world and its people today, just as He has always dealt with us when similar conditions existed.

GRAPH NUMBER I

The History of Israel

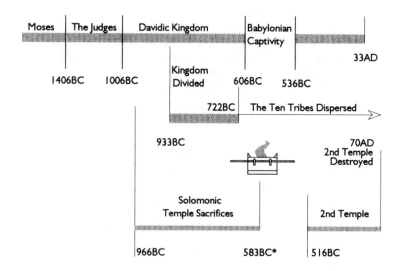

* Conservative dating places the destruction of the Temple of Solomon at 586BC. However, Jeremiah 41:5 shows Levitical sacrifices continuing to be offered long after that date:

> Jer 41:5 That there came certain from Shechem, from Shiloh, and from Samaria, *even* fourscore men, having their beards shaven, and their clothes rent, and having cut themselves, with offerings and incense in their hand, to bring *them* to the house of the LORD.

Jer 41:5 is positioned at the end of the governorship of Gedeliah, and Gedeliah was elevated to that post after Nebuchadnezzar sacked Jerusalem in 586BC. The sacrifices above were offered seven to ten months later. After Gedeliah's time, Jews were taken captive to Babylon only once more:

> Jer 52:30 In the three and twentieth year of Nebuchadnezzar, Nebuzar-adan the captain of the guard carried away captive of the Jews seven hundred forty and five persons: all the persons *were* four thousand and six hundred.

Nebuchadnezzar's 1st year was 606-605BC, and this final captivity took place in the 23rd Year of Nebuchadnezzar, so we have scriptural support that 583BC was the date of the abolition of Levitical sacrifices. 606BC - 23 = 583BC.

When Are We?

CHAPTER 1

When it is evening, ye say,
It will be fair weather: for the sky is red.
And in the morning, It will be foul weather to day:
for the sky is red and lowering.
O ye hypocrites, ye can discern the face of the sky;
but can ye not discern the signs of the times?

MAT 16:2-3

Though the Holy Spirit spoke through prophets and apostles over a 1500 year period, the plan of God was fixed in eternity, Psa 119:89. The Bible, including all the prophetic books, is about that whole plan. God sees all creation from His eternal perspective. If we could look at our 6000 years or so of recorded history as God does, we would see a broad completed tapestry. On that tapestry would be everything that has ever happened, or ever will happen. Time and space are creations of God, and He stands outside them all:

Isa 45:12 I have made the earth, and created man upon it: I, *even* my hands, have stretched out the heavens, and all their host have I commanded.

Man, however, is bound by time and space. We are physically placed on a material world and, as time is reckoned, in the closing decade of the 2nd Millennium AD. The Lord told us about all of this in the Bible, and so far, the Lord has partitioned his dealings with man into three different spiritual epochs, each lasting about 2000 years. Three separate time frames. In each of these eras, God revealed Himself to man in a different way.

1. 4000BC to 1446BC: The years before Moses, called the Pre-flood Era and the time of the Patriarchs. In this era the Lord worked through individual men and women.

2. 1446BC to 32AD: The years between Moses and the cross, sometimes called the Age of the Law. During this era, the Lord worked primarily through the nation of Israel.

3. 32AD to the present: The Christian Era. In this epoch the Lord is working through the Gentile church.

Those are clearly three distinctly different times, and in each, the Lord revealed Himself to man differently. But different as those times may be, in each the Lord provided a method by which man could be found pleasing in His sight:

1. In the Pre-flood Era, man could be found pleasing to God without knowing the Levitical code, and without knowing who the future Savior of mankind would be. According to Bible record, all they knew back then was to make an altar of uncut stone and offer an animal sacrifice upon it. Read the accounts of Abel, Enoch, and Noah in the first six chapters of Genesis. Notice that "Enoch walked with God, and he was not, for God took him" (Gen 5:24). Enoch had no Scripture, yet Enoch was taken up alive into heaven, being found perfect in God's eyes 3000 years before the cross. Since he had no knowledge of the law, nor of Jesus' name, his being found perfect in God's sight could not have had much to do with his doctrine. He had none to speak of.

2. A thousand years later, under the Levitical code, man could also be found pleasing to God without knowing who his Messiah to come would be. Read about Moses, Elijah, Jeremiah, Daniel and the rest of the prophets, all of whom lived hundreds of years before the cross. During that era, Elijah, too, was taken up alive into heaven, and during Jesus' ministry on earth, we saw Moses and Elijah on the mount of transfiguration, covered with the glory of God (Mar 9:2-8). Neither of them knew who Jesus was during their lifetimes (1Pe 1:10-11), so their perfection in the Lord's sight didn't have much to do with their doctrine, either.

3. Today, we too, can be found perfect in God's eyes, but now we know how. We were born after the cross and have the

whole Bible, the whole counsel of God. We know man can be found acceptable to God only through the shed blood of His Son, the Lord Jesus. Because of our knowledge of the cross, we now know that we are delivered from the power of darkness and transferred into the kingdom of God's dear Son (Col 1:13) the moment we come to the Lord. Those are not just high-sounding theoretical phrases. We are literally placed into a real, spiritual kingdom of the Lord Jesus that exists today. 1Co 1:30 declares that we have Christ's righteousness imputed unto us right now, and Eph 2:6 further states that we are even now seated in the heavenlies with Him.

There you have three different God-ordained and totally biblical doctrinal systems (two before the cross, and one after), yet under each one it was possible for man to be found pleasing to God. How can that be? Is it possible to be saved without knowing who Jesus is? Well, the blood of bulls and goats never saved anyone (Heb 10:4). Those early sacrifices, and the temple sacrifices which followed them, were mere symbols -- for ancient man -- of the sacrifice of a Messiah yet to come (Heb 10:10). Old Testament saints didn't know it, but they were saved by the blood of Jesus, just like we are (1 Co 10:1-4). No one, in any time, can come to God except through the blood of His Son, Jesus!

Even though we see the cross at a given point in history, God the Father does not. God sees His Son as ". . . the Lamb slain from the foundation of the world" (Rev 13:8). The moment Adam sinned, creation would have ended in a thunderclap if God had not already seen the shed blood of His Son. As an absolutely Holy God, the Lord could not have looked on Adam's one original sin if He had not already seen Jesus hanging on the cross.

If we view God's plan of redemption from His eternal viewpoint, when a man was born or under which God-ordained doctrinal system he was raised loses all its importance. These different eras are different revelatory times, not special ages in which the plan of salvation was changed. Throughout all time, salvation has always been by grace through faith in God (Eph 2:8-9, Jas 2:23, Heb 11:1-31), regardless of the method by which the Lord willed to reveal Himself to man. Since Jesus died in eternity, salvation has always been through His sacrifice. In God the Father's eyes, the shed blood of Jesus transcends time and has always been the only acceptable atonement for man's sin!

The Christian Era is just one segment of God's overall plan of salvation. It is natural for us to think that *we,* and *our* era, are *the* centerpieces of all creation, but in God's eternal eyes, no one, and no time, is of more importance than any other (Psa 145:8-9). The Lord loved the people of the ancient pre-flood world just as much as He loves you and me.

> Acts 10:34-35 ... Of a truth I perceive that God is no respecter of persons: But in every nation he that feareth him, and worketh righteousness, is accepted with him.

With those doctrinal principles in place, we should be able to look at our own era a little more objectively. Throughout the Christian Era, the brethren have gone through a lot, and once again the children of God are going to fall on hard times. Israel is now isolated, and the United States is in economic, military, and social decline. Individual liberties are being rapidly eroded, anarchy is in divers places, and a new totalitarian state may soon rise right here under the guise of "a new order." Knowing how short man's memory is, Satan doesn't need to change his methods too much to deceive people. Only fifty years ago, Hitler called his Nazi regime a "new order," and today, a reconditioned and repackaged "new order" is being sold to the world.

But the causes of past horrors are all forgotten, and many Christians are again embracing the works of the dragon and making them part of our daily lives. Abominably degenerate rock stars have become the heros of our children and the rebels of the 60s are the guardians of our schools.[1] The National Education Association has even declared that

---

[1]This isn't a brand new thing that just happened. In 1970, Dr. Paul Brandwein, a consultant for the Elementary and Secondary Education Act Title III, wrote, "Any child who believes in God is mentally ill." In 1973, Dr. Pierce of Harvard University in an address to 2000 public school teachers in Denver, Colorado declared: "Every child who enters school at the age of five is mentally ill, because he comes to school with allegiance toward our founding fathers... our elected officials... toward the preservation of this form of government, patriotism, nationalism, sovereignty . . . All of that proves the children are sick . . ." *Sovereignty,* Ken Bohnsack (P.O. Box 782, Freeport, IL, 1983)

fundamental Christians are their enemies. Prayer has been taken from public schools, and the loathsome sins of Sodom are being whitewashed as an equally acceptable "alternative lifestyle." The laws which give us our liberty are being used by the wicked to promote depravities of every kind.

Disregarding numerous Scriptures, a majority of "Christian" teenagers are sexually active, and teenage pregnancies have mushroomed.[1] Among middle school children are many avowed satanists, and an ever increasing number of our youth are practicing spiritists, witches, or warlocks. Some juveniles are even involved in satanic ritual abuse and blood sacrifices.[2] According to many Christian school teachers, this generation of children has no conscience. No conscience at all. Do you realize what that means? It means that the gentle Spirit of God is not working in the hearts of the unsaved like He used to. That Spirit of Jesus, which for nineteen centuries restrained lawlessness in the world, has been taken out of the way:

> Gen 6:3 And the LORD said, "My spirit shall not always strive with man."

> 2Th 2:7 For the mystery of iniquity doth already work: only he who now letteth [*restrains*] will let [*restrain*][3], until he be taken out of the way. And then shall that Wicked be revealed, whom the Lord shall consume with the spirit of his mouth, and shall destroy with the brightness of his coming.[4]

---

[1] Act 15:20, 15:29, 21:25, Rom 1:29, 1Co 6:13, 6:18, 10:8, Gal 5:19, Eph 5:3, Col 3:5, 1Th 4:3

[2] The threat of death or injury by satanists to therapists treating victims of satanic ritual abuse was a major topic at 1994 American conventions of clinical psychologists.

[3] The English definition of "let" has changed since the KJV was translated. The Greek word translated "let" in this verse is Strong's No. G2722. katecho, kat-ekh'-o; from G2596 and G2192; to hold down (fast), in various applications (lit. or fig.):--have, hold (fast), keep (in memory), possess, retain, seize on, stay, take, withhold. So in this case, the NASB "will restrain" is a better rendering.

[4] Throughout this book, explanatory words are sometimes inserted into a Scripture quote in italics and brackets: [*example*]. They may be from different translations or they may be just a clarification or explanation
(continued...)

The children of the martyrs have listened to the voice of the serpent, and godless, television-trained degenerates are our masters. In our government, graft and special interests rule, and the Clinton administration considers sexual depravity to be the norm, with rulings coming down from the Justice Department which allow child pornography. As if all that were not enough, New-Agers, with a one-world agenda, are diligently undermining our national sovereignty,[1] so the psalmist's lament still rings true:

Psa 11:3 If the foundations be destroyed, what can the righteous do?

Christians have forgotten about repentance and have replaced godly sorrow for sin with raised hands and "praise songs," as if a "Praise you, Jesus" or a new charismatic style of worship could make our woefully self-centered lives acceptable to the Holy One of Israel. Polls taken ten years ago indicate that up to 85% of pastors from all denominations deny from one to all five of the basic tenets of the faith, and a recent poll indicates that less than 20% of today's pastors believe that Jesus really died on the cross.

Act 20:29-30 For I know this, that after my departing shall grievous wolves enter in among you, not sparing the flock. Also of your own selves shall men arise, speaking perverse things, to draw away disciples after them.

One pastor acquaintance, returning from a Baptist Seminary in the Southeast, declared that he was the only evangelical in his class and that the professors would not speak to him, for fear that he was a spy from the conservative faction of the convention.

But should this come as a surprise? If you were Satan, where would be the most effective place for you to put your

---

[4](...continued)
of a word or phrase within the verse. These italicized words and phrases do not appear in the original Bible texts.

[1] Humanists are also undermining our Christian foundations. John Dunphy wrote in the (1980) Humanist Magazine, "The classroom must and will become an arena of conflict between the old and the new - the rotting corpse of Christianity, together with all the adjacent evils and misery, and the new faith of Humanism" *Sovereignty*, Ken Bohnsack (P.O. Box 782, Freeport IL, 61032).

servants? In the seminaries and behind the pulpits, of course, and that is exactly where the enemy has placed them:

> 2Co 11:13 For such are false apostles, deceitful workers, transforming themselves into the apostles of Christ. And no marvel; for Satan himself is transformed into an angel of light. Therefore it is no great thing if his ministers also be transformed as the ministers of righteousness; whose end shall be according to their works.

Well did the Lord say:

> Luk 18:8 Nevertheless when the Son of man cometh, shall he find faith on the earth?

Those are the church realities in the United States today. On the world scene, Amsterdam, Holland, the home of the Anabaptist martyrs, has become a cesspool of iniquity. A witch in Zurich, Switzerland, knows only two Christians, and they don't live there. She met them in the train station, while they were touring Europe.[1] The USSR has collapsed, and her break-away states are selling nuclear arms to radical Islamic states. Iran and Pakistan now have nuclear arsenals and the delivery systems with which to get those weapons to any target in the world.

Islamic fundamentalism is spreading throughout the Arab world, into Europe and England, and Islam has become a major force among the Black youth in America. Many American prison populations are controlled by Black Muslims, even to the point where the safety of Christian inmates is now in question. Mohammedans living in this country provide 60% of the funding for terrorists in Israel, the Hamas. Meanwhile, these same duplicitous Mohammedans, while claiming to be our friends, have killed thousands of Christians in Somalia and Nigeria, over 1,000,000 Christians in the Sudan -- many by crucifixion -- and millions more throughout the rest of the world.

> Dan 8:25 . . . he shall cause craft to prosper in his hand; and he shall magnify *himself* in his heart, and by peace shall destroy many:

---

[1] The woman, dressed in all black, came up to a Christian family who was touring Europe and asked, "Where is your spiritual aura? You are the only people I have ever seen without a spiritual aura."

But all of that is far away, and Islam could never be a danger here, right? Of the immigrants now entering this country, 14% are Islamic, and if the Church continues to decline at its present rate, within a decade, Mohammedans could be the largest religious voting block in the United States. They will very soon outnumber the Jews here. Even as we write, Islamic fundamentalists are holding secret meetings in such unlikely places as Tampa, Los Angeles, and Kansas City, plotting terrorist acts against our nation. Many people are homeless and hungry, and wars are everywhere. We seek for peace where there is no peace . . .

Those are the spiritual realities in our world today. Those are the problems we now face. The little flock that would give their all for Jesus -- the true Church -- weeps over all this. We know by the Spirit of God that we have lost our blessed land. Greed has destroyed our crystal rivers and our endless forests. Our bountiful wildlife has been decimated, and the passenger pigeon is no more:

> Rev 11:18 (*excerpts*) . . . and thy wrath is come, and the time . .
> that thou shouldest destroy them which destroy the earth.

This haven of rest that God gave to the persecuted saints of the Middle Ages has been turned over to the agents of Lucifer. Many saints have a little ache their hearts that won't go away. They know the dreadful conclusion of all this:

> Eze 9:3-7 (*excerpts*) And the LORD said, "Go through the midst of the city . . . and smite: let not your eye spare, neither have ye pity: Slay utterly old and young, both maids, and little children, and women . . . and begin at my sanctuary." And he said unto them, "Defile the house, and fill the courts with the slain: go ye forth." And they went forth, and slew in the city.

The Lord did not give that prophecy to Ninevah, or to Babylon, or to some other godless Gentile land. He gave it to His people Israel, and on down through time that message is to the Church, to us. For surely, the same conditions exist today. Like Israel we have turned from the Lord, not in word or in worship, but in mind and heart:

> Isa 29:13 (KJV), Amo 5:21 (NASB) Wherefore the Lord said, "Forasmuch as this people draw near me with their mouth, and with their lips do honour me, but have removed their heart far from me, and their fear toward me is taught by the precept of men . . .

I hate, I reject your festivals, Nor do I delight in your solemn assemblies."

Many are saying, "Oh joy, Jesus is coming soon and we are going to be taken up before the bad times ahead," but all the remnant can do is stand with the prophets and cry:

Isa 13:6-8 Howl ye; for the day of the LORD *is* at hand; it shall come as a destruction from the Almighty. Therefore shall all hands be faint, and every man's heart shall melt: And they shall be afraid: pangs and sorrows shall take hold of them; they shall be in pain as a woman that travaileth: they shall be amazed one at another; their faces *shall be as* flames.

Mic 7:2 . . . for the good *man* is perished out of the earth: and *there is* none upright among men: they all lie in wait for blood; they hunt every man his brother with a net.

"Dear God, please help us. Defend your little flock this one more time." With all that looming on the horizon, what is the Lord's plan for the "seven thousand men who have not bowed the knee to Baal," His remnant church?

In one town in the Midwest, a Christian brother is building an underground shelter, with hidden entrances, that will hold 30 people or more. "I don't know why I am building it this large," he says. "There is only my wife and myself." In a town close by, another brother is being led of the Lord to store long-term food for 30 people or more. He doesn't know why he is doing that either. In a little seacoast town, a third brother is building an ocean-going ship in his little shipyard. He has been led to build it far stronger than any vessel he has ever built before, with massive watertight bulkheads throughout the whole ship. "I believe it of the Lord that this ship is going to be sorely tried," he says. "I think it is going to be used to carry Jews and Christians to Israel." He knows of another brother down the coast from him who has been led of the Lord to do a similar thing.

These are not isolated incidents. Other serious brethren have built island or mountain retreats, stocked to the rafters with food and fuel, or have been given ships or busses with which to transport believers. So what is this all about? Are these just another group of bunker-mentality, doomsday eccentrics, or might there be something going on prophetically that needs looking into? Is there a new move of the Holy Spirit of God here that has nothing to do with present-day charismatic phenomena? To see if there is, maybe we need to take a look at the whole Christian Era, and see what the Lord has told us about the events to come during this age.

THE TIME OF THE GENTILES

Just before Jesus went to the cross, He told His disciples what they could expect to happen in this final major time frame of God's plan. Known to us as the "Olivet Discourse," this talk is Jesus' chapter-long prophecy about the Christian Era. It is recorded for us in all three of the synoptic Gospels: Mat 24, Mar 13, and Luk 21. Though these accounts all agree, each Gospel gives us some important information that is not contained in the other two:

(1) Mat 24:31 - Matthew states that the elect are gathered at the sound of a "great trumpet."

(2) Mar 13:14 - Mark declares that the Abomination of Desolation is an "it," and not a "him."

(3) Luk 21:24 - Luke defines the "time of the Gentiles."

Now please study those verses in your own Bible, and consider what Jesus had to say in each of them because they strongly influence what we believe about the seven-year tribulation, replacement theology, and a host of other doctrines we hold today. For instance, we hear a lot about the dispensations of "Law" and "Grace," but in Luk 21:24, Jesus defines a different kind of time for us, a "time of the Gentiles":

> Luk 21:21-24 (*excerpts*) Then let them [*the Jews*] which are in Judaea flee . . . And they [*the Jews*] shall fall by the edge of the sword, and shall be led away captive into all nations: and Jerusalem shall be trodden down of the Gentiles, until the times of the Gentiles be fulfilled.[1]

So what is this time of the Gentiles? When Jesus spoke those words (in 32 or 33AD), Jerusalem had been under the

---

[1]The Jews had a short period of self-rule under the Maccabees that began in 167BC. However, the Maccabean period does not appear to be prophetically significant. The Davidic monarchy was not reestablished, and the Jews were in continual conflict with the Syrian Greeks. This conflict continued until Rome conquered the Holy Land in 65BC.

control of various Gentile governments for 638 years. Historic record shows that Gentile control of that city began when Nebuchadnezzar of Babylon sacked Jerusalem in 606BC. Gentile rule continued under Medo-Persia, Greece, and later Rome, who governed the Holy Land during Jesus' lifetime.

But continual Jewish rebellions led to Titus the Roman's attack on Jerusalem in 70AD. Jesus foretold that destruction in the verses quoted above. Note however, that he also spoke of a Jewish dispersion to follow Titus' victory, and a time of Gentile domination of Jerusalem to follow that. Look at the tense of the verb "shall be led away captive." Shall be is future to when Jesus spoke.

Shortly after Titus destroyed Jerusalem, the Jews were indeed dispersed among the nations, and they remained dispersed throughout the whole world until this very century! As a matter of historic record, Gentiles ruled Jerusalem through the 1st, 2nd, 3rd, 4th, 5th, 6th, 7th, 8th, 9th, and 10th centuries. The 11th and 12th century crusaders were also Gentiles. Gentiles continued to rule Jerusalem through the 13th, 14th, 15th, 16th, 17th, 18th, 19th, and 20th centuries, right on up until 1967AD. Throughout the whole Christian Era, Gentiles have always ruled Jerusalem. "And Jerusalem shall be trodden down of the Gentiles . . . *until* ." As a matter of historic reality, the city of Jerusalem did not again come under Jewish control *until* after the Six-Day War, June 6th, 1967, "*until* the times of the Gentiles be fulfilled." The only people who are not Gentiles are Jews, and as of June 6th, 1967, the Jews again govern Jerusalem, for the first time in 2573 years! Like it or not, that is reality:

> *Over in the Holy Land is a nation called Israel. It is filled with a people called Jews, many of whom are looking for their Messiah, and they fit that Luk 21:24 prophecy right to the letter.*

Before the Six-Day War, we could argue about what the Lord meant by the "time of the Gentiles," but not anymore. From our vantage point in history, we can see the Jews in control of Jerusalem with our own eyes. Consequently, it is apparent that the Lord was naming the total time of Gentile rule in the Holy City as "the time of the Gentiles." Do we grasp the impact of this fulfillment of prophecy?

Brethren, the time of the Gentiles is over. It's over! If the time of the Gentiles is over, then Gentiles will never again rule Jerusalem, and God's eyes are again focused on the physical seed of Abraham who have returned to the Holy City and their promised land.

GRAPH NUMBER 2

 THE TIME OF THE GENTILES, LUK 21:24

606BC, Gentiles take Jerusalem	Jerusalem Restored, 1967AD
Total time of the Gentiles, 2573 Years	

> Luk 21:24 And they [*the Jews*] shall fall by the edge of the sword, and shall be led away captive into all nations: and Jerusalem shall be trodden down of the Gentiles, until the times of the Gentiles be fulfilled.

But if the "time of the Gentiles" is really over, *when* are we now? What kind of time are we in? So far, we have only seen three different epochs and a "time of the Gentiles," but there must be another kind of time because we are still here. Both the Jews and the Church are still on earth. Searching Scripture from beginning to end, there seems to be only one other time that could come after the time of the Gentiles:

> Dan 12:4 But thou, O Daniel, shut up the words, and seal the book, even to **the time of the end**...

> Dan 12:9 And he said, Go thy way, Daniel: for the words are closed up and sealed till **the time of the end**.

Since we are no longer in the time of the Gentiles (and we sure have to be in some kind of time), we are probably in Daniel's "time of the end," or the "end times" as the NASB translates it. As a result....

We are probably the last generation this present Earth will ever see and the end of all things is at hand.

DISCERNING FALSE DOCTRINES

In Dan 12:9, God declared, by His sovereign Word, that He sealed the book of Daniel until the time of the end. That doesn't sound so earth-shattering, does it? How significant can it be that a relatively obscure Old Testament prophet was sealed until the time of the end? This important:

If the "Time of the End" began in 1967, and Daniel was sealed until the "Time of the End," then all views theorized out of Daniel before 1967 are at best incomplete, and at worst heretical.

Here is the point: Most of the end-time views held by the Church today were theorized from studies made in Daniel hundreds of years ago. If God sealed Daniel until the "time of the end," and the "time of the end" began in 1967, then our present end-time views are wrong, and if they are, we could be basing the last few decisions we will ever make on this planet on theoretical events that are never going to happen. Let's look at an example.

Manuel de Lacunza

CHAPTER 2

I am against them that prophesy false dreams,
saith the LORD, and do tell them,
and cause my people to err by their lies,
yet I sent them not, nor commanded them:
therefore they shall not profit this people at all.

JER 23:32

Probably the Church's most widely held end-time position is that of a coming Great Tribulation period that will supposedly precede the return of the Lord. Few know the origin of that eighteenth century creed, and the Seven-Year Great Tribulation view is generally accepted as an established fact.

But just having an explanation for a puzzling Bible verse doesn't prove that the explanation is right. Back in the 1700s, when the Seven-Year Tribulation idea was thought up, they could also explain diseases. Everyone "knew" that diseases were caused by night humors. At bedtime, folks would board their homes up tight, draw the curtains shut around their high-off-the-floor, four-poster beds, huddle under the covers, and hope that they didn't catch a pox or the bloody flux by morning. They had an explanation for disease, all right, but their explanation was dead wrong.

Therein lies the problem. As popular as the Seven-Year Tribulation view may be, it could also be dead wrong because it has no direct scriptural support. That's right: it has no direct scriptural support. Oh, there are verses we can interpret to mean a seven-year tribulation, all right, but there is not one single verse in the Bible that states we are going to have a seven-year tribulation period at the end of this age. We just assume that we are going to have one.

But despite its weakness, thousands of pastors teach it, and millions of churchgoers believe it. Hundreds of little side doctrines have also sprung from that view, and we now worry about whether we are going to be taken to be with the Lord during a pre-trib, mid-trib, or post-trib "rapture." Unbelievable as it may sound, that whole seven-year idea is based on a 200 year-old questionable interpretation of a prophecy -- from guess where -- the book of Daniel. Few there are who question this view, but it had a very dubious beginning.

Back in the 18th Century, there was a Spanish family living in Chili named the de Lacunzas. In 1731, they had a baby boy whom they named Manuel. After fifteen years at home, young Manuel boarded a ship bound for Spain. He wanted to join holy orders and become a Jesuit priest. Twenty-one years later, the Jesuits were expelled from Spain because of their brutality, and "Father" Manuel de Lacunza y Diaz was forced to leave the country. He made his new home in Imola, Italy, where he remained for the rest of his life.

While in Imola, Lacunza claimed to be a converted Jew named "Rabbi Ben Ezra." Under that alias, he wrote a book entitled *The Coming of Messiah in Glory and Majesty*. In it, Lacunza theorized that the Church would be "raptured" (taken up to be with the Lord) 45 days before Jesus' real return to Earth. During that 45 days (while the Church was in heaven with the Lord), God would judge the wicked who were still remaining on Earth.

That Jesuit "Rabbi" theorized the earliest mini-tribulation, pre-trib rapture view on record! He derived his view from a faulty interpretation of the 1290 and the 1335 days of Dan 12:11-12. We now know his view to be faulty because we have the true fulfillments of those prophecies in the new nation of Israel, and we can prove with certainty what those days really mean. You will read about those fulfillments later on in this book. De Lacunza died in Imola in 1801, and that should have been the end of his theory

But after his death, Lacunza's views were taught in Spain, and in 1812 his book was published in Spanish. Fourteen years later it was translated into English by a Scottish radical named Edward Irving. Lacunza's view could also have died right there, for most in England thought Irving to be a heretic.

But then, this "tribulation period" idea began to spread. In that same year, Mr. J. N. Darby, founder of the Plymouth Brethren, wrote that he had "come to an understanding of a new truth." Later in his letters, Darby admitted that he had been influenced by the writings of de Lacunza.

However, Darby was not satisfied with Lacunza's rather simplistic 45-day tribulation idea, so he devised a more complex theory. It appeared to him that the last week (Dan 9:27) of Daniel's 70 Weeks had yet to be fulfilled, so he suggested a 2000-year gap between the 69th and 70th Week. Darby then theorized that the 70th Week was about a future Seven-Year Tribulation period that would take place at the end of the Christian Era! And there you have it . . . the very beginning of the Seven-Year Great Tribulation idea.[1]

From that springboard, by sundry leaps of logic, Darby supposed that the temple would be rebuilt and that animal sacrifices would be reinstituted. An antichrist was supposed to appear and rule the world for seven years. After three and a half of them, this antichrist would presumably turn against the Jews, stop the sacrifices, and start Armageddon. It went on and on in a profusion of unsupported conjectures, all based upon one shaky foundation: the dubious validity of Darby's 2000 year gap idea, and the seven-year great tribulation theory he conjured up from Dan 9:27!

If J. N. Darby hadn't visited the United States, the seven-year trib theory could have died right there, too. After all, there weren't very many Plymouth Brethren. But while in the States, Darby met C. I. Scofield. Scofield was so charmed by the Lacunza-Darby creed that he wanted to include it in an

---

[1] Dr. Harry Ironside of Moody Bible Institute, himself an ardent supporter of the Lacunza-Darby-Scofield eschatological scheme, admitted in his *Mysteries of God*, p.50: ". . . until brought to the fore through the writings of . . . Mr. J. N. Darby, the doctrine taught by Dr. Scofield [*the Seven-Year Tribulation*] is scarcely to be found in a single book throughout a period of 1600 years. If any doubt this statement, let them search, as the writer has in measure done, the remarks of the so-called Fathers, both pre- and post-Nicene, the theological treatises of the scholastic divines . . . the literature of the reformation . . . the Puritans. He will find the 'mystery' conspicuous by its absence." Yes, indeed, this "mystery is absent," because the Bible doesn't teach it.

annotated Bible he had in the works. Sound Bible scholars of the day such as A. J. Gordon, W. G. Moorhead, Charles R. Eerdman, and others tried to dissuade him. Three noted members of Scofield's revision committee even resigned because of Scofield's unswerving support for the Lacunza-Darby view, but their voices were not heard. The seven-year view remained and Lacunza-Darby was incorporated into the notes of the now world-famous *Scofield Bible*.

In the following decades, the *Scofield Bible* became the most widely read Bible in the English language, and that annotated Bible was the primary vehicle by which the Seven-Year Great Tribulation view was spread throughout the whole English-speaking church. Scathing reviews have been written against Scofield's Bible by various respected scholars of the day, but many others presumed Scofield's notes to be all but inspired. Even today, some folks think a commentator's notes below the line are as valid as the Scriptures above it.[1]

It is impossible to believe that a major end-time doctrine of the Protestant world began in the mind of a Jesuit priest who wrote under an assumed name and claimed to be a converted Jew. But the historic record of the origin of this creed is unassailable. John Bray, who did the research, has even offered a large cash reward to anyone who can find an earlier or different source.[2]

Some have questioned the importance of knowing the origin of this doctrine, but in any court of law, the jury is entitled to know the credibility of the witness. So the Church has every right to ask, "Would a priest from an organization

---

[1] Dr. T. T. Shields humorously commented: "From a position of entire ignorance of the Scripture to a position of oracular religious certainty -- especially in eschatological matters -- for some people requires but from three to six months with a Scofield Bible" *The Gospel Witness* (Toronto Canada, April 7th, 1932).

[2] A copy of the Irving translation of Lacunza's work may still be found in Oxford University, Oxford, UK. The Church is indebted to evangelist John Bray who researched the origin of the Seven-Year Tribulation doctrine. His book, *The Origin of the Pre-Tribulation Rapture Teaching,* was one of the author's sources for this data (John Bray Ministry, P.O. Box 90129, Lakeland, FL 33804). I have just heard that a slightly earlier and somewhat similar view has been unearthed; however, I have not seen any documentation on this new find.

known at the time for its brutality, masquerading as a Jewish Rabbi, be a credible witness on spiritual matters?"

Ironside of Moody Bible Institute fully supported the view but later in life stated that it was "full of holes." Dallas Theological Seminary and other centers of dispensational thinking also promoted it. Since then, there have been a host of weighty rebuttals by conservative theologians, but few clear-headed scholars have bothered to refute the de Lacunza-Darby-Scofield view scripturally, in a language the everyday saint can understand.[1]

Many a seminary student has tried to reconcile the plain assertions of Scripture with the Great Tribulation position, but to no avail. Eventually, the seminarian just accepts it and, after becoming ordained, goes out to teach Lacunza-Darby-Scofield in his church. Rarely does he seriously question the quivering foundation upon which he is trying to build: the questionable opinions of the Jesuit "Rabbi" who started it all.

Evangelicals of many denominations have championed the seven-year view. But the view is so counter to the plain statements of the Bible itself, particularly the last trumpet, that one wonders how it has managed to command so many ardent supporters. In some more radical positions, there are several different "raptures," which one you are "raptured" up in supposedly depending upon how sanctified you are, or which "kingdom" you are in. Those doctrines display a gross misunderstanding of the basic plan of salvation.

We do not get to heaven earlier or later on the basis of our works, good or ill. Works accomplish nothing in relation to salvation. We are either totally cleansed by Jesus' blood and are going to Heaven, or we are not and going to Hell. If God counts even one sin against us, we are in an eternal world of hurt. We go to Heaven on the strength of the imputed

---

[1]Albertus Pieters wrote, "From start to finish it [the *Scofield Bible*] is a partisan book, definitely, both openly and under cover, an instrument of propaganda in favor of an exceedingly doubtful eschatology . . . If Darby and his school are right, the entire Christian church for eighteen-hundred years, was wrong on a vital part of the Christian faith" *Candid Examination of the Scofield Bible,* Albertus Pieters, (Union City, PA, Bible Truth Depot, 1932) pp25, 27.

righteousness of Jesus Christ and in the power of His shed blood only! To Him be all the glory.

> 2Ti 4:3-4 For the time will come when they will not endure sound doctrine; but after their own lusts shall they heap to themselves teachers, having itching ears; And they shall turn away their ears from the truth, and shall be turned unto fables.

Now it has been almost 200 years since de Lacunza's adventure into theoretical theology, and new evidence has come to light. In 1948, the new nation of Israel was born. In 1967, Jerusalem was freed from Gentile governmental control for the first time in 2573 years. The Jews are home, as the Lord told us they would be in numberless Old and New Testament Scriptures. We can now show conclusively that all the Scriptures used to formulate the de Lacunza-Darby view, including the 70th Week (Dan 9:27), have been fulfilled in those almost unbelievable current events. Lacunza came up with his original idea from the 1290 and 1335 "days" of Dan 12:11-12. Maybe now would be a good time to look at what those prophecies really mean.[1]

---

[1] When the Seven-Year Tribulation doctrine was first taught, the new nation of Israel had not yet been established and Jerusalem had not yet been restored. Consequently, we must be careful not to speak ill of brethren who taught these errors unwittingly. These earlier brethren had less fulfilled prophecy than we do on which to base their doctrines.

But there is no excuse for us to continue to teach error. Prophetic fulfillments within the Holy Land in the last 50 years now prove the Seven-Year Tribulation view to be false. The Lacunza-Darby-Scofield dispensational end-time scenario just isn't true. As a result, it does not address today's realities nor prepare the brethren for what lies ahead.

The 69 Weeks

CHAPTER 3

Remember the former things of old;
for I am God, and there is none else;
I am God, and there is none like me,
Declaring the end from the beginning,
and from ancient times
the things that are not yet done.

ISA 46:9-10

Just about now, you are probably saying to yourself, "This is all very interesting, but what does this have to do with the survival of a remnant church?" Well, in the last two thousand years, many schools of thought have developed about what is going to happen on Earth just before the Lord returns. Since Daniel wasn't opened until the end-times, none of them could be right. However, the Jews returning to the Holy Land in 1948, and Jerusalem being freed of Gentile domination in 1967, place us in the end-times and opens a new understanding of the prophetic Scriptures that was hidden from the Church throughout the Christian Era.

How can this be important to our survival? Well, the time of trial is very close, "the hour of temptation[1] which shall come upon all the world" (Rev 3:10), and the decisions we make during God's hour of trial will be important to our survival. How we make those decisions depends on what we believe is going happen during that time.

---

[1] Temptation: *peirasmos*, pi-ras-mos'; from G3985; a putting to proof (by experiment [of good], experience [of evil], solicitation, discipline or provocation); by implication, adversity--temptation, trial.

So back to the subject. The whole idea of a great tribulation at the end of this age began with Lacunza's belief that the Church would be taken up at the end of the 1290 days of Dan 12:11, and would return to earth 45 days later at the beginning of the 1335 days of Dan 12:12. But are those "days" in Daniel really ordinary 24-hour days, or could they represent some other duration of time? There are sound scriptural reasons to believe that they really symbolize years, and here is how we can prove it.

DANIEL RECEIVES A MESSENGER

In 536BC, Darius the Mede conquered Babylon. Daniel and many of his people had been captive in Babylon since 606BC, a captivity that had lasted 70 years. Daniel knew from the book of Jeremiah that his time of captivity should be over:

> Jer 29:10 For thus saith the LORD, "That after seventy years be accomplished at Babylon I will visit you, and perform my good word toward you, in causing you to return to this place."

The night Babylon fell must have been some kind of night. Earlier, Daniel had interpreted the handwriting on the wall, and Belshazzar had promoted him to be the third ruler in the empire. The walls of Babylon were impregnable, and there was plenty of food in store. The Babylonians couldn't run out of water because the whole Euphrates River ran through the city, under the city walls. They were so confident in their defenses that they never even considered the possibility of invasion. So they were feasting and drinking and having a fabulous revel, or so they thought (Dan 5:1-4). But up river from the city, Darius had dug a canal that diverted the whole Euphrates River, and he marched his army into the city on a dry riverbed. The Babylonians weren't even watching. It was an easy victory, and King Belshazzar was slain (Dan 5:30).

In this new Medo-Persian Empire, Daniel was again just an ordinary citizen. What would happen to his people under this new regime? His promotion to the post of chief satrap by Darius and his being thrown into the lions' den were still some time in the future.

Daniel went home to read Scripture, and pray. He had now been a captive in Babylon for 70 years. That prayer of his wasn't some little "Thank you for our food, in Jesus' name,

Amen" kind of prayer. He fasted and sat in sackcloth and ashes, probably for days (Dan 9:3). He may have thought a long time about what he was going to say, and then written down his prayer, for, surely, this is one of the most eloquent and touching prayers in all Scripture. Here is part of what Daniel prayed:

> Dan 9:16-19 O Lord, according to all thy righteousness, I beseech thee, let thine anger and thy fury be turned away from thy city Jerusalem, thy holy mountain. Because for our sins, and for the iniquities of our fathers, Jerusalem and thy people are become a reproach to all that are about us. Now therefore, O our God, hear the prayer of thy servant, and his supplications, and cause thy face to shine upon thy sanctuary that is desolate, for the Lord's sake. O my God, incline thine ear, and hear; open thine eyes, and behold our desolations, and the city which is called by thy name: for we do not present our supplications before thee for our righteousnesses, but for thy great mercies. O Lord, hear; O Lord, forgive; O Lord, hearken and do; defer not, for thine own sake, O my God: for thy city and thy people are called by thy name.

Daniel confessed his sins and the sins of his people. This wonderful man of God knew that he, and the rest of the Jews, deserved nothing from the Lord, any more than we do. But because of God's great mercy, and because of His prophecies through Jeremiah, weren't the 70 years of captivity over?

While Daniel was praying, the Lord sent the angel Gabriel to comfort him, and because the 70 years of captivity were indeed over, to tell him of a new and different 70: a seventy of sevens:

> Dan 9:24-26 Seventy weeks [*or sevens*] are determined upon thy people and upon thy holy city, to finish the transgression, and to make an end of sins, and to make reconciliation for iniquity, and to bring in everlasting righteousness, and to seal up the vision and prophecy, and to anoint the most Holy. Know therefore and understand, *that* from the going forth of the commandment to restore and to build Jerusalem unto the Messiah the Prince *shall be* seven weeks [*or sevens*], and threescore and two weeks [or sevens]: the street shall be built again, and the wall, even in troublous times. And after threescore and two weeks [*or sevens*] shall Messiah be cut off, but not for himself.

The Bible is a historic book. It was written at a specific place in time and refers to events that take place in time. The same is true of Bible prophecy. Every Bible prophecy was given at a point in time and would be fulfilled at another point in time. Those points in time are usually stated in Scripture, as they are in Daniel's 70 Weeks. "From the going forth of the commandment" is a definite starting point, and "and after the three score and two weeks" is a definite fulfillment point. But if we are to understand how long those weeks are, we need to see if the prophesied events have taken place, and how long a time passed between the starting and fulfillment points of the prophecy.

There are a lot of things to consider in understanding the 70 Weeks. First of all, they are divided into two sections: 69 Weeks and One Week. Let's look at the 69 weeks first. To whom are they written and what are they about? They are to the Jews, and about Jerusalem. What does v.24 tell us will be accomplished in these 69 sevens?

1. "Finish transgression."
2. "Make an end of sin."
3. "Make reconciliation for iniquity."
4. "Bring in everlasting righteousness."
5. "Seal up vision and prophecy."
6. "To anoint the most Holy."

When will they take place, and what is the time frame? We are told to start counting time after a decree is sent out to restore Jerusalem, and that it will be a time of trouble.

There were four restoration decrees granted by the Medo-Persian Empire. But almost 100 years after Gabriel spoke to Daniel, a special decree was granted to Nehemiah by Artaxerxes I. This decree was the only one *recorded in Scripture* which gave the Jews permission to restore Jerusalem and rebuild its walls, and since Scripture relates to Scripture, we should start counting time from this decree.[1] Just as Daniel predicted, Nehemiah had lots of trouble wall-building. The people living around Jerusalem tried to stop him every way they could. Neh 4:1-23 shows that they even tried to get the

---

[1] The whole book of Nehemiah is about the events which followed the Artaxerxes I decree. Furthermore, the events recorded in Nehemiah perfectly match Daniel's prophecy of them. The dating of this decree is firm at 445-444BC.

government to come down on him, just like the unsaved and pseudo-Christians come down on true Christians today.

The Messiah is Jesus, of course, and He was crucified in 32 or 33AD. He didn't die for Himself, but for the sins of the world (1Jo 2:2). Are these 69 weeks 69 sevens of years? If so, we have 69 x 7 = 483 years.

The Lord usually spoke to His prophets in a language they could understand. Daniel was a Jew, probably of the royal family (2Ki 20:18), and the Jews had their own 360-day Levitical year. Since our history is recorded in solar years of 365.24 days, we need to convert 483 Hebrew years to solar years: 483 x .9857 = 476 solar years.

Artaxerxes' decree, 444BC + 476 years = 32AD, the cross right to the year!

GRAPH NUMBER 3

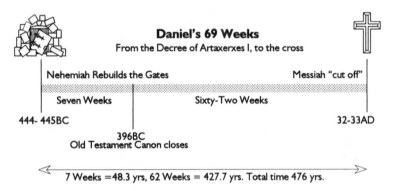

Daniel's 69 Weeks
From the Decree of Artaxerxes I, to the cross

Nehemiah Rebuilds the Gates   Messiah "cut off"

Seven Weeks   Sixty-Two Weeks

444- 445BC   32-33AD

396BC
Old Testament Canon closes

7 Weeks =48.3 yrs, 62 Weeks = 427.7 yrs. Total time 476 yrs.

Note: All our historical dates are recorded in Solar years, so for O.T. prophecy it is necessary to convert from the Hebrew year of 360 days to the solar year of 365.24 days. That conversion factor is .9857.

The cross, right to the year. But what about those six points which were supposed to be fulfilled during these 70 weeks? Aha! All but one were fulfilled at the cross. Did not Jesus (1) finish transgression eternally, (2) make an end of sin, (3) make reconciliation for iniquity, (4) bring in everlasting righteousness, and (6) anoint the Most Holy with His own precious blood?[1] Of course, praise the Lord! Point (5), however, was left out: "Seal up vision and prophecy." This is where those peculiar 7 weeks and 62 weeks come in:

> *7 x 7 Hebrew years = 48.3 Solar years. 444BC - 48.3 is 395.7BC, Malachi written.*

Malachi was inspired to write the last book of the Old Testament in about 396BC. The Scripture to the Jews was complete, and no more was written until the New Testament era! So Old Testament vision and prophecy were indeed "sealed up." As one dear Rabbi lamented in about 200BC, "The Holy Spirit has departed from Israel," and until this very day, the Jews, as a nation, have not been permitted to see any further. The Lord has blinded their eyes so they could not recognize Jesus as their Messiah (Rom 11:8, 2Co 3:15).

So what have we learned so far? Not only that 69 Weeks were fulfilled at the cross, but also that those "weeks"were not ordinary weeks of days, but weeks of years. Every single day of those 69 weeks represented a year, and we can prove it through known historical events. There are even three verses in Scripture which back up the day=year interpretation.

---

[1] Incredible as it may sound, it appears that the archeologist Ron Wyatt may have found the Ark of the Covenant. According to Mr. Wyatt, the Ark was hidden in a cave under Golgotha -- Gordon's Calvary -- probably in the field that Jeremiah purchased from his cousin just prior to the fall of Jerusalem to Babylon in 586BC. "And I bought the field of Hanameel my uncle's son, that *was* in Anathoth, and weighed him the money, *even* seventeen shekels of silver" (Jer 32:9). From the Word of the Lord to him, Jeremiah knew that Jerusalem was about to fall, so he appears to have placed the Table of Shewbread, the Altar of Incense, and the Ark of the Covenant in that cave and walled them up. The cave was forgotten, and it seems that these articles have remained secreted ever since.

If this find can be confirmed, it explains a previously inexplicable prophecy: "and He shall anoint the Most Holy." During the crucifixion, Jesus' side was pierced, and the rocks beneath the cross rent (Mat 27:51). According to Wyatt, the Ark was directly under where the Lord was crucified, and it appears that Jesus' blood ran through the fissure in the rock and fell on the Mercy Seat. If so, then in accordance with Dan 9:24, Jesus did indeed "anoint the Most Holy" with His own precious blood. Videotapes and various newsletters are available from Ron Wyatt (Wyatt Archeological Research, 713 Lambert Dr. Nashville, TN 37220).

THE DAY=YEARS

Captive with Daniel in the province of Babylon was a priest named Ezekiel. He was the prophet inspired by the Lord to write the canonical book that bears his name. As we can show from Dan 9:2, Daniel read Scripture in his devotions. He studied Jeremiah, so no doubt he also studied the rest of the scriptures that were available to him including the books of Numbers and Ezekiel. Within those two books are three verses which gave him the insight he needed to understand the prophetic day=year principle:

> Num 14:34 After the number of the days in which ye searched the land, even forty days, each DAY for a YEAR, shall ye bear your iniquities, even forty years, and ye shall know my breach of promise.

> Eze 4:5-6 For I have laid upon thee the YEARS... according to the number of the DAYS, three hundred and ninety days ... so shalt thou bear the iniquity of the house of Israel. And when thou hast accomplished them ... and thou shalt bear the iniquity of the house of Judah forty days: I have appointed thee each DAY for a YEAR.

A day for a year.[1] Here, in the only two places it appears in the Bible, the Lord shows Daniel that one prophetic day is equal to one of our earthly years. ONE DAY = ONE YEAR! Using this day=year unit of measure to interpret his prophecies, Daniel could not only understand the 69 weeks of Dan 9, but also the 1290 and 1335 days of Dan 12. If we use the same unit of measure that Daniel did, we too should be able to understand those day=years.

Now we have touched on this before, but it is so important we are explaining it more fully here. Daniel was raised under Jewish law (the Levitical code), and the Jews had a twelve-

---

[1] This is not a new concept in the Church. In 1569, the great Anabaptist theologian, Thieleman van Braght, wrote in *Martyrs Mirror,* pages 21-24: ". . . a thousand two hundred and threescore days, which, reckoned according to prophetic language means as many years . . . let it be reckoned as it may, say we, as a very long period of time . . . ."

Two hundred years later, Matthew Henry, in his *Commentary on the Whole Bible,* came to the same conclusion (Vol VI, page 1157, column 1, para. 2): ". . . if the beginning of that interval could be ascertained, this number of prophetic days, taking a day for a year, would give us a prospect of when the end might be."

month calendar of thirty days each, for a year of 360 days. That was Daniel's calendar, so it is correct to use a 360-day year to interpret Old Testament prophecies like his. But since our records of ancient history are all in Solar Years of 365.24 days, we do need to convert those Hebrew 360 day=years to fit our records. Please see the below graph for details.

The Apostle John, however, lived his whole life in the Christian Era, under a Gentile Roman government, and his book is primarily to the Gentile church. Consequently, it is proper to for us to use the Gentile solar calendar of 365.24 days to interpret John's prophecies.

GRAPH NUMBER 4

THE DAY = YEAR PRINCIPLE

| One Day | = | One Year |

(In the O.T., Hebrew 360 day. In the N.T., Solar 365.24 day)

After the day=year revelation was given to Ezekiel, when "days" are spoken of in a prophetic sense, they should be viewed either as Hebrew or Solar years unless context clearly dictated otherwise. The day=year interpretation is scriptural, and it is not hermeneutically sound to view prophetic days differently unless an intervening Scripture annulled that principle.

Hebrew Year = 360 days, or .9857 Solar year: ONLY for interpreting Old Testament prophecy.. Daniel used the Hebrew calendar.

Solar Year = 365.24 days: ONLY for interpreting New Testament prophecy. John was under Roman rule and used the solar calendar.

Photo courtesy of Biblical Archeology Review

The Temple Mount as seen from the North. The Mohammedan memorial, the Dome of the Rock, stands in its center as it has for 1300 years. Circled in the lower right is a little, unimposing cupola, the Dome of the Tablets. Late archeological evidence indicates that the Holy of Holies in both the Solomonic and the 2nd Temple was located here, some 330 feet northwest of the Dome itself. The Dome is positioned in what was once called the Court of the Gentiles.

Daniel's 1290 Days

CHAPTER 4

Be not ye like your fathers,
and like your brethren,
which trespassed against the
LORD God of their fathers,
who therefore gave them up to desolation,
as ye see.

2CH 30:7

When this study of Bible prophecy was begun fifteen years ago, what I really had in mind was finding scriptural support for the *Seven-Year Great Tribulation* doctrine. I was just as convinced as everyone else that there was going to be one, so the biggest surprise in my life came when I couldn't prove the seven-year tribulation view from the Bible. Major pillars of that view are the "days" of Dan 12:11-12. If you will remember, that is where Lacunza got his 45-day tribulation idea in the first place. Now we know that those days probably ought to be looked at as years. But if they are prophetic years, how can we know when they began or if they have ended? For that we need to go back to the time when the Lord gave that prophecy to Daniel.

In the third year of Cyrus the Persian (533BC), "a thing was revealed unto Daniel . . . but the appointed time was long: and he understood the thing, and had understanding of the vision" (Dan 10:1). It was about the future of Daniel's people, the Jews then in captivity. The Babylonian empire had fallen some three years earlier and Daniel was now a very old man, probably in his nineties. He had been a captive in Babylon for 73 years, and the Jews had just begun their trek back from captivity to the Holy Land.

It was then that the Lord gave this dear old saint the final vision of his prophetic ministry (Dan 10:1 - 12:13). A major part of this prophecy is a detailed account of the Medo-

Persian and Greek domination of the Jews in the Holy Land during the next 400 years, but in the final chapter of Daniel there is a very curious passage which includes this verse:

> Dan 12:11 And from the time that the daily sacrifice shall be taken away, and the abomination that maketh desolate set up, there shall be a thousand two hundred and ninety days.

Curious, indeed. Could these days be just ordinary twenty-four hour days, or are they years, like they were in the 69 weeks? If they are years, what is an "abomination that maketh desolate?" Depends on who you are talking to. But since the verse refers to the "daily sacrifice" and those sacrifices were offered at the temple in Jerusalem, then temple sacrifices would have to be involved. This abomination would have to be something to do with God's temple that would defile it and make it impossible for the priests to offer sacrifices there. An idol on the temple grounds, an unclean sacrifice, or the worship of a false god would do it.

The Lord required the Jews to be quite uncompromising about the temple and its contents. In fact, Levitical law states that anyone who desecrated the temple was to be stoned with stones until he was dead. But in defiance of this, in 168BC, the Greek king, Antiochus Epiphanies, sacrificed a pig on the altar of burnt offering. That started the Maccabean revolt, and it has been known ever since as an "abomination that made desolate."

Afterward, the priests had to perform extensive purification of the altar before they could again offer sacrifices to the Lord there. As you remember from Old Testament history, priests were not authorized to sacrifice anywhere else. To the Jew, an Abomination that makes Desolate is anything that keeps them from offering sacrifices to the Lord on the temple site. It was true in Daniel's time; it is true now. God has not changed that definition in over 2800 years.

But to which abolition of sacrifices is the Lord referring in this prophecy to Daniel? Now please, let's not try to make a New Testament doctrine from this Scripture. The addressees are clearly defined. This prophecy is in the Old Testament, in Hebrew, to the Jews, and about the Holy Land while Gentile powers would be ruling there. Context refers to "thy people" (Dan 12:1). Daniel was a Jew and the prophecy was given to him, so it is to and about the Jews. We have no reason to believe that the Lord was telling Daniel about some abolition of sacrifices that might take place 2500 years later, at the end of the Christian Era.

Sacrifices were suspended three times in the Old Testament: once before Daniel, once during Daniel's Babylonian captivity, and once, about four hundred years later, by the Greek king Antiochus Epiphanies. So to which event do you suppose the Lord is referring? Well, when and to whom was this prophecy given? To Daniel in 533BC. Result: we have every reason to believe that the Lord was referring to the sacrifices which were abolished during Daniel's own lifetime: an abolition of sacrifices to which Daniel could relate.

Was it at the time of destruction of the temple? Not likely. Nebuchadnezzar destroyed the temple in 586BC, but Jeremiah tells us that temple sacrifices continued long after the temple was burned:

> Jer 41:5 . . . there came certain from Shechem, from Shiloh, and from Samaria, even fourscore men . . . with offerings and incense in their hand, to bring them to the house of the LORD.

This journey to the temple from Shechem, Shiloh, and Samaria took place at the end of the governorship of Gedaliah. That was seven to ten months *after* the temple was destroyed. So there still had to be some purified priests in Jerusalem who were carrying on. Two more years pass, then in the very last chapter of Jeremiah we read:

> Jer 52:30 In the three and twentieth year of Nebuchadnezzar, Nebuzaradan the captain of the guard carried away captive of the Jews seven hundred forty and five persons: all the persons were four thousand and six hundred.

The year was 583BC. Remember 583BC; you will see it again.

Nebuchadnezzar ascended the throne of Babylon in 606-605BC. Twenty-three years later is 583BC. The Babylonians took the nobles, the artisans, and priests captive. They left the poorer people in the land. Therefore, this final captivity of 583BC is a scripturally supportable time for the sacrifices to have been abolished. There were apparently no purified priests left in the land who could offer sacrifices. What a devastating experience this must have been for God's people in captivity.[1]

Oh, how the Jews repented. From the Babylonian captivity to this day, they have not departed from the Lord their God. As a conquered people in exile, they had 70 years of regret, and they never forgot it. Even today, with an annual feast, the Jews commemorate their restoration from captivity. Their repentance is poignantly recorded in this short quote from an unknown psalmist:

> *By the rivers of Babylon, there we sat down.*
> *Yea, we wept, when we remembered Zion.*
> *We hanged our harps*
> *upon the willows in the midst thereof.*
> *For there they that carried us away captive*
> *required of us a song; and they that wasted us*
> *required of us mirth, saying,*
> *Sing us one of the songs of Zion.*
> *How shall we sing the LORD's song in a strange land?*

PSA 137:1-4

Though he was hundreds of miles away from Jerusalem, Daniel knew all about these new hostages. Another group of Jewish captives being brought back to Babylon by Nebuzaradan, captain of the king's guard, could not have escaped Daniel's notice. He was daily in King Nebuchadnezzar's court. Oh, how it must have hurt that saintly man to hear of sacrifices being stopped, and of the Lord's temple in utter ruin. We can prove that the temple site was abandoned during Daniel's lifetime from Dan 9:17 and Ezr 3:2-3. With that historic background in place, let's look at Dan 12:11 again:

> Dan 12:11 And from the time that the daily sacrifice shall be taken away [*is abolished, NASB*], and the abomination that maketh desolate set up, there shall be a thousand two hundred and ninety days.

---

[1] For further details, please refer to Graph No.1 on p18. It cannot be positively proven from these verses that sacrifices were abolished in 583BC. However, there are N.T. prophecies that pin us to this date. These prophecies are fully discussed in later chapters.

Sacrifices were abolished in 583BC. When God gave this vision to Daniel in 533BC, sacrifices had already been abolished for 50 years. Looking back, Daniel could see that nothing of any special significance had taken place 1290 literal days after the sacrifices had been abolished, so the Lord must been speaking here of something other than 24 hour days. Yet Daniel "understood the vision" somehow (Dan 10:1). How could he have understood the vision if nothing of spiritual significance had taken place 46½ years earlier? He understood it because he was a very astute man who put together when sacrifices had been abolished with some other Scriptures he already knew:

> Eze 4:6 . . . and thou shalt bear the iniquity of the house of Judah forty days: I have appointed thee each day for a year.

With the day=year unit of measure applied to his prophecies, Daniel could understand. He remembered when the regular evening and morning sacrifices were abolished in 583BC. He looked from that time on down 1290 years into the future. He saw that an unbelievable abomination was going to trespass on the temple mount. One that would make it desolate. An abomination that would defile it beyond belief, and prevent all future sacrifices. What could that terrible thing be? Daniel could not know, but we can.

1290 Hebrew years (1271.5 solar years) after 583BC is exactly 688AD. From 685AD to 705AD, Abd el Malik built the Dome of the Rock, a memorial to Mohammed, on the temple mount! Thus, we now have a positive identification:

The Dome of the Rock is the Abomination of Desolation![1]

That is not a coincidence, nor suppositional theology. The date of the construction of the Dome of the Rock is a provable

---

[1] Some will argue that sacrifices could have been abolished a year or two earlier, or a couple of years later than 583BC, as suggested by the author. But none argue that they were abolished earlier than the destruction of the temple (586BC), nor more than ten years later. The Dome of the Rock and Mosque of Omar were under construction on the temple mount for 20 years, from 685AD to 705AD. Leaving the widest latitude for scholarly argument, that 20-year window cannot be circumvented.

historic fact that you can find for yourself in any good encyclopedia or world history.

This interpretation fits the words of Dan 12:11 exactly and fits history right to the year. How can the Jews offer sacrifices to the Lord, on His holy Mountain, while a structure to *the* false prophet remains there?

GRAPH NUMBER 5

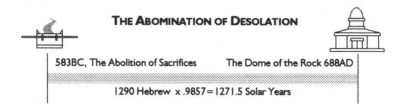

THE ABOMINATION OF DESOLATION

583BC, The Abolition of Sacrifices   The Dome of the Rock 688AD

1290 Hebrew x .9857 = 1271.5 Solar Years

Dan 12:11 And from the time *that* the daily *sacrifice* shall be taken away, and the abomination that maketh desolate set up, *there shall be* a thousand two hundred and ninety days.

Note: Biblical day=year prophecies have a beginning date in history specified by context, and now we can see their historic fulfillments. In Mar 13:14 the Abomination of Desolation is referred to as an "it" not a him, and this dome, a Mohammedan structure, has now stood on God's temple mount for over 1300 years. There are now over a billion and a half people in that false religion, so Mohammed could certainly qualify as the false prophet of Rev 19:20.

Over in Israel today, the Hasidic Jews know they can't. That is why there is such an interest among the conservatives in Jerusalem about tearing it down. It is no secret to them that the Dome of the Rock is an abomination that makes desolate. In the following chapters we will see how the New Testament fully supports this identity of the Dome of the Rock as the Abomination of Desolation. Now don't forget 688AD and the Dome of the Rock. We're going to run into that date, and the Dome, again and again.

Monchs and Days

CHAPTER 5

Behold ye among the heathen,
and regard, and wonder marvelously:
for I will work a work in your days,
which ye will not believe,
though it be told you.

HAB 1:5

From our position in the closing days of the 20th century, we can just begin to see a little of God's exquisite plan. The Abomination of Desolation is not an antichrist in our future. It is a building that has stood on Mount Moriah for over 1300 years. Just like the Lord said to Habakkuk, we wouldn't have believed Him if He had told us about it in advance, and now that we can see it, we can still hardly believe it.

FIGURES AND ALLEGORIES

The "days" and "weeks" we have studied so far were not about literal 24 hour days. Instead, the Lord was using "days" and "weeks" in a figurative way, to depict years. With those two examples of figurative language now understood, this might be as good a time as any to discuss the biblical principles used by scholars everywhere to interpret figurative and allegorical Scriptures.

Most of the Bible was written in plain language. But God's plan, as recorded in Scripture, embraces many writing styles: prose, poetry, some literal, some figurative. The historic books, poetic books, the gospels, and the epistles are primarily literal and should be accepted verbatim. They usually need no special interpretation and should be understood as actual historic accounts. They are not "oral traditions" nor "stories," as the liberals would have us believe.

However, some Scripture is visionary and allegorical. All the way back to Joseph's time, biblical visions used allegorical language (Gen 37:5-9). Peter's vision of the sheet full of unclean beasts is a New Testament example of an allegorical vision (Act 10:9-23). An allegory is usually an imaginative little tale on one subject, used to illustrate a concealed truth. But unless the Lord intended a message to stay hidden over time, biblical visions *(sometimes called apocalyptic visions)* were usually interpreted by the prophet himself.[1]

Using an earthly writer's tale as an illustration, Aesop's Fables, like the "Tortoise and the Hare," have a hidden allegorical message. In that story, Aesop's hidden message was that slow and steady was better than brilliant but unpredictable. Reading an allegory is like receiving a message in code. The fact that the message is in code makes it no less meaningful, but you do need to decipher the code.

That principle is also true for biblical allegories. Much of Daniel and Revelation, and all of Jesus' parables, are allegorical. It is just as wrong to insist on a literal interpretation for an allegorical message as it is to allegorically interpret a historic record. Here are the two important points:

1. *An allegorical interpretation of literal language will lead to faulty doctrine!*

2. *A literal interpretation of allegorical language will also lead to faulty doctrine!*

Both errors lead to big-time heresy, just as church history shows. If we fail to interpret God's allegories figuratively, we totally miss the Lord's message. Interpreting biblical allegories literally, and vice versa, is one of the reasons there are so many maniacal end-time doctrines around.

So how can we know the difference? How can we tell when a passage of Scripture should be literally or allegorically

---

[1] Now, Brethren, I know the difference between an allegory and figurative language, such as a metaphor or simile or a personification or hyperbole, in which words are used in a nonliteral way to achieve an effect beyond the range of ordinary language. But to keep this book from becoming bogged down with grammatical minutia, when any type of figurative language is encountered, it will usually be addressed as "allegorical" or "figurative," regardless of its exact nature.

interpreted? The Bible itself tells us. Most figurative passages in the Bible contain sign posts that tell us they are figurative: the kingdom of Heaven is *like*, or *like unto*, or *as*, a wedding feast, or a mustard seed, or a pearl of great price, or a king going to a far country, or a sower going forth to sow, etc. Now the kingdom of Heaven is not literally a wedding feast, a king in a far country, a mustard seed, a pearl, or a sower. It is only *figuratively likened* unto one!

Only a small portion of the Bible is figurative, but recognizing those passages as figurative is of major importance to us because end-time prophecies are written in that way. Apocalyptic books such as Daniel and Revelation are visionary in nature. These prophetic books were written in symbolic language because the Lord intended their messages to be hidden, not because they are unimportant.[1]

IT'S ON THE WRONG ROCK

That the 1290 days of Daniel (when interpreted figuratively) fit one incident in history is not sufficient evidence to prove that we should use a day=year interpretation for all biblical prophetic days, not even when the 1290 days hits an event as remarkable as the construction of the Dome of the Rock on Mount Moriah, right to the year. However, in Daniel's 70 Weeks, we saw conclusively that 69 sevens were sevens of years which were fulfilled at the cross. If that is the yardstick the Lord used in one part of Daniel, where is our scriptural support to change yardsticks later on in Daniel, or later on in the rest of the Bible, for that matter?

It would be poor theology, indeed, to leave a divinely ordained system which we can show works, and try to interpret "days" in some other way, particularly since we would have to go directly against God's assertion, "I give you a day for a year." To stay lined up with God's Word, we should at least look for a historic day=year fit for the rest of the prophetic "days" in Scripture.

---

[1] The word "apocalyptic" is usually defined as a symbolic or visionary style of writing. Many books in the Bible contain apocalyptic elements, but Ezekiel, Daniel, Zechariah, and some of Isaiah have major passages written in that form. Revelation is almost totally apocalyptic in style.

Let's start this by doing a little time travel. Let's imagine ourselves on the Isle of Patmos in the 1st century, looking at the world about us through the eyes of the Apostle John as he writes Revelation. In the 100 years that followed the crucifixion, the Jews were in a state of revolt against their Roman rulers. That wasn't anything new. They had been in rebellion ever since the Roman occupation began in 65BC. Army after army had been sent to the Holy Land to quell the continual uprisings. Losing all patience, Rome, sending her best general, finally came against Jerusalem itself. In 70AD, after a lengthy siege, Titus and his legions sacked the city. An estimated 1,500,000 Jews fell to the sword and famine, and the beautiful 2nd Temple was torn down to bedrock. It had taken 45 years to build, but stone by stone the Romans threw it into the valleys of Tyropoeon and Kidron. Finally, "not one stone stood upon another," just as Jesus had foretold.

Thirty-eight years earlier, Jesus had warned His disciples of this coming devastation in a prophecy that is recorded in three places, Mat 24:2, Mar 13:2, and Luk 21:6. The Christians in the city were aware of Jesus' prophecy, and just prior to that city's destruction, they all fled Jerusalem in haste. Early church records assert that no Christians were left in the city, and that no Christian life was lost during the ensuing massacre.[1] The demolition of the temple was so complete that even the memory of its exact location was lost. Then, except for that short-lived temple of Jupiter, the Lord's temple site remained in rubble for over 600 years.

However, beginning 685AD, the Mohammedan governor of Jerusalem, Abd el Malik, cleared the temple mount to bedrock. He used the local people to do so, including the Christians and Jews still living in the city. They found two solid rock promontories. One they named "as-Sakhra," and

---

[1] According to Tacitus, the city was crowded with 600,000 visitors. After five months the walls were battered down, the Temple burned, and the city was made desolate. Josephus states that over 1,000,000 Jews were killed and 95,000 taken captive, Henry Halley, *Halley's Bible Handbook* (Grand Rapids, MI, Zondervan, 1965) pp. 655-656. Eusebius writes, "On the other hand, the people of the church in Jerusalem, were commanded by oracle given by revelation to those in the city who were worthy of it, to depart and dwell in one of the cities of Perea, which they called Pella." *Ecclesiastical History*, Book 3, v. 5, ln. 3-4.

over as-Sakhra they built the Mohammedan memorial, the Dome of the Rock, the actual construction of which began in 688AD. You remember the numbers from the last chapter:

1290 Hebrew years (1271.5 Solar years) after 583BC is 688.5AD! 583 + 1271.34 = 688.66.

Over another promontory (an unusually flat stone about 300ft north and slightly to the west of as-Sakhra), a little, unimposing cupola was constructed that they aptly named "The Dome of the Spirits," or "The Dome of the Tablets." Having no science of archaeology in those days, guess what?

They built the Dome of the Rock on the wrong rock!

I don't know how you feel as you read that line, Brethren, but I remember how I felt fifteen years ago when I first understood it. I sat at my desk, stunned for a moment, and them just leaned back and roared with laughter. I ran the numbers again and again, praising God. As-Sakhra has no historic or spiritual significance whatsoever. The Dome of the Rock is right in the middle of what was once the court of the Gentiles. Even ceremonially unwashed Canaanite slaves were allowed to go into the court of the Gentiles. You didn't have to be a priest, or a Levite, or even a Jew to go there.[1]

The House of the Lord, where only the sons of Aaron could enter, stood over that little flat rock some 300ft north of where the Dome now stands. We know exactly where the temple stood because of holes drilled in the bedrock that are spaced on the sacred cubit.[2] The sacred cubit could be used only in the temple itself, and these holes pinpoint the exact location of the House of the Lord.

---

[1] How spiritually appropriate their building on the wrong rock has proved to be. There is only one rock on which to build, the rock Christ Jesus. Mohammed is not just a little false prophet; he is probably THE false prophet of Rev 19:20! There are about 1,000,000,000 people in that false religion today and, worldwide, Mohammedans now outnumber Christians. God help the world when Islam gains the military power to be a threat to the West.

[2] The Hebrews had two units of measure for the cubit: the ordinary cubit of about 18 in., and a sacred cubit, "a cubit and a span" of about 21½ in. The sacred cubit was used only in temple construction.

GRAPH NUMBER 6

Location of the Solomonic Temple

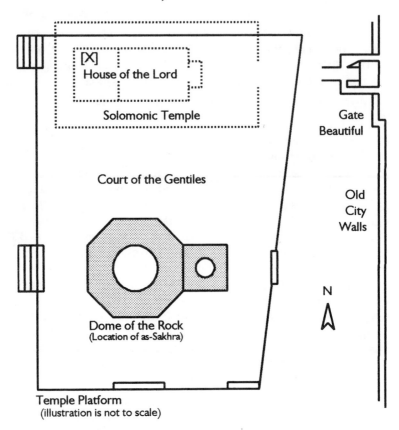

Temple Platform
(illustration is not to scale)

[X] Location of the flat bedrock, now under the Dome of the Tablets.

This sketch of the Temple Mount shows the Mohammedan *Dome of the Rock* to be some 330 feet south of the sites for both the Solomonic and 2nd temples. The dotted line shows the location of the Temple of Solomon. Notice that it faces East and is directly in line with the Golden Gate. The 2nd temple (not shown) was in exactly the same location, but was turned on its axis somewhat more easterly. In both temples, the flat bedrock, now under the little Dome of the Tablets, was part of the floor of the *Kodesh ha- Kodashim*, or Holy of Holies.

The *Kodesh Ha-Kodeshim*, the Holy of Holies, was directly over that little flat rock marked [X] on the drawing. Bathed in Shekinah Glory, that flat rock had been the resting place of the Ark of the Covenant: "God's dwelling place, and the footstool of His feet, forever." It was exactly on an East-West line with the Golden Gate.[1] The very gate through which Jesus walked on His way to teach in the temple. Now, for the first time ever, we can discern the meaning of a baffling allegorical verse in Ezekiel:

Eze 42:20 He measured it by the four sides: it had a wall round about, five hundred reeds long, and five hundred broad, to make a separation between the sanctuary and the profane place.

That spiritual wall of separation, probably guarded by holy angels, has stood on the temple mount for 1300 years, and we haven't seen it. The Dome of the Rock is 300ft to the South of the temple. That Dome is not now, and never has been, over the old temple site. The Dome was, is, and, as long as it stands, shall be right in the middle of the Court of the Gentiles.

THE 42 MONTHS

Isn't it wonderful to know that by permitting the temple's total destruction, the Lord protected His Holy of Holies from the profanity of having a memorial to a false god, and *the* false prophet, built over it? Of more importance, if the Mohammedans had not built on the wrong rock, it would be impossible for this next quote to be fulfilled. Now look carefully at the language and see how perfectly it fits the situation on God's holy hill today:

Rev 11:2 But the court which is without the temple leave out, and measure it not; for it is given unto the Gentiles: and the holy city shall they tread under foot forty and two months.

"Leave out the court . . . it has been given to the Gentiles!" The Dome of the Rock is in the court, and it is a Gentile structure. So we now have the location. Then we read that Jerusalem shall be under Gentile control for 42 months. Farfetched as it may seem, could those 42 months be turned into days, and looked at as years? It was day=years in the Old

---

[1] Temple Foundation Located, *Biblical Archaeology Review*, Mar. 1983.

Testament, and there is no Scripture anywhere that does away with that interpretation. So let's try for a historic fit using day=years.

A Solar year is 365.24 days. Since there are 12 months in a year, dividing by 12 gives us a month of 30.44 days. Rev 11:2 speaks of 42 months, so 42 x 30.44 gives us roughly 1278.5 days. If they are years, when do they begin and when do they end? We need the historical setting again.

On the 6th day of June, 1967, at the end of the Six-Day War, General Moshe Dayan and a tough, hard-bitten contingent of Israeli commandos stood before a wall of ancient stones. Their shoulders were shaking, and tears were streaming down their faces. They were at the Wailing Wall in East Jerusalem, that Holy Place from which they had been exiled so many centuries before. They were crying thanks unto God for restoring their ancient city to them. There they solemnly swore: "Never again shall we be driven from this place." For the first time in 2573 years (from 606BC to 1967AD) the Jews were in control of their Holy City. Could that touching moment be the historic end of, "and they [*the Gentiles*] will tread under foot the Holy City for 42 months?"

1967AD - 1278.5 = 688.5AD . . . the Dome of the Rock!

GRAPH NUMBER 7

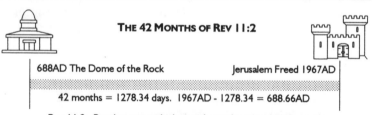

THE 42 MONTHS OF REV 11:2

688AD The Dome of the Rock   Jerusalem Freed 1967AD

42 months = 1278.34 days. 1967AD - 1278.34 = 688.66AD

Rev 11:2 But the court which is without the temple leave out, and measure it not; for it is given unto the Gentiles: and the holy city shall they tread under foot forty *and* two months.

Note: Please study Rev 11:2 carefully. This interpretation fits Scripture and history too well to be ignored. "And the holy city shall they tread underfoot forty and two months." Forty-two months is 1278.34 days , and it is exactly 1278 years from the beginning of the construction of the Dome of the Rock until Jerusalem was again under Jewish control. Then, "Leave out the court . . ." The Dome of the Rock is in the Court of the Gentiles, 300 feet south of the temples.

In the 1290 days of Dan 12, the Lord took us from 583BC, and the abolition of sacrifices in Daniel's time, to 688AD and the Abomination that makes Desolate, the Dome of the Rock. Then in the 42 months of Rev 11:2, the Lord shows us the accuracy of that interpretation. He takes us from the restoration of Jerusalem in 1967, right back to 688, and the Dome of the Rock. We come to 688, and that dome, right to the year, from both directions. As a result, from the Lord's view, the central event to take place in Jerusalem during the time of the Gentiles was the building of the Abomination of Desolation on the footstool of His feet. And it is not just the numbers that work. Look at how this fits the very words of Scripture:

(1) "Sacrifices abolished."
(2) "Abomination set up."
(3) "Leave out the court."
(4) "Holy city tread under foot for 42 months."

This many factors coming together can't be just a numerical and verbal fluke, can they? Writing it off as coincidence is statistically unreasonable, and there are other fulfillments using the same yardstick still to come.

THE TIME OF JACOB'S TROUBLE

When God unlocks a book and opens our eyes, He does so in such a way that it cannot be reasonably refuted. Using the day=years again, the Lord gives us proof upon proof:

> Rev 12:1-5 And there appeared a great wonder in heaven; a woman clothed with the sun, and the moon under her feet, and upon her head a crown of twelve stars: And she being with child cried, travailing in birth, and pained to be delivered. And there appeared another wonder in heaven; and behold a great red dragon, having seven heads and ten horns, and seven crowns upon his heads. And his tail drew the third part of the stars of heaven, and did cast them to the earth: and the dragon stood before the woman which was ready to be delivered, for to devour her child as soon as it was born. And she brought forth a man child, who was to rule all nations with a rod of iron: and her child was caught up unto God, and to his throne.

Who is this woman, and who is the man child? When we read His description, there is only one Person in all eternity who matches that portrait. Who will rule all nations with a rod of iron?[1] Who descended from Heaven, and who ascended up into it again?[2] Who now sits at the right hand of the throne of God?[3] None but Jesus Christ the Righteous. That makes the woman Israel, and the 12 stars the 12 tribes. The dragon would then be Satan, who tried to defeat the Lord at the cross, and the fallen stars would be the fallen angels.[4]

> Rev 12:6 And the woman fled into the wilderness, where she hath a place prepared of God, that they should feed her there a thousand two hundred and threescore days.

During the Christian Era the Jews were dispersed into the nations.[5] For centuries the Jews have been hounded from country to country, made slaves of: were robbed, beaten, and murdered wholesale, as in Nazi Germany . . . but never again. God has promised that never again would the Jews suffer anything like that holocaust in which 6,000,000 of the physical seed of Abraham were murdered:

> Jer 30:3-8 And these are the words that the LORD spake concerning Israel and concerning Judah. For thus saith the LORD; We have heard a voice of trembling, of fear, and not of peace.
>
> Ask ye now, and see whether a man doth travail with child? wherefore do I see every man with his hands on his loins, as a woman in travail, and all faces are turned into paleness? Alas! for that day is great, so that none is like it: it is even the time of Jacob's trouble, but he shall be saved out of it.

A more moving account of the atrocities of the Nazi gas chambers would be hard to imagine. There, in the winter snow, stood line after line of naked Jewish men, their hands in front of them to cover their nudity. Shivering bodies, numb

---

[1] Rev 19:15 And out of his mouth goeth a sharp sword, that with it he should smite the nations: and he shall rule them with a rod of iron:

[2] Eph 4:10 He that descended is the same also that ascended up far above all heavens, that he might fill all things.

[3] Col 3:1 If ye then be risen with Christ, seek those things which are above, where Christ sitteth on the right hand of God.

[4] Rev 1:20 tells us that the stars are the "aggelos" or messengers (Strong's No. G32). That same Greek word is also used in Rev 12:4. Aggelos, pronounced "anglos" is usually translated angels.

[5] The wilderness is the Gentile world, Eze 20:35.

with cold, beatings, and starvation. Faces pale, they shuffled slowly into extinction. As Your Son hung naked on the cross so long ago, so now it has happened unto Your people, O God. But that is all in the past now. The time of Jacob's trouble is over. The Lord has broken Satan's yoke from off their neck, and the Jews will never be in bondage again.

> Jer 30:7 For it shall come to pass in that day, saith the LORD of hosts, that I will break his yoke from off thy neck, and will burst thy bonds, and strangers shall no more serve themselves [*make slaves*] of him.

As of 1948, the Jews are no longer dispersed in the nations. On May 15th of that year, Israeli Prime Minister, David Ben-Gurion, stood on the floor of the Knesset and declared the new nation of Israel to be a sovereign state. That is a historic fact which no one can deny. As of 1948, the woman, Israel, is no longer in the wilderness, and if she isn't, then Rev 12:6 should be fulfilled.

From the 6th verse we see that this woman Israel will be in the wilderness 1260 days. Is this years again? In this instance, the Lord gave us prophetic days straight out with no complicated mathematics.[1] Even a 2nd grader can figure this one out:

1948 - 1260 = 688AD . . . and the Dome of the Rock!

It was exactly 1260 years from the construction of the Dome of the Rock to the establishment of the new nation of Israel. These day=years are "so great a cloud of witnesses" (Heb 12:1), that it would take a closed mind indeed to deny the fulfillment of these prophecies in the Dome of the Rock and new nation of Israel.

How come we couldn't see it sooner? God planned it that way, and He even told us so. Remember in Dan 12:9, when the Lord stated that this book was sealed until the time of the end? Until the new nation of Israel and a free Jerusalem became historic realities *(which began the time of the end)*, there was no way to decipher these days. We didn't have the

---

[1] In New Testament times, the Jews were under Roman rule and the 365.24 day Roman year was in common usage. Consequently, it would be an error to use a 360 day Hebrew year to interpret NT prophecies. It is correct use the 365.24 solar year to interpret all NT prophecies.

Photo courtesy Biblical Archeology Review

We are filled with reverence and awe when we realize that surrounding the now exposed bedrock under this little cupola, was the Holy of Holies of the temple of Solomon. On this rock once stood the Ark of the Covenant. When Solomon erected the temple in 966BC, this very space was filled with the Shekinah glory of God. The Ark was "lost" during Nebuchadnezzar's siege of Jerusalem. Jewish tradition states that the prophet Jeremiah took the Ark and the original tabernacle through a secret tunnel under Jerusalem and buried them on Mount Nebo. We now believe the Ark was buried in a cave under Golgotha.

end-time historic pins to show that Revelation's day=years affirmed the 1290 days of Daniel.

You realize that in the Seven-Year Tribulation view, every one of these "days" is supposed to represent either the first or the last half of the great tribulation. They are even considered by many folks to be pillars of that view. But obviously, that is not what those "days" are about at all. They are about the Dome of the Rock, Jerusalem and the Holy Land. They are about the restoration of the people God gave the land to in the first place: the physical seed of Jacob.

GRAPH NUMBER 8

THE 1260 DAYS OF REV 12:6

688AD, The Dome of the Rock   New nation of Israel, 1948AD

1260 years, no conversion. John used the Solar calendar.

Rev 12:6 And the woman fled into the wilderness, where she hath a place prepared of God, that they should feed her there a thousand two hundred *and* threescore days.

Note: Before 688AD, both Christians and Jews could freely worship in Jerusalem, and on the temple mount. They were not prophetically in the "wilderness" of the nations until the Mohammedans made it unsafe for them to worship in that city. That is why the 1260 days begin in 688AD.

This goes against some of the popular "replacement" and dispensational theologies of today, but how can we deny the evidence of our own eyes? An Israeli flag, complete with the star of David, flies over the battlements of Jerusalem, and Jews by the millions have returned to the land. That's not guesswork theology, folks; that's reality.

Two Witnesses

CHAPTER 6

Can a woman forget her sucking child,
that she should not have compassion
on the son of her womb?
Yea, they may forget,
yet will I not forget thee.

ISA 49:15

We can't go to Revelation with our end-time doctrines in place and expect the Holy Spirit to teach us anything from that book. The Two Witnesses of Rev 11:3-7 are good examples of why. Most believe these witnesses to be Moses, Enoch, or Elijah, but could they be somebody else entirely?

> Rev 11:3 . . . and I will grant authority to my two witnesses, and they will prophesy for twelve hundred and sixty days, clothed in sackcloth."

If the Lord ever intends for us to know who those witnesses are, there should be a sound scriptural way to discover their identity, and there is. The Lord tells us exactly who they are, but He tells us in figurative language. He tells us these witnesses are olive trees and candlesticks:

> Rev 11:4 These are the two olive trees, and the two candlesticks standing before the God of the earth.

Hummm . . . olive trees and candlesticks. What can those figures mean? Well, taking the day=year principle of Eze 4:5-6 into consideration, those two witnesses would have to witness for 1260 years. No one in this age lives 1260 years, so unless the Lord's Two Witnesses are a pair of elderly olive-bearing olive trees and two ancient, oil-dripping golden candlesticks, then, like it or not, we are dealing with figurative language.

Candlesticks and olive trees are used figuratively in Zec 4, but the figures within that chapter were defined for us as things that existed during Zechariah's time (the Jewish leader Zerubbabel being one of them). So on the basis of the definitions in Zec 4, could Zerubbabel and "the two anointed ones" be the Two Witnesses of Rev 11? Not very likely. We see no end-time reference to a personage like Zerubbabel in the New Testament, and Revelation does not call the two witnesses of the Christian Era "anointed ones." However, since Zechariah's two anointed ones are not clearly identified, they might possibly be an Old Testament reference to the Two Witnesses in Revelation 11.

This all sounds very confusing. To sort it out we probably need to apply some of the rules of hermeneutics. Now, hermeneutics is not a discipline we play games with to fit our doctrines. It is a sound study of how to interpret either the spoken word or a written document. Hermeneutics has some excellent, time-tested rules. Among them is the rule of "scriptural adjacency." That rule states: When you read a verse you don't understand, first study the surrounding verses, then the chapter, then the book in which that chapter appears, then the testament which contains that book, and finally, relate the verse to the whole Bible. That is one of the rules, and it is a good one.

We don't go to the Old Testament for definitions of New Testament allegories when there are New Testament definitions that fit perfectly!

In Rev 11:4 quoted above, the Two Witnesses of the Christian Era are described as olive trees and candlesticks. To find the correct definition for those figures, we should find the closest contextual address which explains them. Lo and behold, right in Revelation we find candlesticks defined for us:

Rev 1:20 The mystery of the seven stars which thou sawest in My right hand, and the seven golden candlesticks. The seven stars are the angels of the seven churches: and the seven candlesticks which thou sawest are the seven churches.

Right in Rev 1:20, candlesticks are defined as churches. If candlesticks are churches in Rev 1, then candlesticks are still churches in Rev 11. The only way they would not be is if the Lord God Himself changed the symbolic meaning of that word somewhere between Rev 1:20 and Rev 11:4. No change of definition appears there -- nor anywhere else in Scripture for that matter -- so the candlesticks of Rev 11:4 are churches. That interpretation is not the product of some clever theologian's overactive imagination. Candlesticks are churches because the Bible itself defines them as such. As a result, if the seven candlesticks of Rev 1 are seven churches, then the two candlesticks of Rev 11 would be two churches.

If the Two Witnesses are two churches, then which two churches would they be? Probably every denomination in the world would like to claim that it surely is one of the Two Witnesses, with all the rest being heretics, of course. But God's churches of the Christian Era are far broader than any sectarian restrictions, and the Olive Trees figure positively identifies these churches for us. Olive trees are not explained for us in Revelation, so we must look elsewhere for that definition.

Still applying the principle of scriptural adjacency, we first try for a definition in the chapter, then the book, and finally in the rest of the New Testament. Four times in the Old, and twice in the New, Israel is defined as an olive tree. The Old Testament verses are included in footnote[1]; however, we still don't use Old Testament definitions of New Testament figures when there are New Testament definitions which fit perfectly. I have taken the liberty of adding a few explanatory words in italics to the next Scripture quote:

> Rom 11:17 And if some of the [*Jewish*] branches be broken off, and thou [*the Gentile church*], being a wild olive tree, wert grafted in among them, and with them partakest of the root and fatness of the olive tree.

> Rom 11:24 For if thou [*the Gentiles*] wert cut out of the olive tree which is wild by nature, and wert grafted contrary to nature into a

---

[1] Jer 11:16 The Lord called your name, "A green olive tree, beautiful in fruit and form;" With the noise of a great tumult He has kindled fire on it, And its branches are worthless.
Isa 17:6 Yet gleanings will be left in it like the shaking of an olive tree, Two or three olives on the topmost bough, Four or five on the branches of a fruitful tree, Declares the Lord, the God of Israel.
Isa 24:13 For thus it will be in the midst of the earth among the peoples, As the shaking of an olive tree, As the gleanings when the grape harvest is over.
Hos 14:6 His shoots will sprout, And his beauty will be like the olive tree, And his fragrance like Lebanon.

good olive tree [*the Jews*]: how much more shall these [*the Jews*],
which be the natural *branches,* be grafted into their own olive tree?

Revelation is a New Testament book, and a New Testament definition for olive trees can be found in the 11th chapter of Romans. According to that whole chapter, the Gentile church is one olive tree, and the Jewish people are the other. As a result . . .

> *One witness is the Jewish people*
> *and the other is the Gentile church!*

If we just accept the scriptural definitions for olive trees and candlesticks, we are not left with too many doctrinal options. Take a realistic look at history. The nation of Israel could not have maintained its identity through nineteen centuries of dispersion, under constant persecution, were it not for the protecting hand of the Lord our God. The Bible itself affirms it. Listen to what Scripture says:

> Jer 31:35-37 Thus saith the LORD, which giveth the sun for a light by day, *and* the ordinances of the moon and of the stars for a light by night, which divideth the sea when the waves thereof roar; The LORD of hosts *is* his name: If those ordinances depart from before me, saith the LORD, *then* the seed of Israel also shall cease from being a nation before me for ever. Thus saith the LORD; If heaven above can be measured, and the foundations of the earth searched out beneath, I will also cast off all the seed of Israel for all that they have done, saith the LORD.

Our eternal Heavenly Father has not forgotten those words. He stated right there that the children of Israel would be a nation before Him *forever.* He has remembered His chosen people all along. That the Lord had plans for the physical seed of Israel throughout all time, including the Christian Era, is confirmed by too many Scriptures to ignore.[1]

---

[1] Gen 17:7 speaks of an unconditional everlasting covenant with the seed of Abraham. Lev 26:44-45 shows that Israel's restoration was not to be conditional. Isa 11:11 speaks of a second restoration of the Jews. Isa 26:20-27:1 speaks of a final hiding of the children of Israel followed by Satan's complete judgment. Isa 27:12-13, in context with the above, speaks of a final regathering of Israel. Jer 30:4-8 speaks of the time of Jacob's trouble and future restoration. Jer 30:18-24 states that a restoration for the tents of Jacob will take place in the latter days, i.e. not

(continued...)

Replacement theology[1] notwithstanding, from the multitude of verses cited in the footnote below, it is apparent that the Lord never intended to forget the physical seed of Israel! Let me tell you just how important that is. If the Jews could not trust the promises God made to them in the Old Testament, then how can the Church trust the promises God made to us in the New? It's comforting to know (despite man's doctrines to the contrary) that our God is an absolutely Holy God who keeps His Word in eternity.

> Psa 33:11 The counsel of the LORD standeth for ever, the thoughts of his heart to all generations.

But if the Two Witnesses are two churches, when are they going to witness? If we stand by the day=year principle, they would have to witness for 1260 years:

---

[1](...continued)
the first restoration of 536BC. Jer 31:35-37 speaks of the permanent nation of Israel. Jer 33:24-26 is a definitive unconditional covenant with Jacob's descendants. Eze 16:60-63 speaks of an unconditional everlasting covenant with the Jews. Eze 37:1-28 speaks of an unconditional future restoration of Israel, followed closely by Armageddon in Exe 38-39. Hos 11:9-10 speaks of a future restoration of Israel from the West. Joe 3:1-3 predicts the restoration of Judah, followed by Armageddon. Amo 9:11-15 speaks of an Israel restored to the land. Zec 8:8 speaks of a post-exilic, unconditional restoration of the Jews to Jerusalem and the land. Zec 10 and 12 are more prophecies of a future restoration of the Jews. Zec 14 speaks of Armageddon, with the Jews in Jerusalem. Luk 21:24 speaks of a dispersion, the time of the Gentiles, and a restoration following. Rom 11:11 states that the Jews have not fallen. Rom 11:17 states that only some of the branches were broken off. Rom 11:17 states that the church was grafted in among the Jews. Rom 11:28 states that the gospel-age Jews are still elect. Rom 11:29 states that God's calling of the Jews is irrevocable. Rev 7:4-9 speaks of the 12 tribes of Israel in the Christian Era. Rev 12:1-6 speaks of Israel in the Christian Era. Rev 15:3 is a passage primarily about the Christian Era; there are two songs, one for the Jews, one for the Gentile church.

[1] Simply stated, Replacement Theology is the belief that the Church, as adopted Israel, has totally replaced the physical seed of Abraham and that God is completely finished with the Jews of the Christian Era. This view holds that during this era, the Church is all the Israel there is. The Scriptures cited in the preceding footnote, plus Rom 11:15, stand directly against such a doctrine.

Rev 11:3 And I will give *power* unto my two witnesses, and they shall prophesy a thousand two hundred *and* threescore days, clothed in sackcloth.[1]

The time of the Two Witness cannot come after the time of the Gentiles because Jesus told us there would be only one generation to follow it: "This generation [*after the time of the Gentiles*] will not pass away until all things are fulfilled" (Luk 21:24, 32). A generation cannot be over 70 years (Psa 90:10), and is usually considered to be 40 years, so we have to look back in history for these 1260 years. The author could find only one 1260 year time period that had any spiritual significance at all during in the whole Christian Era:

1948AD - 1260 = 688 AD and the Dome of the Rock! [2]

And this fits history perfectly! As of 1948, the Jews are no longer witnessing in the nations. The Abomination that maketh Desolate was set up in 688, and the Jews were driven into the "wilderness" of the nations at that time.[3] Now, 1260 years later, there is a new autonomous nation of Israel, and the Jews are back in the Holy Land again. So the Jewish people are one of the Two Witnesses of the Christian Era.

THE OTHER WITNESS

We can see 688 to 1948 as the time of Jewish witness, but what about the Church? How can the church's time of witness be over since we are still here? Well, look at what has happened to the Church since 1948. Because of our careless

---

[1] "Clothed in sackcloth" was an Old Testament symbol for mourning, of humbling oneself before the Lord, or of being in repentance for sin.

[2] Since there have been Hebrew believers all the way back to Abraham's time, and the Church has existed since Pentecost, why do the 1260 days start in 688 AD? Before that date, both Jew and Christian were free to worship in Jerusalem, even on the temple mount itself. After 688 the Mohammedans persecuted the Christians and Jews and drove them out of the land. That is when the most final of all the dispersions of the Jews took place. By now we should begin to get the picture. God's Word is eternal, and regardless of what nation ruled in the Holy Land, that old temple site was always of inestimable importance to the Lord.

[3] Eze 20:35 "And I will bring you into the wilderness of the people," shows the Gentile nations to be the wilderness.

disobedience of the Word, and the apathy and sin which have followed, much of the Gentile church has now fallen into apostasy.[1] The fall into satanism and immorality within the Christian nations quickened in 1948, and the western church has done little to slow that decay.[2]

Most churches in this country are terminally ill, many have already fallen away, and Europe is much worse. They

GRAPH NUMBER 9

     THE TWO WITNESSES OF REV 11:3-4

688AD, The Dome of the Rock	New nation of Israel, 1948AD
1948AD - 1260 Days = 688.66AD	

Rev 11:3-4 And I will give *power* unto my two witnesses, and they shall prophesy a thousand two hundred *and* threescore days, clothed in sackcloth. These are the two olive trees, and the two Candlesticks standing before the God of the earth.

Note: Before 688, both Christians and Jews could freely worship in Jerusalem, and on the temple mount. They were not prophetically in the nations until the Mohammedans made it unsafe for them to worship in that city. That is why the time of the Two Witnesses began in 688.

---

[1] Apostasy, as usually defined, means a departure from the truth to such a degree that the lost can no longer hear the Gospel of Jesus Christ, and cannot come to the Lord through the message that is preached.

[2] Many elders or deacons within mainline churches are occultists or satanists (*see Footnote 2 on page 197*). Furthermore, in 1948, The National Council of Churches (to which your own church probably belongs) joined the World Council of Churches. That organization has a declared goal of causing social change rather than teaching the gospel of Jesus Christ. That is what "Liberation Theology" is all about. It is further reported that through them, millions of dollars from mainline denominational churches (your tithes included) have gone to buy guns to support various insurgent "liberation fronts" in the third world. From the above, it is apparent that the Gentile hurch has fallen into apostasy.

are beyond reach, "the sin unto *spiritual* death."[1] Since our battle is really spiritual, one is inclined to wonder if the coming destruction of the Church may not be more spiritual than physical. If so, we are frighteningly close to that hour:

> Rev 11:7 And when they [*the Two Witnesses*] shall have finished their testimony, the beast that ascendeth out of the bottomless pit shall make war against them, and shall overcome them, and kill them.

One way or another, in the final hours of this age, the Two Witnesses are going to be destroyed. Read Rev 11:7 in any translation you like. They all predict the violent end of the Church. How can that be? Didn't Jesus promise that the gates of Hell would not prevail against His church? Yes, but the true Church that remains now is only a remnant . . . a few hairs hidden in a hem of the Lord's garment (Eze 5:3). Truth has fallen in the street (Isa 59:14).

For the first time since the invention of the printing press, books on astrology, satanism, and the occult are outselling the Bible, and the consciences of our people have been seared, as with a branding iron (1Ti 4:2). This will eventually lead to a worldwide rejection of the Bible and of the Lord. As the spiritual decay deepens, a ruthless and devastating evil will be unleashed upon this planet, and it will come with an intensity unknown since the flood. It has already begun.

What is the Remnant Church supposed to do when conditions become unbearable? Scripture indicates that we will be united with the faithful Jews, standing in steadfast array against the enemies of the Lord:

> Isa 11:13-14 The envy also of Ephraim shall depart, and the adversaries of Judah shall be cut off: Ephraim shall not envy Judah, and Judah shall not vex Ephraim. But they shall fly upon the shoulders of the Philistines toward the west; they shall spoil them of the east together.

The above verse is the answer. We have not covered it as yet, but will do so in a later chapter.

---

[1] 1Jo 5:16 "If any man see his brother sin a sin which is not unto death, he shall ask, and he shall give him life for them that sin not unto death. There is a sin unto death: I do not say that he shall pray for it."

Timeless Covenant

CHAPTER 7

Do not abhor us, for thy name's sake,
do not disgrace the throne of thy glory:
remember, break not thy covenant with us.

JER 14:21

How can the Jewish people be one of the Two Witnesses of the Christian Era? Can they be one of God's witnesses and still be lost? Since "there is no other name under heaven, given among men, whereby ye must be saved" (Act 4:12), and they don't recognize Jesus as their Messiah, what has been the spiritual condition of the Jewish people during the Christian Era? Well, first of all, were the Jews ever really saved as we understand it? Were Old Testament saints "born again" like New Testament Christians are? There are some dispensational and covenantal theologians who would argue the point, so let's bring some Scripture to bear on the issue.

In His discussion with Nicodemus, recorded in John 3, Jesus put a name to what happens in the human heart when we first turn to the Lord. He called it being "born again." When Jesus talked with Nicodemus, the cross was still in His future, yet right here He made a doctrinal statement that many think applies only to the Church:[1]

> JOH 3:3,10 Jesus answered and said unto him, Verily, verily, I say unto thee, Except a man be born again, he cannot see the kingdom of God ... Art thou a master of Israel, and knowest not these things?

Jesus had not yet gone to the cross, and Nicodemus was still under the Levitical code. The Church was still in the

---

[1] Joh 3:3, 3:7 and 1Pe 1:23 are the only verses in the Bible where this experience is so named.

future, yet the Lord expected Nicodemus to know what being born again was all about. Now how could Nicodemus possibly be expected to understand the born-again principle before Jesus died on the cross? He could only have understood it if Old Testament believers *could* be born again before the cross. Nicodemus should have known, as did a scribe of his own time, that it wasn't correct doctrine, but a changed heart that resulted in salvation:

> Mar 12:32-33 And the scribe said unto him, Well, Master, thou hast said the truth: for there is one God; and there is none other but he: And to love him with all the heart, and with all the understanding, and with all the soul, and with all the strength, to love his neighbour as himself, is more than all whole burnt offerings and sacrifices.

The Old Testament is full of verses which declare that faith, rather than sacrifice, is the central aspect of salvation.[1] The whole 11th chapter of Hebrews teaches that Old Testament saints were saved by faith. They were not justified by the Levitical code, nor by the deeds of the law. Old Testament believers were given a changed heart before the cross, were born again, just like Christians are after the cross. This is a major issue in some churches, so please make an effort to understand the argument. It will be important to your spiritual well-being, as well as aid you in your future comprehension of the Bible.

Since Jesus said, "Except a man be born again he cannot see the kingdom of heaven," Noah, Abraham, Moses, David, Elijah, Job, Daniel, and the rest of the great Old Testament saints had to be born again, or we will not see them in Heaven. We saw Moses and Elijah, in their glorified bodies, on

---

[1] Here are four of many Old Testament verses which stress faith unto salvation above ritualistic observance:

Gen 15:6 And he believed in the LORD; and he counted it to him for righteousness.

Hab 2:4 Behold, his soul which is lifted up is not upright in him: but the just shall live by his faith.

Psa 51:16-17 For thou desirest not sacrifice; else would I give it: thou delightest not in burnt offering. The sacrifices of God are a broken spirit: a broken and a contrite heart, O God, thou wilt not despise.

Mic 6:8 . . . what doth the LORD require of thee, but to do justly, and to love mercy, and to walk humbly with thy God?

the Mount of Transfiguration, before the cross, so we can prove they were born again, unless we wish to believe that God would permit His glory to radiate from the faces of the unsaved. Obviously, those elder brethren had changed hearts, and a changed heart is what being born again is all about.

> Eze 36:26 A new heart also will I give you, and a new spirit will I put within you: and I will take away the stony heart out of your flesh, and I will give you an heart of flesh.

Old Testament or New, there is no difference in how a soul is born again. The only difference is doctrine, and doctrine is determined by how the Lord willed to reveal Himself to man at a given time. Old Testament saints and Christians have different doctrines, but the method of salvation is the same. True saints have always been born again "by grace through faith," regardless of the era in which they lived.

> 1Co 10:1-4 I would not that ye should be ignorant, how that all our fathers were under the cloud, and all passed through the sea. And were all baptized unto Moses in the cloud and in the sea; And did all eat the same spiritual meat; **And did all drink the same spiritual drink: for they drank of that spiritual Rock that followed them: and that Rock was Christ.**

We said all that to get to this: When Jesus went to the cross, there were Old Testament, believing Jews, spread throughout the whole known world. They were in Africa, Spain, England, and even as far away as India. If they were true believers, they must have been born again. Elect, just like you and I are (Rom 11:28). Many of them must have been unaware of Jesus' ministry, death, and resurrection.

So here is the question: Did those dispersed Jews lose their salvation the moment Jesus went to the cross and they suddenly and unknowingly came into the Christian Era? If we believe that, then we are saying a man is saved by his doctrine, rather than by his heart condition. Rom 11:28 states, ". . . as touching the election, they [*the Jews*] are beloved for the father's sakes."

If a Jew, under God's covenants given to him through the patriarchs and prophets, could be saved by faith in his coming Messiah for one millisecond into the Christian Era, then a Jew *in that same spiritual condition* can be saved under those same covenants a thousand, or even 1900 years later.

The only way that would not be true is if salvation is based upon where we are positioned in history, and the correctness of our doctrine. Numerous times in the Old Testament the Lord speaks of His everlasting covenant with the children of Israel, including the following verses:[1]

> Gen7:7 And I will establish my covenant between me and thee and thy seed after thee in their generations for an everlasting covenant, to be a God unto thee, and to thy seed after thee.

> Psa 105:8-10 He hath remembered his covenant for ever, the word which he commanded to a thousand generations . . . And confirmed the same unto Jacob for a law, and to Israel for an everlasting covenant.

If faith in God's Old Testament covenant was good enough to save Moses and Elijah, then it is good enough to save a Jew today *if* -- and it is a big *if* -- the Holy Spirit has not revealed to that Jew that Y'shua is his Messiah.[2] When the Holy Spirit does so, the Jew needs to recognize God's Son as his Messiah and Lord just as we do.[3]

---

[1] Not for a second is the author suggesting some sort of Jewish universalism. It was only a remnant who had not bowed the knee to Baal in Elijah's time, and there is no reason to believe it is more than a remnant today. Not all those who claim to be Jews have the circumcision of the heart any more than all those who go to church are Christians.

[2] Some have suggested that it is impossible for a Jew in this age not to know about Jesus. If we were dealing in the natural realm, the author would agree, but we are not. God blinded their spiritual eyes (Rom 11:8), and only He can cause them to see again! If the Lord blinded their eyes during the Christian Era so that they would be lost, then He broke faith with the Patriarchs, and His many covenants to Israel are null and void. Num 23:19 states, "God is not a man, that he should lie; neither the son of man, that he should repent: hath he said, and shall he not do it? or hath he spoken, and shall he not make it good?"

[3] It is no easier to tell if a Jew is saved than it is to tell the spiritual condition of a Gentile. But, if the Holy Spirit reveals to a Jew that Jesus is his Messiah, he is no longer blind. If a Jew then rejects the Lord, he is as lost as any Gentile who does. A witness to the Jews is as necessary as it is for the Gentile. If a Jew already has the circumcision of the heart (Rom 2:28-29), and the Holy Spirit takes the veil away, the believing Jew WILL turn to Y'shua. Why? Because, the same Spirit that takes the veil away will point him straight to God's Son. Only the Lord knows the heart condition, (1Sa 16:7).

So is it possible for a Jew in this information age to be unaware that Y'shua[1] is his Messiah? Jesus gave us a marvelous parable in Luke which explains it very clearly:

> Luk 5:33-39 (*excerpts*) And they said unto him, Why do the disciples of John fast often, and make prayers, and likewise the disciples of the Pharisees; but thine eat and drink? And he said unto them, Can ye make the children of the bridechamber fast, while the bridegroom is with them?. . . And he spake also a parable unto them; No man putteth a piece of a new garment upon an old; if otherwise, then both the new maketh a rent, and the piece that was taken out of the new agreeth not with the old. And no man putteth new wine into old bottles; else the new wine will burst the bottles, and be spilled, and the bottles shall perish. But new wine must be put into new bottles; and both are preserved.

The Pharisees were questioning why the disciples did not keep the Jewish traditions. Jesus replied that the children of the bridegroom did not fast while the bridegroom was present, speaking of Himself and the disciples. He then likened the gospel to new wine, and the Jews to old wineskins. Jesus went on to say that He would not put the new wine of the gospel into the old wineskins of the Jewish people, lest He destroy them both. Jesus concludes with the categorical statement that He did not will for the old bottles to perish, so new wine was put in new wineskins, *and both are preserved*. That is a mystery indeed. How can a Jew be preserved if he does not understand the gospel? Let's see how God accomplished it. He promised Moses He would:

> Lev 26:33-45 (*excerpts*) I will scatter you among the heathen, and will draw out a sword after you . . . And they that are left of you shall pine away in their iniquity in your enemies' lands . . . And yet for all that, when they be in the land of their enemies, I will not cast them away, neither will I abhor them, to destroy them utterly, and to break my covenant with them: for I am the LORD their God . . But I will for their sakes remember the covenant of their ancestors, whom I brought forth out of the land of Egypt in the sight of the heathen, that I might be their God: I am the LORD.

---

[1] Strong's No. H3091. Yehowshuwa', yeh-ho-shoo'-ah; or Yehowshu'a, yeh-ho-shoo'-ah; from H3068 and H3467; Jehovah-saved; Jehoshua (i.e. Joshua), the Jewish leader: Jehoshua, Jehoshuah, Joshua. Compare H1954, H3442. Transliterated into Greek as Jesus, many Jews spell His name in the abbreviated Hebrew form of Y'shua or Yeshua.

ELECTION FOR BOTH COVENANTS

Throughout the centuries, the Holy Spirit has kept the Jew under the law (2Co 3:14, Gal 5:2-3). As stated before, for the Jew, the Old Testament is all the Bible there is. To him, the Messiah is still to come, and oh, how he longs for His appearance, just as we do. The Jew believes in Him and trusts in Him because of the promises of God given to him in the Old Testament. Can his faith be in vain? The Bible tells us, if we only have ears to hear it:

> Rom 11:8-11 (According as it is written, God hath given them the spirit of slumber, eyes that they should not see, and ears that they should not hear;) unto this day. I say then, Have they stumbled that they should fall? God forbid: but *rather* through their fall salvation *is come* unto the Gentiles, for to provoke them to jealousy.

> Rom 11:24-25 For if thou [*the Gentile church*] wert cut out of the olive tree which is wild by nature, and wert grafted contrary to nature into a good olive tree [*the Jews*]: how much more shall these, which be the natural *branches,* be grafted into their own olive tree? For I would not, brethren, that ye [*Gentiles*] should be ignorant of this mystery, lest ye should be wise in your own conceits; that blindness in part is happened to Israel, until the fulness of the Gentiles be come in.

> Rom 11:28-29 As concerning the gospel, *they* [*the Jews*] *are* enemies for your sakes: but as touching the election,[1] *they* [*the Jews*] *are* beloved for the fathers' sakes. For the gifts and calling of God *are* without repentance. [*are irrevocable, NASB*]

Note the two groups of people in those verses: *We* and *They.* Language is meant to communicate, and in no language known to man are *we* and *they* the same group of people. These are two distinctly different bodies of people. From context, these two groups are the Jewish people and the Gentile church. According to Rom 11:28, one of these two groups is the enemy of the Gospel. The Church is not the enemy of the Gospel, so the other group must be, and that other group is the Jewish people.

But despite their enmity to the truth of the gospel, wonder of wonders, they are still elect. Hear that: the Jews are still

---

[1] Strong's No. 1589. ekloge, ek-log-ay'; from G1586; (divine) selection: chosen, election.

elect. That is not a suppositional doctrine; Rom 11:28-29 states they are still elect, and the following verses affirm it:

> Rom 11:30-32   For as ye [*the Gentiles*] in times past have not believed God, yet have now obtained mercy through their [*the Jews*] unbelief: Even so have these [*Jews*] also now not believed, that through your mercy [*shown to the Gentiles*] they [*the Jews*] also may obtain mercy. For God hath concluded them all [*both Jews and Gentiles*] in unbelief, that he might have mercy upon all.

Those Scriptures lead us to this point: If the Church is "elect," and Israel is "elect," wherein lies the difference between us? Only in our historic position, and the accuracy of our doctrine (*neither of which saves us*). The Old Testament saints knew their Messiah was coming, even though they did not know who He was going to be. They were born again, even though they did not know His identity. They were saved by faith in the same Messiah that you and I are, and not by their doctrine. Praise God we are not saved because our doctrines are perfect, but because Jesus is the perfect atonement for our sins, and His blood is perfect even for the Jew who does not know His name.

Over the years, I have watched people dance all around Rom 11:24-32. I know several brethren who even heatedly declare, "I don't know what those verses mean, but they certainly don't mean what they say," thus putting the doctrines of men above the Word of God. Why not believe just what these verses say? Is the Bible the Word of God, or isn't it? I fear our traditions are so firmly entrenched that only a major disaster, or the return of the Lord, will change them. Throughout the Christian Era, we have been trying to make Gentiles out of Jews, but we have it backwards. Israel was not grafted into the Church; the Church was grafted into Israel.

Brethren, in Rom 11:25, we were commanded not to become "wise in our own conceits" toward the Jews because we were given the gospel while they were not. We went ahead and got arrogant anyway, and it has resulted in our blindness, too. We've been thinking all along that we had it all, while the Jews were without hope. It isn't so, but unless we permit the Holy Spirit to take the scales from our eyes, we will remain hopelessly blinded to God's overall plan.

BLINDNESS UPON ALL

Looking at the big picture, why did the Lord decree a spiritual blindness upon the Jews? If the Jewish people had come to know Jesus as their Messiah, they would have been absorbed into the Church, and Jews would have disappeared from the face of the earth. That doesn't sound so bad, does it? How significant can that be?

> *If the Jewish nation had accepted Y'shua as their Messiah, then Israel, as a separate people, would have ceased to be, and the host of Old and New Testament prophecies we have been looking at in this book could never have been fulfilled.*

The fulfillment of every prophecy we have discussed so far, plus a hundred more, depended upon the Jews not knowing that Jesus is the Messiah! Like the Lord said to Habakkuk, if God had told us what He was going to do in advance, we still wouldn't have believed Him.

But despite their not recognizing God's dying Son as their Messiah, the Lord put His merciful hand over the eyes of His beloved people Israel, and saved them. Do we even begin to grasp the caring and forgiving nature of our Heavenly Father? All He had to do for them to be lost was simply nothing . . . just nothing. Instead of that, He blinded them so they could not sin against a knowledge of the truth.[1] Oh, what it has cost those precious people. What sufferings they have endured throughout the centuries because of their inability to see the Savior who went to the cross for them.[2] Spiritually, they suffer still, looking dimly ahead, through darkened Old Testament eyes, for the coming of their beloved Messiah.

> Rom 11:33-36 O the depth of the riches both of the wisdom and knowledge of God! how unsearchable are his judgments, and his

---

[1] Heb 10:26 For if we sin wilfully after that we have received the knowledge of the truth, there remaineth no more sacrifice for sins, But a certain fearful looking for of judgment and fiery indignation, which shall devour the adversaries.

[2] Certainly many of the Pharisees rejected the Lord so as to be lost, but not all. Nicodemus and Joseph of Arimathea are notable exceptions. Nor would it surprise the author to see Gamaliel in Heaven. He defended the brethren in Acts 5:37-39, and that he feared the Lord is unquestionable.

ways past finding out! For who hath known the mind of the Lord? or who hath been his counsellor? Or who hath first given to him, and it shall be recompensed unto him again? For of him, and through him, and to him, are all things: to whom be glory for ever. Amen.

The Lord desires a more open heart from the Church than we have yet displayed. He wants us to understand the Jews so we can be careful and loving to our brethren afar-off, moving them to jealousy so they will come to His Son.

However, most Jews believe that Christians hate them. They may not show it up front, but down inside the Jews believe it, and not without good reason. Terrible things have been done to Jews in the name of Jesus. It is a deplorable fact that so-called Christians have persecuted the Jews throughout the centuries, and it continues to this very day in some parts of the world. As a glaring example, Nazi Germany's extermination efforts were based on the pretext that Jews killed Jesus. Result: the Church reinforced the Jew's blindness. We mistreated the Jews until they didn't want to accept the Lord and then blamed them because they didn't. Unless we show the Jews that we love and understand them, we have little hope of leading them to God's Son.

Brethren, our spiritual eyes have been dulled. Don't you see that you and I killed Jesus? Jesus died because you and I sinned. When Jesus hung on the cross, He looked down through time and saw your sins and mine. When He said, "Father forgive them, for they know not what they do," He was speaking of your sins and mine for which He died.

Blindness is upon Israel until the fullness of the Gentiles is come in (Rom 11:25). Maybe that day is at hand because many thousands of Jews are now turning to the Lord. But the Lord has yet to take the scales from the eyes of all, and some Jews still look to Moses and the prophets.

In Heb 7:1-9, we read about Abraham giving tithes to Melchizedek (the Lord Jesus). Father Abraham did so for all those who would proceed from his loins: for his children throughout all generations to come (Heb 7:1-10). Now what was Melchizedek's response to Abraham? He set a table before him, and on that table, bread and wine (Gen 14:17-20). Bread and wine . . . the same communion that Jesus served the disciples at the last supper. Oh, the richness of the foreknowledge of God. Do we have eyes to see what the Lord Jesus did through Abraham, and for his physical seed forever? As Abraham gave tithes for the children of Israel yet to be born, so, in like manner, Jesus (as Melchizedek) had communion with all the children of Israel yet to be born, and our God is a covenant-keeping God.[1]

The verses we have studied so far show us three things:

1. How close we are to the return of the Lord.

2. That most of Bible prophecy has already been fulfilled.

3. That the Jews have been God's partners with the Church throughout the Christian Era. They have been the keepers of the oracles of God (Rom 3:2).

There is a lot more scriptural support for the end-time concepts we have studied so far. Some of it is hidden away in the Hebrew and Aramaic words: *iddan* and *moadah*. Twice in Daniel, those words are used in a prophetic sense.

---

[1] Most denominations believe that the Jews of the Christian Era who are blind to the fact that Jesus is their Savior are lost. Nonetheless, the scriptural evidence to the contrary is so strong that the author wonders how the Church has been able to champion that position.

Time, Times, & a Half

CHAPTER 8

But if ye turn unto me,
and keep my commandments, and do them;
though there were of you cast out
unto the uttermost part of the heaven,
yet will I gather them from thence,
and will bring them unto the place
that I have chosen to set my name there.

NEH 1:9

So far, all prophetic days have been shown to be years. But day=years are not the only kind of prophetic time in the Bible. Twice in Daniel, and once in Revelation, there is the expression "time, times, and half a time." We will look at the times in Daniel first:

> Dan 7:25 And he shall speak great words against the most High, and shall wear out the saints of the most High, and think to change times and laws: and they shall be given into his hand until a time and times and the dividing of time.

> Dan 12:7 And I heard the man clothed in linen, which was upon the waters of the river, when he held up his right hand and his left hand unto heaven, and sware by him that liveth for ever that it shall be for a time, times, and an half; and when he shall have accomplished to scatter the power of the holy people, all these things shall be finished.

What can *time* mean? Is a *time* a year like the day=years? One thing is for sure: a *time* is not a year. Here is how we can know it, for sure. God gave us "a day for a year." He did not give us a *time* for a year.

The Hebrew word for day is *yom*. The Hebrew and High Syriac words for *time* as used in Dan 7:25 and 12:7 are *iddan* and *moadah*.[1] Surely, the creator of the universe knows the difference between iddan, moadah, and yom. Of course, and He gave us a yom for a year, not an iddan or moadah for a year. So *iddan* (time), and *moadah* (time), probably mean something else. Lets call these time durations "X."

What about the cryptic way in which these words are used, "time, times, and the dividing of a time?" How many "times" are we dealing with here? As is true of English, Hebrew is full of idiomatic language. For instance, the Hebrew idiom "cut off" means to kill. "Ate the pieces of" means to bring malicious accusations against, and so on. Can "time, times, and the dividing of a time" also be an idiom? Let's see if we can find Scriptural support for that hypothesis:

> Job 33:14 For God speaketh once, yea twice, yet man perceiveth it not.

> Job 40:5 Once have I spoken; but I will not answer: yea, twice; but I will proceed no further.

> Psa 62:11 God hath spoken once; twice have I heard this; that power belongeth unto God.

Here we see the same idiomatic style. The words are different, but the form is the same. *Once* is one, and *twice* is only one more, for a total of two: 1+1=2. That's just one of many Hebrew idioms in the Old Testament. A singular *one* followed by a plural *twice* is only two. In the same way, a singular *time* followed by a plural *times* might be only two. Only two! If the Lord had said, "time, yea times" we might have seen it right away.

Now let's employ the same idiomatic language to interpret time, times, and half a time. *Time* = one; *times* = one more, for a total of two times. Add a *half a time* and we have two and a

---

[1] DAY= H3117. yowm, yome: from an unused root mean. to be hot; a day (as the warm hours), whether lit. (from sunrise to sunset, or from one sunset to the next. TIME= H5732. 'iddan, (Chaldean), id-dawn': from a root corresponding. to that of H5708; a set time. TIME= H4150. mow'ed, mo-ade'; or mo'ed mo-ade'; or (feminine) mow'adah (H2 Chron. 8 :13), mo-aw-daw': from H3259; prop. an appointment, i.e. a fixed time or season.

half times, or 1+1+½=2½.[1] That is pretty simple, isn't it? So why have people been saying that "time, times, and half a time" are three and a half years? Who knows? Probably because it fits the Seven-Year Great Tribulation scheme so well. Students of Hebrew have told me that their grammar does not support 3½ as a correct translation of that idiom.

All right, so "time, times, and half a time" are two and a half times. But if a time isn't a year, how long is it? Daniel understood day=years, but he didn't understand *time*. Why? Because day=years were defined for him in the Old Testament Scriptures. Time was not. In fact, *time* was not defined until late in the New Testament epistles:

> 2Pe 3:8 But, beloved, be not ignorant of this one thing, that one day [*Greek word, hemera*] is with the Lord as a thousand years, and a thousand years as one day.

On the surface that doesn't look like much of a definition for time, does it? It certainly doesn't work in English. But something is wrong here. God has already given us a definition for day. He has already told us a day is a year. Is the Lord changing His definition of prophetic days here?

No, we can prove that the day=year interpretation is still in force by the 42 months and 1260 days of Revelation 11 and 12. So what we have here in 2Pe 3:8 is this: an "X" with the Lord is as a thousand years, and a thousand years is as an "X." How do we solve for "X"? By doing a word study in Greek, the original language of the New Testament.

The Greek word translated "day" in 2Pe 3:8 is *hemera*, (ἡμέρα).[2] *Hemera* is an ambiguous word sometimes translated: period, moment, season, year, and, guess what . . . *Time*. So what is the correct translation here? Well, in Greek, context often determines translation. But in the verse above, the correct translation cannot be established with certainty because context does not suggest the correct word. Under-

---

[1] Sorry about this 1+1 stuff. I know I am getting down on the kindergarten level, but this seems to be the easiest way to explain it.

[2] Strong's No. G2520. hemera, hay-mer'-ah: feminine. (with G5610 implied) of a der. of hemai (to sit; akin to the base of G1476) several days were usually reckoned by the Jews as inclusive of the parts of both extremes; fig. a period (always defined more or less clearly by the context): age, + always, forever, judgment, (day) time, while, years.

standably, the translators went with "day," which is the most common usage, but that may not be correct. *Hemera* is translated *time* in four verses in the KJV, and twelve in the NASB. So *time* is a very acceptable translation. Is it possible that the duration of "X" is a thousand years?

If *time* is a thousand years, and we have 2½ of them, then "time, times, and half times" could be 2500 years. Thus far, we have only a supposition. But that is all we had for day=years until we started plugging them into history. Let's see if there is an exact 2500 year historic fit that fulfills the Bible's description of these *times* right to the year.

After Nebuchadnezzar of Babylon died in 562BC, three of his sons ruled for a couple of years each. The kingdom was very unstable. Daniel must have been walking on eggs to avoid the plots and political intrigue in the Babylonian court. Though the archives don't tell us about it, reading about those Middle Eastern empires from secular sources gives us a picture of what was going on there. Heads must have been rolling all over the place. The Lord protected our brother Daniel in that dangerous environment. Many of his fellow rulers in Babylon hated him and plotted his death (Dan 6:4-13).

Then in 555BC, a nephew of Nebuchadnezzar seized the throne. His name was Nabonidus, and he proved to be an able ruler. However, he couldn't stomach the Babylonian court life, so three years later, in 552, he chose a close relative, Belshazzar, to rule the empire for him. Then Nabonidus spent the rest of his life wandering around Arabia, doing archeological digs and writing poetry.[1]

During these turbulent times, the Lord gave Daniel the vision of four great beasts coming up out of the sea.[2] Scripture tells us when this was to the year, "In the 1st year of Belshazzar" (Dan 7:1). In pictorial language, the vision then

---

[1] To date, there is no direct archeological evidence for 552BC being the 1st year of the Belshazzar's regency. However, that date can supported by correlating evidence about the reign of Nabonidus. John Walvoord, *The Key to Prophetic Revelation* (Chicago, Moody Press, 1971) p. 115 accepts a 553BC Belshazzar dating, and most authorities recognize a one to three year ambiguity in Old Testament dating.

[2] The sea is the peoples of the Earth (Rev 17:15): "The waters which thou sawest . . . are peoples, and multitudes, and nations, and tongues."

describes the four great kingdoms that were to rule in the
Holy Land during the time of the Gentiles. At the end of that
prophecy, the Lord tells Daniel about *times*:

> Dan 7:25 And he shall speak great words against the Most High
> and shall wear out the saints of the most High, and think to change
> times and laws: and they shall be given into his hand until a time
> and times and the dividing of time.

Sometimes our doctrine gets messed up because we don't
think about to whom the Lord is speaking, and when. In this
instance, the Lord is speaking to Daniel in 552BC. In Daniel's
day, who spoke out against God? Then, as now, Satan speaks
out against God. Who were the saints in Daniel's time? The
Jews, of course. So from 552BC, when this prophecy was given,
the Lord is telling Daniel that the Jews would be under satanically controlled Gentile powers for two and a half times, or
possibly 2500 years. From Daniel's time, the Holy Land would be
ruled by strangers far into the future. Let's run that up and
down the framework of history and see what it fits. Since the
definition for time was given in the New Testament, we don't
even need to convert from Hebrew to solar years to fit our
calendar. A simple subtraction will do just fine:

2500 - 552BC = 1948AD, and new Israel!

GRAPH NUMBER 10

Time, Times & ½ a Time, Dan 7:25

552BC, 1st Year of Belshazzar	New Israel, 1948AD

Exactly 2500 years

Dan 7:25 And he shall speak *great* words against the most High, and shall
wear out the saints of the most High, and think to change times and laws:
and they shall be given into his hand until a time and times and the
dividing of time.

Just a lucky hit? If that is not the correct interpretation,
then it has to be one of the most remarkable coincidences in

all of recorded history. It fits Scripture and history, right to the year. But remarkable as that fulfillment of prophecy may be, we would still have only a theory if it was the only 2500 year *time* period that fit antiquity. The Lord is so kind. When He takes the blinders off, He gives enough proof for us to know for sure that we are headed in the right direction.

At the end of Daniel's prophetic ministry, the Lord gave him another vision containing *times*. This prophecy also includes the 1290 days which led us to understand that the Dome of the Rock is the Abomination that makes Desolate. The full story of this later vision is recorded in the 10th through the 12th chapters of Daniel. This vision may be dated to the third year of Cyrus the Persian, or 533BC:

> Dan 10:1 In the third year of Cyrus king of Persia a thing was revealed unto Daniel, whose name was called Belteshazzar . . .

Daniel was a very old man now. He knew he was going to be with the Lord soon. The temple mount had been abandoned and sacrifices abolished during his own lifetime. He knew that an Abomination of Desolation was going to stand on that beloved temple mount in less than 1300 years. Would the Jews ever control Jerusalem again? Of course. Many Old Testament Scriptures told him so. But when? The Lord told him, right to the year, but then hid it so that no one would know when that time would be, until it happened:

> Dan 12:7 And I heard the man clothed in linen, which was upon the waters of the river, when he held up his right hand and his left hand unto heaven, and sware by him that liveth for ever that it shall be for a time, times, and half; and when he shall have accomplished to scatter the power of the holy people, all these things shall be finished.

Cyrus had given a decree that would permit the Jews to return to their homeland three years earlier. They had begun their trek back to the Holy land, and soon they would begin to build the 2nd temple. That temple stood until 70AD, when the Jews were driven from the land again. But God knew the end of this second dispersion, too. He knew that at the end of it, the Jews would return to the Holy Land one more time and again control Jerusalem. When was the vision given? In 533BC, the third year of Cyrus. So this "time times, and half a time" should begin in the third year of Cyrus:

2500 - 533BC = 1967AD and Jerusalem freed!

The Lord even worded the last phrase of that prophecy in such a way that it would be difficult to miss His intent: ". . . and when he shall have accomplished to scatter [*or shatter, NASB*] the power of the holy people, all these things shall be finished." As of 1967AD, His holy people, the Jews, were no longer scattered among the Gentiles. They have their nation again, and their power is shattered no longer.

GRAPH NUMBER 11

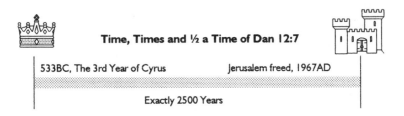

Time, Times and ½ a Time of Dan 12:7

533BC, The 3rd Year of Cyrus	Jerusalem freed, 1967AD

Exactly 2500 Years

Dan 12:7 And I heard the man clothed in linen, which *was* upon the waters of the river, when he held up his right hand and his left hand unto heaven, and sware by him that liveth for ever that *it shall be* for a time, times, and an half; and when he shall have accomplished to scatter the power of the holy people, all these *things* shall be finished.

Note: When the Jews again took control of Jerusalem in 1967, the "scattering of the power of the holy people" was over. Daniel was a prophet to the time of the Gentiles. Daniel's prophecies were, in the main, fulfilled in 1967AD. This does not include the last half of Dan 8, which directly states that it is a vision of "the ultimate time of the end."

A SEASON AND A TIME

As additional evidence, there is a third *time* in Daniel (unnoticed at first) which proves that *time* should be understood as a thousand years. The four beasts of Daniel 7 are generally understood by the Church to be the great Gentile empires that would rule in the Holy Land during the time of the Gentiles. The fourth beast, Rome, fell in 476AD (more on this last empire in a later chapter). The Mohammedans came on the scene soon after. But the Mohammedans were not granted world dominion like the empires which came before them; however, the Lord did permit them to rule in the Holy Land for a "season and a time":

> Dan 7:11-12 I beheld *even* till the beast [*Rome*] was slain, and his body destroyed, and given to the burning flame. As concerning the rest of the beasts, they had their dominion taken away: yet their lives were prolonged for a season and time.

If time is 1000 years, and there are four seasons, then a season of time would be about 250 years. 1000+250=1250. Remembering that a season is not an exact number and could fluctuate a week or two either way, this "season and time" fits history well, indeed.

> *New Israel became a nation a "Season and Time,"*
> *(1260 years) after the Dome of the Rock was built.*

We have seen three examples, from Daniel alone, of *time* fitting history, when it is understood to be a thousand years. Consequently, it is unrealistic to hold that prophetic *times* could mean anything else.

Brethren, I'll accept a 1000-year "time" fit as a coincidence once, but not three times. These solutions using 1000 years for "X" can be pinned, right to the year, to three different incidents which have pin dates in our own time.[1] They were not fulfilled from events that just happened last week, either. They are tied to three events in antiquity. That is a statistical impossibility! So we no longer have just a theory; we have a scripturally and historically supportable doctrine.

In *times* and day=years, we have a solid empirical argument, a prophetic jigsaw puzzle in which all the pieces interlock with each other. We can argue about the placement, color, or shape of each piece, but when the whole puzzle is put together, we can stand back and view a completed picture. A prophetic picture, in which all the pieces fit perfectly, is not so easy to discredit. If it is not of God, it will crumble back into its original pieces on its own; however, if it

---

[1] There is a further message in Dan 12:7: "all these things shall be finished" shows that all events predicted in Daniel's last vision, including "Michael standing up," were fulfilled by 1967. This brings to an end the contention that Dan 11:36-45 is about some future tribulation period or a coming antichrist. These verses are all fulfilled.

is of God, it will remain and flourish, no matter who comes against it (Act 5:35-39).

These day=year and *time* prophecies are truly remarkable. They show the sovereignty of a timeless God over the affairs of men in a way that is difficult to dispute, and they do so over eons of time. Despite the best efforts of the enemy and the complexity of 2500 years of history, God not only fore-knew the events that would take place, but also sovereignly managed history in such a way that they would occur in His chosen location, at His chosen time, right to the year.

But as interesting as these times may be, the Lord did not put them in His Word just to make the Church feel good about itself when it finally understood them. The historic fulfillment of Daniel's *times* enables us to understand Revelation's *times*, and Revelation's *times* show us what happened to the ten tribes of northern Israel after Shalmaneser of Assyria dispersed them into Mesopotamia in 725-722BC, and knowing what happened to those ten tribes is of importance to the Remnant Church. Who and where are they? That story appears to be hidden in the folk religions of isolated tribes like the Karen, Yalu, Rengma, and Lahu.

One More Time

CHAPTER 9

They shall come with weeping,
and with supplications will I lead them:
I will cause them to walk
by the rivers of waters
in a straight way,
wherein they shall not stumble:
for I am a father to Israel,
and Ephraim is my firstborn.

JER 31:9

Deep in the mountainous interior of Irian Jaya, formerly Dutch New Guinea, there lives a tribe of natives called the Yalu. They were one of the most isolated peoples on the face of the earth yet they had a very formalized blood sacrificial system. They had a law of Ten Commandments called the *wene malalek* and a holy ground called an *osuwa*. That *osuwa* was surrounded by a stone wall. Any man not consecrated to the spirits of *kembu*, or any woman who trespassed on that ground, would be killed. Within the *osuwa* was a sacred building called the *kembu-vam*. It had two rooms, an outer room where the priests of *kembu* held ceremonies, and an inner room which held the sacred stone. The stone was never allowed to be moved by one man, but had to be carried by four men at its four corners. Pigs were slaughtered and roasted in the court outside the *kembu-vam*, and priests, with awesome ceremony, took pig fat into that holiest of rooms and anointed the sacred stone.[1]

---

[1]The foregoing account is from pages 76-80 of Don Richardson's *Lords of the Earth* (Ventura, CA Regal Books, 1977).

Though unbelievably corrupted, the parallels of the Yalu folk religion to the Levitical code are so inescapable that one has to ask: Where did they get all that?

In Burma, there was a tribe of people called the Karen who worshiped the God Y'wa. Their prophets declared that they once possessed a book of the law but had lost it many centuries before. Sacred songs passed down from generation to generation, reminded them of their lost law:

Omnipotent is Y'wa; Him have we not believed.
Y'wa created men anciently.
He has a perfect knowledge of all things.
Y'wa created men at the beginning.
The earth is the treading place for the feet of Y'wa.
And heaven is the place where He sits.
He sees all things and we are manifest to Him.

Y'wa formed the earth originally.
He appointed food and drink.
He appointed the "fruit of trial."
Mu-kaw-lee deceived two persons.
He causes them to eat of the fruit of the tree of trial.
They obeyed not; they believed not Y'wa . . .
They became subject to sickness, aging and death . . .

O children and grandchildren,
If we repent of our sins,
And cease to do evil - restraining our passions -
And pray to Y'wa. He will have mercy upon us again.
If Y'wa does not have mercy on us, there is no other one
*   who can.*
He who saves us is the only one - Y'wa.
O Children and grandchildren! Pray to Y'wa constantly.
By day and by night.[1]

Y'wa is just too close to Yahweh, the Hebrew name for God, to be coincidental. And what about the "fruit of trial" and prayer? Those traditions do not appear to be founded in the

---

[1] Don Richardson, *Eternity in Their Hearts* (Ventura, CA, Regal Books, 1981) pp.77-79, cites from *The Gospel in Burma,* Wylie, p. 6, and *The Karen Apostle*, Mason, p. 97-99.

New Testament Gospel, but upon a knowledge of Old Testament law. Again we have to ask: Where did they get all that?

The Lahu of northern Burma had a tradition that *Gui'Sha*, the Creator of all things, had given their forefathers His law written on rice cakes. The Rengma tribe in India believed that the Supreme Being gave His words to their forefathers written on animal skins *(which, by the way, is what the Mosaic law was written on)*. But according to their traditions, the forefathers of the Rengma people had been careless with the skins and dogs had eaten them.[1]

These examples are not unique. The native religions of almost every isolated people on earth contain haunting memories, in varying detail, of an earlier knowledge of the true God, or of His Law. So, once again we ask; where did all this knowledge come from? To find out, we may again need to go back into the history of the children of Israel.

Jacob, named Israel by the Lord, was Abraham's grandson. Jacob had twelve sons, among whom was Joseph, and those twelve men became the fathers of the twelve tribes of the nation of Israel. After the death of Jacob, Israel's twelve tribes remained in Egypt for 430 years. They fled Egypt in 1446BC, and were in the wilderness for another 40 years. After Joshua's conquest of Canaan, they lived in the Promised Land, under judges, for another 300 years. Then, during the judgeship of Samuel, the people demanded a king.

God first gave them Saul, then David, and with David began the line of kings through which Jesus would be born. But the kingdom remained unified for only two generations. If you read the account carefully, it appears that Solomon, the wisest man who ever lived, had a son who was really incapable. Rehoboam's decision to raise taxes caused a revolt, so during Rehoboam's reign the Davidic kingdom divided.

God separated the ten northern tribes from Judah and Benjamin, and the twelve tribes became two separate nations: Israel in the North, and Judah in the South. Jerusalem remained the capital of Judah and Samaria became the capital of Israel.

---

[1] Ibid pp. 85-91

Northern Israel was in continual rebellion to the Lord, putting itself in constant conflict with Judah and the other nations that surrounded them. Finally, in 748BC, Tiglath-pileser of Assyria made northern Israel a vassal state and took captives off to Assyria. In 725BC, Shalmaneser began a major deportation of Israel, and put Samaria under siege. Samaria itself fell in 722BC, and all the inhabitants of Israel were then relocated near the Caspean Sea (north of what is now Iran) and were never heard from again. This all happened just as Moses prophesied it would:

> Neh 1:8 Remember, I beseech thee, the word that thou command-edst thy servant Moses, saying, *If* ye transgress, I will scatter you abroad among the nations:

GRAPH NUMBER 12

Hiscory of the Ten Tribes

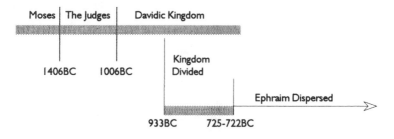

Lev 26:32-33 And I will bring the land into desolation: and your enemies which dwell therein shall be astonished at it. And I will scatter you among the heathen, and will draw out a sword after you: and your land shall be desolate, and your cities waste.

Why did God ever allow this to happen? Were the Israel-ites not part of God's chosen people? Didn't the everlasting covenant God made with Abraham include them? The prophet Isaiah saw what was going on around him and lamented:

> Isa 63:17 O LORD, why hast thou made us to err from thy ways, *and* hardened our heart from thy fear? Return for thy servants' sake, the tribes of thine inheritance.

The fall of northern Israel was not just an unfortunate accident in history. It was an integral part of God's eternal plan, and the Lord told His people about it in advance.

Just before Israel fell, the Lord sent the prophet Hosea to prepare His people for the calamity that was about to befall them. Hosea prophesied from about 750-722BC, and he was to the ten northern tribes what Daniel was to Judah. He foretold what would happen to Israel *after* the northern kingdom was taken into captivity. Read the prophet carefully, and you will see that the destruction of Israel and Samaria is fixed. It is going to fall to Assyria, no matter what. Hosea is not a call to repentance to save the northern kingdom. Instead, the prophet is describing the Lord's plan for the ten northern tribes *after* they disappeared.

In the verse below, we begin to see the everlasting love our Heavenly Father has for His wayward Israelites. While they were figuring ways to rebel against Him, God was putting a long-term plan in motion to save them: a plan spanning thousands of years. The following verse is in that setting. Israel is about to go into captivity when God tells them:

> Hos 1:10 Yet the number of the children of Israel shall be as the sand of the sea, which cannot be measured nor numbered; and it shall come to pass, that in the place where it was said unto them, Ye are not my people, there it shall be said unto them, Ye are the sons of the living God.

That is a paradoxical Scripture. Note the tense of the verb, "shall be." Shall be is future to when it was written. Israel is about to go into captivity never to be heard from again, and the Lord tells them that they are going to be numerous beyond count. Furthermore, He tells them that no one will know that they are His Israelites. Nonetheless, they will be called the sons of God. Isn't that mystifying?

> Hos 2:19-20 And I will betroth thee unto me for ever . . . I will even betroth thee unto me . . . and thou shalt know the LORD.

The Lord then declares that this lost and scattered people will be His bride, a bride whether they know it or not. Impossible from man's standpoint, but an accomplished fact from God's. But there is more. If we picture in our minds how seed was sown in the old days, we can also understand this unique Old Testament figure of the sower:

> Hos 2:23 And I will sow her [*Israel*] unto me in the earth; and I
> will have mercy upon her that had not obtained mercy; and I will
> say to them which were not my people, Thou art my people; and
> they shall say, Thou art my God.

Taking from his bag of grain, an ancient farmer would
cast seed evenly over every square foot of his field with a side-
wise motion of his arm. That is what the Lord did with Israel.
He scattered Israelites all over His great field, the earth, from
South Africa to China. Oh, my Brethren, God scattered the
seed of Israel over the whole world, from Terra del Fuego to
the tip of Siberia.

Descendants of the lost tribes of Israel are everywhere,
and God did not disperse them to lose them. In spite of their
scattering, the Lord declares that He will have mercy on them.
Here, at the end of the 20th century, it is only one hundred
generations since God made an everlasting covenant with
Abraham. Since the very hairs of our heads are numbered,
surely the Lord has no trouble remembering every one of
Israel's descendants. The prophet Amos spoke of this continuing covenant with a dispersed Israel, but it is in figurative
language:

> Amo 9:9 For, lo, I will command, and I will sift the house of Israel
> among all nations, like as *corn* is sifted in a sieve, yet shall not the
> least grain fall upon the earth.

Now let's put it together. The Creator of the universe loves
everyone who has ever lived on this earth. In eternity, He saw
and planned the history of the world and all its inhabitants.
God didn't have just a little local plan to deal with a few
Israelites during the Old Testament era. The Lord sees all
creation from eternity, and He is very good. Everything God
does is good; the Lord scattered the ten tribes of Israel abroad
for a good reason, and not just as a judgment upon His
wayward people. To see why Israel was dispersed, we need to
stand outside our 20th century mind-set and look back on
Earth's 6000 years of recorded history from God's eternal
perspective.

Remember, earlier in this chapter, how bits of the true
faith were spread among the primitive peoples of the world?
Apostate as northern Israel became, there were still men
within it who retained some knowledge of YHWH and of His
law. Taking a broad view of history, it appears that 700 years

before Jesus was born, the Lord spread the children of Israel over the whole earth for the express purpose of sharing the knowledge of the true God that they still held. To prepare the hearts of the Gentile peoples of the world for the coming of Messiah and the preaching of the Gospel. Now we can see the literal fulfillment of a verse that is usually spiritualized away:

> Rom 11:25-26 Blindness in part is happened to Israel, until the fulness of the Gentiles be come in. And so all Israel shall be saved.

What does that verse say? That the Gentiles have to come to the Lord Jesus if all Israel is going to be saved. But when the Gentiles do come to Jesus . . . *ALL Israel shall be saved!* Do you see what that verse could mean if taken literally? Despite the dispersion of the ten lost tribes, it could mean that God intended to save the Israelites all along, and in the Christian Era there is only one way the Lord would do so: by leading them, through His Spirit, to His Son the Lord Jesus. Everyone in the Church may not be a direct descendant of Jacob, but from Amos 9:9 and the other verses we have studied, I think it appropriate to believe that all the dispersed descendants of Israel will be saved and in the Church.

No matter where you are on this planet, if you have come to the Lord with a humble heart, it is very possible that you are a physical descendant of one of the lost tribes of Israel, and as such you could be the physical brother or sister of every other believer on Earth. Greetings, then, my brother or sister, in the name of our Lord and Savior, Jesus Christ.[1]

---

[1] Because parallels to prominent historic Israelite figures like Abraham, Moses, and David do not appear in most native religions, Don Richardson (author of *Eternity in their Hearts* and *Lords of the Earth*) questions whether these religions originally sprang from Hebrew roots. But those beliefs could have been passed down by oral tradition. Over the 2700 years that Israel has been dispersed, almost any amount of corruption or omission could have taken place. The importance of their great historic figures would have lessened as the memory of their deeds was lost in antiquity. If a culture barely remembers that it once had a "lost book," it seems unlikely to me that they would remember who wrote it, or what it contained.

EPHRAIM, WHERE ARE YOU?

Now we have discussed all Israel, but whatever happened to the tribe of Ephraim? Joseph had two sons, Manasseh and Ephraim. Our historic setting for the following quote is with them, in Egypt, at Israel's bedside 3700 years ago. The great seven-year famine is long past. Jacob is old and full of years. He is almost blind, and now he is about to die.

Jacob (Israel) called his twelve children around him to give them his final blessing. Joseph and his two sons were ushered in first. Joseph came in herding his boys before him, just as any parent would do when he wants you to notice his children:

> Gen 48:13 And Joseph took them both, Ephraim in his right hand toward Israel's left hand, and Manasseh in his left hand toward Israel's right hand, and brought them near unto him.
> 14-16 And Israel stretched out his right hand, and laid it upon Ephraim's head, who was the younger, and his left hand upon Manasseh's head, guiding his hands wittingly; for Manasseh was the firstborn. And he blessed Joseph, and said, God, before whom my fathers Abraham and Isaac did walk, the God which fed me all my life long unto this day, The Angel which redeemed me from all evil, bless the lads; and let my name be named on them, and the name of my fathers Abraham and Isaac; and let them grow into a multitude in the midst of the earth.
> 17-18 And when Joseph saw that his father laid his right hand upon the head of Ephraim, it displeased him: and he held up his father's hand, to remove it from Ephraim's head unto Manasseh's head. And Joseph said unto his father, Not so, my father: for this is the firstborn; put thy right hand upon his head.
> 19 And his father refused, and said, I know it, my son, I know it: he also shall become a people, and he also shall be great: but truly his younger brother shall be greater than he, and **his seed shall become a multitude of nations**.

So the half tribe of Manasseh would become a great people, but sometime in the future, the descendants of the half tribe of Ephraim would become a multitude of nations. From Old Testament history, Ephraim never did become a multitude of nations. So if they didn't do so *before* they were taken captive, Ephraim would have to do so *after* they were absorbed into the Gentile world. Obviously, the tribe of Ephraim is not out there claiming they're Israelites, so they must not even know who they are. Where has the Lord hidden them, and can it be proven biblically?

Ephraim, as the warrior tribe, was the most powerful in northern Israel. In fact, that tribe was so influential that Ephraim's name was sometimes used to refer to all ten of the northern tribes of Israel. When the Lord tells us He will not give Israel up, He makes special reference to Ephraim, so Ephraim probably has some special prophetic significance.

> Hos 11:8-10 (*excerpts*) How shall I give thee up, Ephraim? how shall I deliver thee, Israel . . . mine heart is turned within me, my repentings are kindled together . . . I will not execute the fierceness of mine anger, I will not return to destroy Ephraim: for I am God, and not man; the Holy One in the midst of thee . . . then the children shall tremble from the west.

They are going to return from the West, and since Ephraim's lands bordered the Mediterranean Sea, wherever they are, west would have to be west of the Holy Land itself!

> Hos 7:8 Ephraim, he hath mixed himself among the people; Ephraim is a cake not turned.

This is one of my favorite verses. The tribe of Ephraim is not only mixed among the nations, but it is also a bread not turned. What can that possibly mean? Well, the ancient Israelites made a pan bread that they baked one side at a time, something like the pancakes we make today. It takes time to bake one side, and more time to bake the other. The Lord in figurative language tells us, at the time of the prophet Hosea, that Ephraim's past is only half the story, one side of the bread. For the future, the cake will need to be turned over and baked on the other side. God is telling us in 725BC, that half of Ephraim's saga was still to be told and that it would take place after their dispersion:

> Hos 9:13-17 (*excerpts*) Ephraim . . . is planted in a pleasant place: but Ephraim shall bring forth his children to the murderer . . .[1] Oh LORD: what wilt thou give? give them a miscarrying womb and

---

[1] "Murderer" in Hebrew is: H2026. harag, haw-rag'; a prim. root; to smite with deadly intent: put to [death], make [slaughter], slay (-er), "Shall bring fourth his children to the murderer (slaughter)" In OT times, Israel "went forth to war." This is probably a figurative reference to warfare, to abortion, or to both.

dry breasts...yea, though they bring forth, yet will I slay even the beloved fruit of their womb . . . and they shall be wanderers among the nations.

Ephraim will be placed in a pleasant land, but in these terrible texts, we see that Ephraim's future would not always be pleasant. A warrior tribe still, they would be involved in foreign wars. Many of their children would die unborn. That would appear to be either abortion or miscarriages. So who and where are they?

REVELATION'S "TIME" IDENTIFIES EPHRAIM

The two "time, times, and half a time" in Daniel were 2500 years, so unless we find a solid scriptural reason to deny it, Revelation's "time, times, and half a time" would also be 2500 years. This 2500 years cannot be in our future because the time of the Gentiles is already fulfilled (Luk 21:24), and according to Luk 21:32, there can be only *one* generation (forty years or so) following the time of the Gentiles. We have to run these 2500 years up and down the fabric of world history to see where they fit.

> Rev 12:14 And to the woman [*Israel*] were given two wings of a great eagle, that she might fly into the wilderness, into her place, where she is nourished for a time, and times, and half a time, from the face of the serpent.

The last we heard of Ephraim was when they were taken captive into Assyria. Samaria, the capital of Israel, fell in 722BC.[1] But the major captivity took place about two years earlier, circa 724BC. Hosea states, "Ephraim is mixed with the nations," and his book was written just before the fall of Samaria. Could 724BC be when Revelation's "time, times, and half a time" began? If so, then this *time* should lead us to a significant year in the history of Ephraim:

2500 - 724BC = 1776AD...The United States became a nation!

Have we seen a temporary regathering of the ten tribes here in America? Is America the pleasant land where Ephraim

---

[1] The language of the verse does not tie us to the date of the destruction of Samaria. "Fly into the wilderness" speaks of the dispersion itself, and would be applicable for any time between 725-722BC.

is planted, and could the people who come from all over the world to seek freedom from tyranny and religious persecution be made up of the descendants of those missing tribes? It certainly appears likely.

GRAPH NUMBERS 13

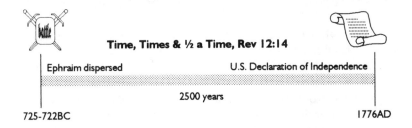

Time, Times & ½ a Time, Rev 12:14

Ephraim dispersed   U.S. Declaration of Independence

2500 years

725-722BC   1776AD

Deu 4:27 And the LORD shall scatter you among the nations, and ye shall be left few in number among the heathen, whither the LORD shall lead you.

Hos 2:15-16 And I will give her vineyards from thence, and the valley of Achor for a door of hope: and she shall sing there, as in the days of her youth, and as in the day when she came up out of the land of Egypt. And it shall be at that day, saith the LORD, that thou shalt call me Ishi; and shalt call me no more Baali.

Note: *Ishi* is Hebrew for husband, *Baali* is Hebrew for master. In the New Testament, the Church has a bride-bridegroom relationship with the Lord.

For years people have been looking for the United States in prophecy. Now that we have found some solid evidence that this nation could contain remnants of Ephraim and the ten lost tribes of Israel, do you suppose anyone will want to believe it? Not on your life. We would rather hang in there with the Seven-Year Tribulation view for which there is *no* biblical or historic evidence whatsoever. But, unless we can think of some other incident of major prophetic importance that took place on or near 1776, the United States becoming a nation is probably what that prophecy is all about. That makes North America and the United States the pleasant and protected land where the Lord hid Ephraim (Hos 9:13).

THE DISPERSION

How some of the children of the ten lost tribes migrated to Europe is a story recorded by others.[1] Suffice to say that the heraldic symbols used by the great houses of Europe have their roots in the titles that Jacob gave his twelve sons. If you question that, ask any authority on heraldry.[2] Those coats of arms that people so proudly hang on their walls are straight out of Gen 49:1-27.

Throughout the Christian Era, the true saints of God were hounded all over Europe. The chronicles of the oppression of the true Church during the middle ages have to be read to be believed. Fox's *Book of Martyrs*, Thielman van Braght's *Martyr's Mirror* (the Anabaptist record), and Broadbent's *The Pilgrim Church* record the sufferings of our forefathers in detail. The true Christians had no settled home in any land, and their very lives were continually at risk. They wandered from place to place or were in hiding from persecution. They had a symbolic valley of Achor *(Achor means trouble)* throughout the middle ages. But the Lord told us it would be like that:

> Heb 13:13-14 Let us go forth therefore unto him without the camp, bearing his reproach. For here have we no continuing city, but we seek one to come.

Then they cried unto the Lord and the Lord hid them from their persecutors and planted them in a very pleasant land. It was rich and fruitful and flowing with milk and honey. The New World was just such a land, and the United States was

---

[1] To avoid any suggestion that the author is using material which is conjectural or lacks red-letter accreditation, only common historic knowledge and the Bible itself were used to support the conclusions in this chapter. However, for those interested in pursuing this line of study, here are a few books on the subject: *One Man's Destiny*, C.R. Dickey (Merrimac MA, Destiny Publishing); *Missing Links Discovered in Assyrian Tablets*, E. Raymond Capt (Thousand Oaks, CA, Artisan Sales); *The Royal House of Britain and Enduring Dynasties*, W. H. M. Milner (Windsor, Ontario, Canadian-British Israelite Association.)

[2] Heraldry is the profession, study, or art of devising, granting, and blazoning coats of arms, tracing genealogies, and determining and ruling on questions of rank or protocol, as exercised by an officer of arms.

founded by Christians fleeing religious persecution. God also told us exactly how that was going to happen:

> Rev 12:15-17 And the serpent cast out of his mouth water as a flood after the woman, that he might cause her to be carried away of the flood. And the earth helped the woman, and the earth opened her mouth, and swallowed up the flood which the dragon cast out of his mouth. And the dragon was wroth with the woman, and went to make war with the remnant of her seed, which keep the commandments of God, and have the testimony of Jesus Christ.

In the verses above we read that Satan would try to destroy the Jews and the Church with a flood of people.[1] But the Lord separated a remnant church and many Jews from their enemies by the Atlantic Ocean. This country grew and prospered and became the hub of the western world. West, West, where have I heard that before?

> Hos 11:10-11 (*excerpts*) They shall walk after the LORD . . . then the children shall tremble from the west...and I will place them in their houses, saith the LORD.

This hemisphere is as far West as you can get. Go any farther and it is called the Far East. In another similarity, the Church, like the Levites, is called to be priests and to come out from the world.[2] God called Levi to be directly in the Lord's service. As priests, they were separated from the rest of the people. God even gave them special cities to live in:

> Num 35:7 . . . cities which ye shall give to the Levites shall be forty and eight cities: them shall ye give with their suburbs.

The Levites had 48 cities; the Continental United States has 48 states. It was not until after the pivotal year of 1948 that other states were added. It was not until after that year that the United States began to lose its influence as the Christian lighthouse of the world. Occasional coincidences happen. But are all of these historic fits just random chance that by some fluke just happen to fit Scripture? That would be difficult for any thinking person to swallow. Here are another couple of "coincidences" of interest.

---

[1] Rev 17:15 defines "waters" as peoples, tongues, and nations.

[2] 2Co 6:14-18, 1Pe 2:5-9, Rev 1:6, 5:10, and 18:4-5.

1. The Lord gave Abraham the covenant of circumcision. Until the last decade, babies were routinely circumcised in the United States. Why us? There is no sound medical reason for this practice.

2. The United States was the first nation to have a five-day work week, thus observing the Sabbath as well as Sunday.

3. Though Jacob had only 12 sons, Joseph's two sons became two tribes. Counting Ephraim and Manasseh, there were then actually thirteen tribes. In America there were only 12 colonies, but the Carolinas were too large to govern in horse and buggy days, so the Carolinas were split into two states, North and South Carolina. Result: As Israel's twelve sons became thirteen tribes, so our twelve colonies became thirteen states.

All that was long ago. Since then the United States has fought a half-dozen foreign wars: bringing her "children forth to the murderer," as foretold in Hosea 9:13. And now, through manifold abortions, we bring our children forth to the murderer in a new and savage way. However, terrible as that may sound, God's eternal plan is still right on schedule.

EZEKIEL'S TWO STICKS

Just before the Lord describes the battle of Armageddon in Ezekiel 38 and 39, He tells us of the restoration of the Jews to the Holy Land in a vision about dry bones. Noting the context, these dry-bones are about 1948 and the new nation of Israel.

> Eze 37:11-12 Son of man, these bones are the whole house of Israel: behold, they say, Our bones are dried, and our hope is lost: we are cut off for our parts . . . Therefore prophesy and say unto them, Thus saith the Lord GOD; **Behold, O my people, I will open your graves, and cause you to come up out of your graves, and bring you into the land of Israel.**

Armageddon follows closely at the heels of this prophecy. How soon will that battle be? End-time pundits notwithstanding, Scripture doesn't say. However, because of where we are in history, can now cross-reference these dry-bones with one of Daniel's final prophecies and get a time pin:

> Dan 12:1-2 And at that time shall Michael stand up, the great prince which standeth for the children of thy people: and there shall be a time of trouble, such as never was since there was a nation even to that same time: and at that time thy people shall be delivered, every one that shall be found written in the book. **And many of them that sleep in the dust of the earth shall awake, some to everlasting life, and some to shame and everlasting contempt.**

That "time of trouble" undoubtedly refers to the Nazi holocaust, in which six million Jews were killed, and though many died, the Jews were indeed delivered into a new land, the new land of Israel. If the verse above was speaking about the final resurrection of the dead, all would have been brought back to life, not just "many." So here is another figurative description of the persecution of the Jews and their ensuing restoration to the Holy Land.

As the Lord put flesh on the dry-bones lying in their graves (Eze 37:11), so those who slept in the dust awoke, to be restored to the Holy Land (Dan 12:1-2). Same event, different allegorical language. As an interesting side note, God tells us that all who came to life (returned to Israel) would not be believers. However, despite their spiritual condition, the Lord is assembling the forces which are going to take a stand for Him in the final battle:

> Eze 37:16 Moreover, thou son of man, take thee one stick, and write upon it, For Judah, and for the children of Israel his companions: then take another stick, and write upon it, For Joseph, the stick of Ephraim and for all the house of Israel his companions:

At the end of this vision, the Lord tells of the division between Jacob's children, between Israel and Judah, and declares that He is going to draw them back together again. Note the two sticks. Simply stated, Ephraim and the ten northern tribes are one stick, while Judah is the other.

Just before Armageddon, God plans to make one stick of them. So are 1948 and 1967 important dates? In those years, the new nation of Israel was born, the time of the Two Witnesses was over, Jerusalem was freed, and all the day=years and time-times were fulfilled. We are in the final generation, and except for an hour of trial and the battle of Armageddon, there is little prophecy left to be fulfilled before Jesus returns. But as we look about us now, something wonderful is about to happen to both the Jews and the ten lost tribes . . . something we have been waiting 2700 years for:

> Isa 11:13 The envy also of Ephraim shall depart, and the adversaries of Judah shall be cut off: Ephraim shall not envy Judah, and Judah shall not vex Ephraim.

Before the end, the Lord will take the stick of Ephraim, now in the true Church, and unite it with the stick of Judah, and we will be one in God's hand.

> Eze 37:19 Say unto them, Thus saith the Lord GOD; Behold, I will take the stick of Joseph, which is in the hand of Ephraim, and the tribes of Israel his fellows, and will put them with him, even with the stick of Judah, and make them one stick, and they shall be one in mine hand.

Within this generation, the true Christians will be united with the Jewish people, and we will be one people again. The Israel of God. Will we be up to the task ahead? Of course not, but now that our hearts can be opened to who Ephraim and Judah are, we can begin to see what our end-time roles will be:

> Zec 9:13 When I have bent Judah for me, filled the bow with Ephraim, and raised up thy sons, O Zion, against thy sons, O Greece, and made thee as the sword of a mighty man.

Judah, now back in the Holy Land, will have only one ally. Ephraim with the rest of the Gentile church is the only true ally that little Israel now has. We are the only candidate left in the world for the title of "the stick of Joseph." The days when the United States would totally support Israel are drawing to a close, as the leaders of our land dip Old Glory in the tar-pit of Arab oil.

You already know in your heart -- because the Holy Spirit has told you -- that there is only a remnant of the true Church left in any western land. As Scripture opens before us, we can see that this remnant is probably from the lost tribes of Israel. As conditions worsen in the United States and elsewhere, we all may soon need to flee to Israel. Either that or be resigned to living behind barbed wire. Don't be lulled to sleep, Brethren. If the Lord does not provide a way of escape, physical persecution is very close at hand for us all:

Rev 12:11-12 And they overcame him by the blood of the Lamb, and by the word of their testimony; and they loved not their lives unto the death. Therefore rejoice, *ye* heavens, and ye that dwell in them. Woe to the inhabiters of the earth and of the sea! for the devil is come down unto you, having great wrath, because he knoweth that he hath but a short time.

Now we better get the rest of those doctrinal skeletons out of our closets. We have to get those pre-trib rapture and seven-year tribulation ideas out of our minds, Brethren, because they aren't going to happen. As perilous as these end-times are going to get, the Remnant Church doesn't want to be basing its future decisions on the bogus vision of an 18th Century Jesuit.

Daniel's 70th Week

CHAPTER 10

But when ye shall see
the abomination of desolation,
spoken of by Daniel the prophet,
standing where it ought not,
(let him that readeth understand)
then let them that be in Judaea
flee to the mountains:

MAR 13:14

Finding the foundations of the Solomonic temple on the old temple platform in Jerusalem, 300 feet or so north of the Mohammedan Dome of the Rock, may be one of the most important archeological discoveries of this century. However, since that discovery, some archeologists have been trying to prove that the old temple of Solomon was located where the Dome of the Rock now stands. These archeologists are not farmers, or from the Scripture itself, they would have clearly seen their error:

> 2Ch 3:1 Then Solomon began to build the house of the Lord in Jerusalem on Mount Moriah, where the Lord had appeared to his father David, at the place that David had prepared, on the threshing floor of Ornan the Jebusite.

The old temple was built over a threshing floor. Note that Scripture calls it a "floor." Floors are flat. Anyone who knows anything at all about threshing grain knows that a threshing floor must be flat! *As-Sakhra,* the craggy stone over which the Dome of the Rock was built, is as prickly as a porcupine. No farmer in his right mind would have attempted to thresh grain on it, particularly when there was an absolutely flat rock, just perfect for threshing, only 300 feet away. So rest fully assured, the temple was not built where the Dome of the Rock now stands.

But since the discovery of the original foundations of the Solomonic temple, recorded in *Biblical Archeology Review,* Mar 1983, the enemy has tried to cover up the evidence. Mohammedans have built over the holes in the bedrock, spaced on the sacred cubit, and archeologists have written lengthy arguments to show that the temple was located where the dome is now. As we have seen, *As-Sakhra* is an impossible location for the temple, both scripturally and agriculturally.

But why is knowing where the old temple was located so important? Because knowing its location enables us to understand the day=years of Daniel and Revelation, and understanding those day=years enables us to understand Daniel's 70th Week.

ON WHAT WING?

Most evangelicals recognize the 69 Weeks of Dan 9:24 as sixty-nine sevens of day=years that were fulfilled at the cross.[1] But the 70th Week was different. It looked to dispensational folk like the 70th Week could not have been fulfilled at the time of the crucifixion, so they figured this "week" had to be seven years that would be fulfilled sometime down in the future. They figured this 70th seven would be a *Seven-Year Great Tribulation* that would take place at the end of the Christian Era, and invented a 2000 year gap between the 69th and 70th seven. Then they figured the days=years of both Daniel and Revelation had to be either the first or last half of the seven year tribulation. It all sounds very reasonable, and many believe in it even today. But, there is one major flaw in the view: It doesn't fit Scripture very well.

We now know those "days" are really day=years, and that they were fulfilled in new Israel. A pivotal insight, because

---

[1] As covered in the chapter, *The 69 Weeks,* when Hebrew day=years are converted to solar years, they fit from the decree of Artaxerxes I which authorized Nehemiah to rebuild Jerusalem, to the cross of Jesus in 32-33AD, right to the year. 483 Hebrew (396 solar) - 444 = 32AD.

understanding Daniel's 70th Week depends on our recognizing the Dome of the Rock as the Abomination that makes
Desolate. Once we see that Mohammedan edifice for what it
really is, then the 70th "week" opens up to us in a new way.
Let's look at Dan 9:26-27 once again. For those who do not
read Hebrew, which includes me, Green's bare-bones, literal,
word-for-word translation might prove helpful:

> Dan 9:26-27 (Green's Interlinear) and its end with the flood and
> until end war are determined desolations and he shall confirm a
> covenant with the many week one and in the half of the week he
> shall make cease sacrifice and offering and upon a wing abomina-
> tions a desolator even until end and that which was decreed shall
> pour out on the desolator.

Unfortunately, there are no punctuation marks in the
original Hebrew. That doesn't sit well with English readers, so
all English translators punctuate as seems grammatically
correct to them. Sometimes we need to go back to the original
text to see if there is an alternate sentence structure which
would enable us to view a passage of Scripture in a different
way. Dan 9:26-27 is one of those cases.

Read the above verses carefully. That's how they appear
in the original Hebrew. If you had not already read the KJV or
the NASB, or been told what those verses mean, what would
"upon a wing abominations a desolator" mean to you? Well
first, let's put a mental comma after "wing," and look at that
phrase again. "Upon a wing, abominations a desolator." Then
ask yourself: "Upon a wing *of what* is this abomination that's
going to desolate be placed?" The translators of the NIV saw
the possibility of a different meaning, and rendered those
verses as follows:[1]

---

[1] Evidence is mounting that modern Bibles (including the NIV and NASB)
were translated from Greek NT texts corrupted in the 3rd Century by the
Egyptian gnostic church. Under UV inspection, it appears that codex
Aleph, codex Bezae, and Papyrus 75 etc., used by Wescott & Hort to edit
the NT Greek, were altered for doctrinal reasons, and do not reflect the
true intent of Scripture. Unfortunately, these textual errors did not come
to light until after most of the modern English translations were made.
Because of these textual errors, the KJV is still the best conservative
translation of the majority text available in the English language today,
and most Bible quotations in this book are from the KJV.

Dan 9:26-27 (NIV) ...And its end will come with a flood; even to the end there will be war; desolations are determined. But He will confirm a covenant with many for one seven, but in the middle of that seven, he will put an end to sacrifice and offering, and one who causes desolations will place abominations on a wing *of the temple*, until the end that is decreed is poured out on him.

Ah-ha, so somewhere in Daniel's future, an Abomination that makes Desolate could be placed "on a wing of the temple." That makes some sense. Sacrifices took place at the temple, so if sacrifices were to be brought to an end, the temple would be where they would have to be abolished.

SHIQQOTS HA SHAMEN

Now let's read the verse which identifies what the Abomination that makes Desolate was going to be:

Dan 12:11 (KJV) And from the time *that* the daily *sacrifice* shall be taken away, and the abomination that maketh desolate set up, *there shall be* a thousand two hundred and ninety days.

We now know for a fact that those 1290 days are years that fit from the abolition of sacrifices in Daniel's time to the Dome of the Rock. The dome is without a doubt the Abomination of Desolation. That's no guess. We can prove it![1] In the above verse, the Hebrew word translated "abomination" is *shiqqots* (Strong's No. 8251), and the Hebrew word translated "desolation" is *shamen* (Strong's No. 8074):

Guess what? In the 70th Week, Dan 9:27, we again find Shiqqots and Shamen, and they are translated in the same way, as "abominations" and "desolations." Both verses tell of an abomination that makes desolate!

So let me ask you, how many *Shiqqots ha Shamen* -- Abominations of Desolations -- are there going to be in Daniel's future? The words are singular, and nowhere in Scripture is there any indication that there is going to be more than one.

---

[1] As we have seen in Chapter 6, the identification of the Dome of the Rock as the Abomination of Desolation is confirmed by the day=years of Rev 11:2-3 and 12:6, and 13:5. The dates are historically unassailable, and the mathematical fit uncontestable.

Archeological evidence *(Biblical Archeology Review, March 1983)* and even a recently found copper scroll place the Solomonic temple 300ft north of the Dome of the Rock, on a direct line with the Gate Beautiful. The Dome of the Rock is located in what was once the Court of the Gentiles, on "a wing of the temple," just as the NIV translates that verse.

So isn't it obvious that Dan 9:27 and Dan 12:11 are about the same Abomination of Desolation? Of course. Daniel's 70th Week is not about some future "Seven-Year Great Tribulation" period as the dispensationalists suppose, but about the Dome of the Rock, built by the Mohammedans, on God's holy mountain back in 688AD. Now here is the point:

Once we recognize the Dome of the Rock as the Abomination that maketh Desolate, then whenever we wish to place Daniel's 70th Week, that week would have to stretch into the past and future from when the Dome was constructed, or from 688AD.

When we see that Daniel's 70th Week is really about the Dome of the Rock, then all support for a future Seven-Year Tribulation period vanishes into thin air because Dan 9:27 is the ONLY verse in the whole Bible from which anyone could even conjure up such an idea. But if the 70th Week isn't about a seven-year trib, then what's it all about?

SHAVUOT AND SHAVUIM

The following is a little scholarly and not all that easy to grasp, but if you want to understand the 70th Week, I guess we'll just have to go through it. If you wonder why this is covered at all, sometimes before a person can hear the truth about what is to come, you have to dispose of the error.

Daniel was placed in Babylon at the beginning of the time of the Gentiles, and he was placed at that particular time for a reason. The Lord was using Daniel to show His people, and the surrounding nations, a prophetic picture of the time that Gentiles would rule the Holy Land. That was Daniel's whole mission, and there is no reason to believe that the Lord departed from that central theme in just one verse. As a result, an interpretation of the 70th Week that fits the history of the Jewish people during the time of the Gentiles would be appropriate. The 70th Week could be a multi-thousand year picture of the total history of the Holy Land during the time of the Gentiles. If it is, the key to understanding that week would be hidden in the unique Hebrew word *shavuim.*

The Hebrew words *shavuot* and *shavua* are translated into English as a week or seven. *Shavuot* and *shavua* are used everywhere in the Old Testament except right here in the book of Daniel. Here Daniel uses a really unusual word for seven, *shavuim*, which is the masculine plural form of *shavuot.* This plural form appears only in Daniel, but even here, *shavuim* is used only four times, three of which are in the 70 Weeks. So why is this unusual plural form of the word for seven used here instead of the usual *shavuot?* Because it IS plural, that's why! The 70th Week is more than just a seven of years -- it is a multiple of sevens of years!

In his book *The Covenant, The Holocaust & The 70th Week*, Dr. David Lurie (a Messianic Jew and Hebrew scholar) concluded that since *shavuim* is a plural word, then the 70th Week must also be plural: an unknown multiple of sevens. According to Dr. Lurie, the form of *Shavuim* itself demands that it be multiplied by something.[1] If the 70th Week requires a multiplier of some sort, we need to ask ourselves: multiplied by how many? Let's look at the Scriptures Daniel knew, such as Gen 2:2-3, Exo 23:10, and Lev 25:1-11, and see what they have to tell us about weeks and multiples.

All the way back to creation, there were weeks of days. Six work days followed by a Sabbath day of rest. Then in Leviticus the Lord also established a week of years. Six work years, followed by a Sabbatical year of rest. Daniel knew full well about both kinds of weeks. He knew his Scripture and was equally familiar with weeks of days and weeks of years.

Further in the Levitical code, the Lord initiates another kind of cycle: a cycle of 50 years. Seven weeks of years (for 49 years) followed by a year of the Jubilee. Within that cycle, every seventh year was a Sabbatical year, with the Jubilee following the 49th sabbatical year *as an extra Sabbatical year!*

---

[1] For Dr. Lurie's exposition of the word *Shavuim*, please see Appendix I. We use the same method of interpretation, but Dr. Lurie and I come to different conclusions about when the 70th Week was fulfilled. Dr. Lurie believes it was fulfilled during the Nazi Holocaust, while I believe the 70th Week refers to the "Time of The Gentiles" (Luk 21:24).

Jubilee was an additional Sabbatical year, with 360 more days of rest. Without question, Daniel knew about this 50 year cycle, and the year of the Jubilee:

THE LEVITICAL CODE

> 1st: Seven years.
> 2nd: Seven sevens of years.
> 3rd: One unique year of the Jubilee.

Seven years, seven sevens of years, and the year of the Jubilee, were plainly spelled out for Daniel by Moses. This cycle of 50 years repeated itself right on down through Jewish history. Now compare that Levitical code with the cycle that Gabriel gave Daniel in the 70 Weeks:

DANIEL'S 70 SEVENS

> 1st: Seven Sevens of years, seven *Shavuim*.
> 2nd: 62 more Sevens of years, 62 *Shavuim*.
> 3rd: One unique Seven multiple, one *Shavuim*.

Note the identical structure. Seven *shavuim*, then a multiple of *shavuim*, followed by one *shavuim*. The Lord used a system with which Daniel was familiar, but changed the numbers. He gave Daniel a 70 instead of a 50, but the structure is the same. This had to be obvious to Daniel. He had been raised under the Levitical code. As Daniel saw it, first there were the well under-stood seven sevens of years, for 49 years. But instead of those 49 years being followed by a Jubilee, as he would have expected, the Jubilee was deferred while the Lord gave Daniel 62 more sevens of years. These 69 sevens of years were then followed by one special kind of seven, a *shavuim,* or plural seven of years. What could that mean? Though the numbers are different, the numeric progression in the Levitical code and Daniel's 70 Weeks are identical. They are compared below:

1st:	A Seven.
2nd:	A multiple of sevens.
3rd:	A unique Jubilee.

1st:	Seven Sevens
2nd:	62 Sevens
3rd:	A plural Seven. The Jubilee was a unique year, *so the 70th Week should also be a unique plural!*

The cycle is the same. Since Jubilee was unique, Daniel would also have recognized the 70th Week as being unique, different *in kind* from the prior 69, and somehow similar to the year of the Jubilee. Daniel was a brilliant man, and the Lord had also given him the gift of interpreting dreams. If we folk 2500 years down the line can see this parallel progression, Daniel, who was brought up under the Levitical code, would have seen it easily.

The next question is this: In what way is the 70th Week similar to the Jubilee? Well, what was the year of the Jubilee like? It was a special sabbatical year for every living thing in the land. Look at this excerpt from Leviticus:

> Lev 25:10 And ye shall hallow the fiftieth year, and proclaim liberty throughout *all* the land unto all the inhabitants thereof: it shall be a jubilee unto you; and ye shall return every man unto his possession, and ye shall return every man unto his family. A jubilee shall that fiftieth year be unto you: ye shall not sow, neither reap that which groweth of itself in it, nor gather *the grapes* in it of thy vine undressed. For it *is* the jubilee; it shall be holy unto you: ye shall eat the increase thereof out of the field.

Besides the forgiving of debts, Jubilee was treated as a year of complete rest for every man and beast, a special kind of super Sabbatical year. *For all practical purposes, Jubilee was an additional year of rest with 360 Sabbaths!*

Since the 70th Week (a unique *Shavuim*) linguistically suggests a multiplier of some kind, is the Lord showing us the correct multiplier through the Levitical statute of the Jubilee? Remember Eze 4:5-6, "I give you a day for a year"? Using that yardstick, could every day of this *Plural* 70th Week actually represent a year? If this is the path the Lord intends for us to pursue to understand this verse, then it is simplicity itself to see how this prophecy fits the history of the Holy Land:

If the 360 day Hebrew Year is our multiplier, then 7 x 360 = 2520 Hebrew Years. Since our history is written in solar years we must convert 2520 x .9857 = 2484 (2483.95).

2484 - 536BC = 1948AD
½ of 2484 is 1242 - 536BC = 706AD

1. From Cyrus' decree to return to the land in 536BC to new Israel in 1948AD is exactly 2484 solar years!

2. The exact middle of that time is 706AD, one year after the completion of Mohammedan work on the temple mount!

GRAPH NUMBER 14

DANIEL'S 70TH WEEK, DAN 9:27

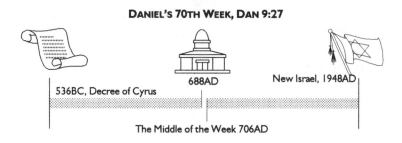

536BC, Decree of Cyrus

688AD

New Israel, 1948AD

The Middle of the Week 706AD

Dan 9:27 "And he shall confirm the covenant with many for one week: and in the midst of the week he shall cause the sacrifice and the oblation to cease, and for the overspreading of abominations he shall make *it* desolate, even until the consummation, and that determined shall be poured upon the desolate."

Note: The Dome of the Rock is "on a wing" of the temple. The "Middle of the week" is not a precise time when used to describe 2484 years; 706AD is also in the "middle of the week."

From the above, it appears that the Lord intends the 70th week of Dan 9:27 to be an overview of the time that Gentiles would rule in the Holy Land, a time that ended in 1948AD. If so, the 70th Week is fulfilled, and there isn't going to be any Seven Year Great Tribulation in our future![1]

---

[1] This is not the only place in prophecy where the Lord used imprecise terms to describe general areas of time. In Dan 7:12, God used "a season and a time" to describe 1260 years. This unusual usage is documented in Chapter 8.

ISRAEL'S BIG PICTURE

Now, that is most of the hard data. But hard data alone will not give us a true picture of Daniel's prophecies. Spiritual truths are involved, and "spiritual things are spiritually discerned." Caught up in our little materialistic lives, we look myopically through darkened spiritual glasses and only see those things historically close at hand. We lose sight of what a great and timeless Being our God really is. We disregard His long range plan.

What concerns this great and inexplicable Being? What is His viewpoint of the happenings on an insignificant little planet orbiting a minor type G2 sun, on the rim of one of the smaller galaxies of His incredibly vast creation? What does this great Being want us to know about Himself and His great plan from the book that He directed His Spirit to inspire?

Well, the Lord knew all of human history, even before Eve gave the first bite of fruit to Adam. God knew that man was going to fall. He permitted a fallen archangel, Satan, to have a devastating influence in the affairs of men (LUK 4:5-6), an influence which continues to this day. The enemy influenced man to depart from God, a condition that a loving and Holy God could not allow to continue under any circumstances. He could have destroyed man, Satan, and the rest of creation right then, but He didn't. That would have been contrary to His loving nature. So to fulfill His eternal purposes, the Lord launched a spiritual war against Satan and the angels who fell with him: a war set in motion through His Son, His holy angels, and the people who love Him.

That is what the Bible is all about. Every word in Scripture is about the children of Israel, about the temple, and about the earthly ministry and the subsequent death and resurrection of God's Son. Every word relates to that enormous spiritual conflict. That spiritual conflict is one of the Bible's central subjects, and all prophecy should be viewed with that prolonged battle in mind. That great conflict will end at a single point in time, culminating in Jesus' final judgment of the forces of Satan.

Because of recently fulfilled prophecy, we Christians can now look back at the cross and beyond, and correlate the scriptural account of that great spiritual conflict with 6000 years of recorded history. Beginning with Abraham, the battle raged around the Children of Israel. To help them, the Lord inspired prophets and historians to write a book to guide them. We know that book as the Old Testament. During its writing, Moses first made the Tabernacle, and later, Solomon built a temple in Jerusalem. It was to be "a house of prayer for all peoples." The Lord declared that temple site to be "the footstool of His feet, forever."

> *In the Old Testament Era, the great spiritual battle not only involved a specific people, the Children of Israel, but it also had a specific battleground -- Jerusalem -- and to be more specific, the Temple of the Lord on Mount Moriah!*

But the Children of Israel fell away from the Lord, and served the Baals, the Ashtaroth, and Molech, the abomination of the Sidonians. So the Lord allowed them to be taken into captivity to Babylon. After seventy years, they were restored to the land, and five centuries later, Jesus died on the cross. After the cross, the Lord added the Church to His forces.

Understanding who the Two Witnesses are, we can now see that the Lord had two human armies fighting for Him during the Christian Era: the Jews and the Gentile church. For His 2nd army, He even had a new book inspired. We know that new book as the New Testament. The battleground for this new army was expanded by Jesus to: "Go ye into all the world, and preach the Gospel to every creature." The Gentile church began, and we can now see that the Church includes the descendants of the long-forgotten ten lost tribes of Israel. So the Church has been the "Israel of God" all along.

But back to God's first army, the Jews. After the fall of the Davidic Kingdom in 606BC, the Lord sent Daniel to encourage His people. The first half of Daniel is to and about the Gentile nations who were to rule in the Holy Land during the Time of the Gentiles. The last half of Daniel is directly to and about the future of the Jews then in captivity to Babylon. If we wish to understand Daniel, we need to recognize to whom it was written, and when!

> *Daniel's prophetic mission was to tell the Jews about their future role in this great ongoing 6000 year spiritual battle, about the coming of their Messiah, about the future of the old temple site, about their holy city*

Jerusalem, and about their beloved land during the "time of the Gentiles."

The Holy Land has always been the Jewish battleground! God has never seen fit to change the battleground for His first army, the physical seed of Abraham. For physical Israel, Mount Moriah remains "the footstool of God's feet, forever!"

At the end of the Babylonian captivity, 536BC, the Jews were restored to the Land for the first time. They were again dispersed by the Romans in 70AD, and have been among the nations ever since. During this era, the Jews have longed for their inheritance. They have wept at the wall. Looking toward Jerusalem for nineteen centuries, the Jews have trusted in God's promise to restore them to their ancient homeland.

> Isa 11:11 And it shall come to pass in that day, *that* the Lord shall set his hand again the second time to recover the remnant of his people, which shall be left, from Assyria, and from Egypt, and from Pathros, and from Cush, and from Elam, and from Shinar, and from Hamath, and from the islands of the sea.

The return of the Jewish people to the new nation of Israel in 1948, and the freeing of Jerusalem in 1967, affirm that prophecy. That is when the Jews were returned to the Holy Land a second time, as foretold by Isaiah the prophet. They have been returned to their old battleground for the final battle of all time, the battle of Armageddon.

Daniel is the one book in the Bible which most clearly defines this age-old battle and the satanic forces against whom we fight. In Dan 10:20, we read of satanic princes who would influence the Medo-Persian and Greek empires and their descendants. These are only two of the fallen angels who have influenced world governments down through the ages: Isa 14:12-21, Eze 28:12-19, Luk 4:5-6, and Rev 13:1, 17:3, and 19:19 are other references to these satanic beings which come readily to mind.

THE SIXTY-NINE WEEKS

In the 69 Weeks, we read about the rebuilding of Jerusalem under Nehemiah, about the coming Messiah, and about how Satan influenced his servants to kill the Lord. Satan did not comprehend why God the Father would send His only beloved Son here, not to rule, but to die for the likes of you and me.

Satan didn't realize that by Messiah's death he would be totally defeated. The enemy didn't understand that we would then be reconciled to the Father, and that we would be "transferred from the kingdom of darkness, into the kingdom of His dear Son" (Col 1:13-14). Satan didn't understand that the cross would enlist a new and even greater army of people to stand against him.

The 70th Week

In the 70th Week, the Lord paints a picture of the future of the temple mount with a very broad brush. God spans two millennia in only 59 words (Dan 9:26-27). Of more importance to Him than the destruction of the temple of Herod in 70AD, was the horror of an abomination that would stand upon the "footstool of His feet" for over 1300 years!

In this 70th "week," the Lord is NOT detailing what is going on in the visible empires of men. Instead, He is telling us of events taking place behind the scenes, in the great spiritual conflict in the unseen spiritual world. We read of fallen angels. We read how *"he"* of Dan 9:27 (probably the satanic prince of Medo-Persia of Dan 10:20, or Satan himself) "would make a firm covenant with many people for one seven," a covenant he would later break. This covenant would obviously be with the Jews and would concern Jerusalem (Dan 9:24). In 536BC, Cyrus the Persian (a Gentile king) gave a decree which allowed the Jews to return to the Holy Land and worship. Ezra rebuilt the temple, and sacrifices were reinstituted.

The Romans destroyed Jerusalem in 70AD, and we read about "the people of the [*spiritual*] prince to come," who would destroy Jerusalem, and about the horrors which would take place then. After the Romans left, Jews and Gentiles could have again worshiped on the temple mount.

Then the Mohammedans took Jerusalem, and the satanic princes of Babylon, Medo-Persia, and Greece had jurisdiction over the Holy Land for a major part of the Christian Era. We read how *"he"* broke the covenant he had made with God's people, and trespassed on God's Holy Mountain. In 639AD, the Mohammedan scourge took Jerusalem and drove the Jews and Christians out of the land, or underground.

"And its end will come with a flood [*of people*]". In 688AD, the Dome of the Rock was placed on the temple mount, some 300 ft. south of where the old Solomonic Temple had been. This would prove to be such an abomination that it would preclude any possibility of future Jewish sacrifices on the temple mount. "And in the midst of the week *'he'* will cause sacrifice and grain offering to cease, and one who causes desolations will place abominations on a wing of the temple." The Dome of the Rock was indeed an abomination that would make desolate, on a "wing of the temple" (Dan 9:27, NIV). With the help of the Mohammedans, those satanic princes continued to control the Holy Land down to the present day.

Until 1948, Satan must have thought he had won the battle for the Holy Land. Then "Michael arose," that angelic prince who is the defender of Daniel's people (Dan 12:1). In 1948, the miracle of new Israel took place, and for the first time in 2554 years, the Jews again controlled the land which God gave to them in perpetuity through His covenant with Abraham, Isaac, and Jacob. Just 19 years later, Jerusalem was freed of Gentile domination for the first time in 2573 years, thus bringing the "Time of the Gentiles" to an end (Luk 21:24). In the prophetic day=years, the Lord is telling us of *three* distinct time frames:

1. From the abolition of sacrifices in Daniel's time, 583BC, to the Dome of the Rock in 688AD.

2. From the Dome of the Rock to new Israel in 1948.

3: From the Dome to a freed Jerusalem in 1967.

Today, Jerusalem's synagogues and churches are again overflowing with the Lord's people (Rev 11:11). Soon, Jesus will return, and with the Sword of His mouth, Messiah, who "was cut off and had nothing," will bring "a complete destruction, poured out on the one who makes desolate." In case you don't feel like looking the numbers up, here they are again:

7 x 360=2520 x .9857=2484 Hebrew Years.

2484-536BC = 1948AD Decree of Cyrus, to new Israel.

1948-1242 (2484/2)=706AD
Construction finished on the temple mount.

So there you have it, the big spiritual picture. Daniel's prophecies are primarily about the time of Gentile control of the Holy Land. The whole spiritual story of the "Time of the Gentiles" is encapsulated in the 70 Weeks. The 70 Weeks begins by telling us of events which took place long before the cross. It continues with Messiah's ministry on earth, and Satan's later trespass on God's mountain. The prophecy of the 70 Weeks culminates with Satan's final destruction, still to come. Truly, "God's ways are above man's ways, and past finding out." These things were impossible to see just a few years ago, but God has been in control all along.

For some, the argument for interpreting the 70th Week as a multiple of seven will not be conclusive enough. Tradition usually wins over deliberation. But when viewed in the light of the identity of the Abomination of Desolation, the day=years, and all the other prophecies which are fulfilled in new Israel, why then, the evidence is overwhelming! Before we discount these things, we really need to scrutinize the alternative.

ALTERNATE DISPENSATIONAL VIEW

By using the imaginary work of an 18th Century Jesuit priest as a spring-board, dispensational scholars have arrived at the end-time views they hold today. Most of these traditional eschatologists believe Dan 9:27 to be about a Seven-Year Great Tribulation that is supposed take place at the end of the Christian Era. As their doctrine goes, at the beginning of that tribulation, the Church will be "raptured" up to be with the Lord. Then Satan incarnate, as antichrist, will supposedly rule the world from Jerusalem, and make an agreement with the Jews. It is then assumed that antichrist will have the temple rebuilt.

To fool everyone into believing that he is a good fellow, it is also thought that antichrist will start the Jewish sacrifices again. But 3½ years later, it is suggested that he will place an image of himself in the temple before which everyone on earth will need to bow down and worship. (By the way, the theory of a first 3½ and second 3½ years of the "tribulation" is based on a faulty interpretation of the day=years, which we can now see were fulfilled in new Israel.) Antichrist is then supposed to stop those Jewish sacrifices, destroy the temple, and persecute everyone within reach -- there are various optional scenarios. Finally, antichrist is supposed to start Armageddon, and so on, all built on a futurist seven-year interpretation of Daniel's 70th Week.

When it can be shown with some certainty that every verse used to support a seven-year tribulation has been fulfilled in new Israel, how can that view possibly stand? Interpreting the 70th Week as a multiple of seven takes us to historically provable incidents which are affirmed by the day=years. Furthermore, the weight of scriptural, linguistic, and historic evidence appears to support the use of a 360 multiplier to interpret the 70th Week.

But as the Lord said through Isaiah, it's "line upon line, precept upon precept, a little here, a little there," and "to him who hath much, more shall be given, but to him who hath not, even what he hath shall be taken away" (Mar 4:25). Which, being interpreted, means: If we grow in the Word, we shall continue to learn more from it. But if we stagnate, we will forget even that which we already know.

The Last Trumpet

CHAPTER 11

When thou art in tribulation,
and all these things are come upon thee,
even in the latter days,
if thou turn to the LORD thy God,
and shalt be obedient unto His voice;
(For the LORD thy God is a merciful God)
He will not forsake thee, neither destroy thee,
nor forget the covenant of thy fathers
which He sware unto them..

DEU 4:30-31

Well, if there isn't going to be a seven-year tribulation at the end of this age, when is the "rapture" going to take place, and when is the Antichrist going to appear? There are so many conflicting ideas tossed about concerning the end-times that we ought to take a truly revolutionary approach. Let's make a little agreement between you, the Lord, and me. Let's take all our commentaries and set them aside for a while. Then let's take the Bible, and only the Bible, and see what it has to tell us about this sequence of events.

Please be patient with me for making this a kind of nit-picking chapter. The I's are dotted and the T's are crossed because if the Scripture verses quoted below really mean what they say, then ALL of our current end-time ideas will need rethinking. Let's begin with a quote that is familiar to almost every Christian:

> 1Th 4:16-17 For the Lord himself shall descend from heaven with a shout, with the voice of the archangel, and with the trump of God: and the dead in Christ shall rise first: Then WE which are alive *and* remain shall be caught up together with them in the clouds, to meet the Lord in the air: and so shall we ever be with the Lord.

All agree that those verses refer to the so-called "rapture" of the Church.[1] In fact, 1Th 4:16-17 is one of the central passages in Scripture that supports the physical return of the Lord Jesus to this Earth. Note the *we*. Paul was speaking to the Church of which he was part, the Church of his time. We have every scriptural reason to believe that *we* also includes us. Every other time *we* is used in reference to the Church, we say that *we* is to us, so let's be consistent and do so now. You and I are the *we*. That's relatively simple, isn't it?

Another thing to note is that Jesus is returning with the trumpet of God. The great trumpet of God will be sounding as Jesus descends from the heavens. Now, the Bible is full of trumpets, including seven in Revelation. So the next logical question is: Which trumpet are we taken up in? Of all the trumpets in the Bible, at which one is the Lord returning?

> 1Co 15:51-52 Behold, I shew you a mystery; WE shall not all sleep, but WE shall all be changed, In a moment, in the twinkling of an eye, **at the last trump**: for the trumpet shall sound, and the dead shall be raised incorruptible, and WE shall be changed.

There it is: the *last* trumpet! Compare this 1Co passage with the 1Th quote above it. In both, the dead in Christ are raised, and in both, trumpets are blown. Notice also that there are three more *we*'s. Here is the point: If the *we* Paul was speaking of in 1Th 4:17 includes us, then so do the *we*'s in 1Co 15:51-52. Believe it or not, there are those who claim that the 1Th 4:16-17 "rapture" is for the Church, while the

---

[1] "Rapture" is in quotes because the author does not find the return of the Lord for the saints so characterized anywhere in Scripture. It is believed to have come from the Latin Vulgate's use of the word "raptao" in reference to this event. By definition, the word "rapture" seems more suitable for the mystery religions than it does for sober Christians looking forward to the most awesome event in all history, the return of Jesus as our God and King. Rapture was probably brought into common usage by Margaret Macdonald, a 15-year-old Scottish visionary of the 19th Century. John Bray, *The Origin of the Pre-Tribulation Rapture Teaching* (P.O. Box 90129, Lakeland, FL 33804, John Bray Ministry, 1981).

1Co 15:52 "rapture" is for the great tribulation saints. Nonsense! There are *we's* in both passages! Either both verses are for us, or neither are. We can't go arbitrarily picking through the *we's* in the Bible on the basis of some doctrine we wish to defend.

So aren't these two passages just different descriptions of the same happening? Of course, and in 1Co 15:52, there is a trumpet again; only this time we know which trumpet it is. We are taken to be with the Lord at the *last* trumpet!

Now, look at that *last* trumpet very carefully. Trumpet is singular, so no other trumpets are blown with it. The *last* trumpet is blown by itself. Also, there are no modifiers such as, "except the trumpets of judgment," or "except the trumpets in Revelation." That needs to be emphasized:

There are NO excepts! Not one Bible trumpet is left out!

GRAPH NUMBER 15

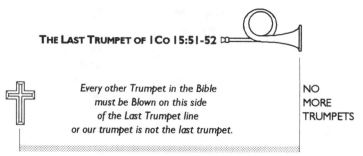

THE LAST TRUMPET OF 1CO 15:51-52

Every other Trumpet in the Bible must be Blown on this side of the Last Trumpet line or our trumpet is not the last trumpet.

NO
MORE
TRUMPETS

The Christian Era

1 Cor 15:51-52 Behold, I show you a mystery; We shall not all sleep, but we shall all be changed, In a moment, in the twinkling of an eye, at the last trump: for the trumpet shall sound, and the dead shall be raised incorruptible, and we shall be changed.

Note: The Last Trumpet draws a line in time. Every event predicted in the Bible must take place either to the right or left of that line. 1Co 15:51-52 leaves no trumpets out, so that includes the trumpets in Revelation.

So we will be taken to be with the Lord at the very *last* heavenly trumpet that will ever sound. The very last trumpet of all time! There are some denominational theologians who declare that this *last* trumpet does not include the seven trumpets in Revelation. Unbelievable as it may sound, they theorize that Revelation's seven trumpets are "special" trumpets of judgment excluded from the firm mandate of 1Co 15:52. There is absolutely *no* Scripture for their view, and it is counter to the plain testimony of the Bible: the declaration that we are taken to be with the Lord at the *last* trumpet!

Our trumpet is either the very *last* trumpet of all time, or 1Co 15:52 is a lie. The Bible is infallible truth, so one more time: We will be taken to be with the Lord at the one and only *last* trumpet of all time! That is just believing what the Word of God says straight out, and it simplifies a doctrinal point that the Church has been arguing about for 70 years.

> Mat 24:21 For then shall be great tribulation, such as was not since the beginning of the world to this time . . . .
>
> Mat 24:29 Immediately after the tribulation of those days . . . the powers of the heavens shall be shaken:
>
> Mat 24:31 And he shall send his angels with a great sound of a trumpet [*a great trumpet, NASB*], and they shall gather together his elect from the four winds, from one end of heaven to the other.

Note the sequence of events:

(1) Tribulation.
(2) After the tribulation.
(3) Great trumpet.

Since our trumpet is the *last* trumpet, this great trumpet either has to be our trumpet, or our trumpet would have to come *after* it! If we are going to stand on our pretribulation rapture position, we have to rewrite Scripture. We have to put Mat 24:31 before Mat 24:21! Think that through. First, a great tribulation. Second, after the tribulation. Third, the great trumpet. It is obvious from MAT 24 that our trumpet-- *the last trumpet* -- comes after the tribulation.

That's not all. Some believe that the Church is "raptured" out at the end of Revelation 3. Why? Because "church," the Greek word ἐκκλησία (*ekklesia*), does not appear after Rev 3. But that doesn't matter because trumpets are recorded all the way through Rev 11. The *last* trumpet in Revelation -- *the 7th trumpet* -- is not blown until Rev 11:15. Since we are taken to be with the Lord at the *last* Trumpet, the 7th trumpet of Rev 11:15 has to be our trumpet, or our trumpet would have to come after that one, too. No matter what our doctrines may have been in the past, the Bible states that our trumpet is still the *last* trumpet of all time.

What does that tell us? Well, first of all, we now have solid scriptural proof that the Church will be on earth through six of the seven trumpets of Revelation. This is not just another end-time theory. If we have ears to hear it, this is what the Word of God proclaims, straight out.

This 7th trumpet in Revelation is obviously a pretty important trumpet, so we need to know next if that trumpet is indeed our trumpet, or does our trumpet come after it? The 7th trumpet itself is blown in Rev 11:15, but what takes place around that trumpet blast is described in chapter ten:

> Rev 10:6-7 . . . that there should be time no longer: But in the days of the voice of the seventh angel, when he shall begin to sound, the mystery of God should be finished, as he hath declared to his servants the prophets.

What a tremendous verse that is. If there is a central Scripture about the second coming of the Lord, this one has to be it! As is true of every other creation of this present age, when the seventh trumpet sounds, time itself will come to an end. This is very important, because understanding that time itself will come to an end affects our end time doctrine.[1]

First, if there is no more time after the 7th trumpet, there isn't any more time for another trumpet to blow. So our trumpet couldn't come after this 7th trumpet. Second, our trumpet can't come before this 7th trumpet either, or our trumpet would not be the last one. So the 7th trumpet of Revelation is our last trumpet. It is the very trumpet at which we, the Church, are taken to be with the Lord!

That trumpet sound is not going to stretch over several years, either. The phrase "when he shall begin to sound" tells

---

[1] The correct definition of the Gr. χρόνος (*chronos*) is "time," and it is so translated in the KJV. The modern translation of *chronos* as "delay" is invalid. Greek has several words for delay, including χρονίζω (*chronizo*) from the same root. If delay had been intended, the Lord chose the wrong Greek word to express it. Though *chronos* appears 185 times in the NT, only in Rev 10:6 have modern translators taken the liberty of rendering *chronos* delay. χρόνος G5550, a space of time, years old, season, space, time, while. *Chronos* represents "delay" only by implication.

us so. At the very first peep out of that trumpet, there will be no more time! Time as a natural phenomenon will cease to exist, and we will be in the eternal Kingdom of God.

The "mystery of God" is the Church in Christ Jesus.[1] So the Church as a betrothed body of believers on Earth will be concluded at this trumpet.

GRAPH NUMBER 16

THE SEVENTH TRUMPET
OF REVELATION 10:6-7 AND 11:15

No More Time
All Prophecy Fulfilled
Mystery of God Finished
Eternal Kingdom of God

Every prophet fulfilled on this Side of the Last Trumpet, including the book of Revelation.

The Christian Era

Rev 10:6-7 . . . there should be time no longer: But in the days of the voice of the seventh angel, when he shall begin to sound, the mystery of God should be finished, as he hath declared to his servants the prophets.

Note: The Greek word translated "time" in Rev 10:6, KJV, is *chronos* (Strong's No. G5550, χρόνος. *Chronos*, khron'-os; a space of time. Greek has perfectly good words for delay, one of which is *chronizo*. (Strong's No. 5549, from the same root, χρονίζω. *Chronizo*, khron-id'-zo; to take time, i.e. linger: delay, tarry). If the Lord intended *chronos* to be understood as delay, (as we see in contemporary translations) then He chose the wrong Greek word to express it. It appears that present-day translators have rendered *chronos* delay for doctrinal, rather than linguistic, reasons.

"As He hath declared to His servants the prophets." Which prophets is the Lord speaking of? We don't see any excluded, so these prophets are all the prophets in the Bible, both Old Testament and New. All prophecy will be fulfilled at this trumpet. Of course, this does not include those few verses

---

[1] Rom 16:25, Eph 1:9, 3:4, 3:9, 5:32, Col:1:27, 2:2.

which refer to the eternal Kingdom of God. That timeless state continues into infinity.

Let's look at the verse where that trumpet blast sounds. The 7th trumpet is blown right in the middle of Revelation, after the Seven Churches, after the Seven Seals, after six other trumpets, and after the Two Witnesses:

> Rev 11:15 And the seventh angel sounded; and there were great voices in heaven, saying, The kingdoms of this world are become the kingdoms of our Lord, and of his Christ; and he shall reign for ever and ever.

The 7th angel sounds, and the Lord reigns forever. Right then, forever! That verse does not allow any time for a tribulation after it blows, or time for a 1000-year millennium either. Why? Because we go straight into the eternal Kingdom of God when that last trumpet sounds. Despite differing doctrines, that is the chronological picture as declared by the Bible. We will show later how Rev 20, the so-called millennium, is an allegory of the Christian Era (*See Appendix II*).

So when is the great tribulation? Matthew 24:21 tells us there was going to be one. Well, who gets tribulation? The Greek word for tribulation is *thlipsis*, also translated affliction and trouble. Thlipsis is used 37 times in the New Testament. In almost every instance, *thlipsis* refers to the suffering of whom? The saints! Here are a couple of familiar verses:

> Joh 16:33 These things I have spoken unto you, that in me ye might have peace. In the world ye shall have [*thlipsis*] tribulation: but be of good cheer; I have overcome the world.

> Rom 12:12 Rejoicing in hope; patient in [*thlipsis*] tribulation; continuing instant in prayer.

> 2Th 1:4 So that we ourselves glory in you in the churches of God for your patience and faith in all your persecutions and [*thlipsis*] tribulations that ye endure.

There are many more. If you need additional evidence, please look them up in your concordance. Generally speaking, the unsaved don't go through *thlipsis*; they are destined for *orgy* or *thumos*, God's wrath.[1] *Orgy* and *thumos* are the two Greek words for wrath. So we the saints do undergo tribula-

---

[1] Rom 9:22, Eph 5:6, 1Th 1:10, Rev 16:19.

tion, but we are not destined unto a final wrath, exactly as 1Th 5:9 tells us, but unto eternal salvation.[1] The wicked are destined unto final wrath, the judgment of the Great White Throne, and the second death. So when is "the great tribulation"? John tells us:

> Rev 1:9 I John, who also am your brother, and companion in tribulation, and in the kingdom and patience of Jesus Christ, was in the isle that is called Patmos, for the word of God, and for the testimony of Jesus Christ.

Oh Brethren, God forgive us for forgetting the terrible suffering the saints of the past have endured. Between two and twenty million Christians were killed by the Roman Empire in tortures unimaginable. The Catholic church killed up to twelve million more during the middle ages. In our own generation alone, the Nazis murdered six million Jews, and up to five million Christians. We don't read *The Pilgrim Church, Fox's Book of Martyrs,* or *Martyrs Mirror* anymore, so we have lost our sense of history. We have lost all memory of sufferings of our forefathers:

> Mat 25:29 For unto every one that hath shall be given, and he shall have abundance: but from him that hath not shall be taken away even that which he hath.

The Lord has taken away our spiritual insight. We have lost sight of the Lord's big spiritual picture. The Great Tribulation of the Church began with the stoning of Stephen, and continued until the time of the Gentiles ended. Here is how we can show that to be so.

From the Scriptures we have studied so far in this book, all defined biblical times have been fulfilled in new Israel. As a result, the Great Tribulation could be an epochal time that has been running throughout the Christian Era. In fact, since the true saints have suffered terribly ever since the cross, the "Great Tribulation" that Jesus speaks of in the Gospels may be His own name for the whole Christian Era.

---

[1] The "but unto salvation" of 1Th 5:9 is much beloved by pre-trib rapturists as proof of their position. However, it is not about a tribulation period at all, but about the eternal salvation of the saints. The verse must be read carefully if we are to grasp what it teaches.

However, at the very end of this end time, there will still be a terribly violent, short period of suffering for the Church. Rev 3:10 speaks of an hour of trial that is to come upon the whole inhabited Earth. That hour is still in our future, and we need to get ready for it.

GRAPH NUMBER 17

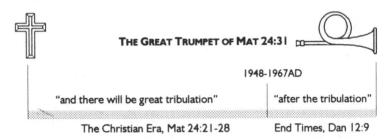

THE GREAT TRUMPET OF MAT 24:31

1948-1967AD

"and there will be great tribulation"   "after the tribulation"

The Christian Era, Mat 24:21-28   End Times, Dan 12:9

Mat 24:21 For then shall be great tribulation, such as was not since the beginning of the world to this time, no, nor ever shall be.

Mat 24:29 Immediately after the tribulation of those days shall the sun be darkened, and the moon shall not give her light, and the stars shall fall from heaven, and the powers of the heavens shall be shaken:

Mat 24:31 And he shall send his angels with a great sound of a trumpet, and they shall gather together his elect from the four winds, from one end of heaven to the other.

Note: In the above verses there are two distinct time periods (A "great tribulation" and "after the tribulation"). Since parallel day=year and times also show two time frames (the "time of the Gentiles" and "the end times"), it is reasonable to believe that they are concurrent and that the time "after the tribulation" began in 1948-1967AD.

Mat 24:21 tells us of a Great Tribulation. V. 29 tells us of a time *AFTER the Tribulation*, closely followed by the gathering of the saints, v. 31. According to Luk 21:24-32 there will be only one generation after the time of the Gentiles. So, when is this time *AFTER the tribulation*? Right now. The time after the tribulation and the end times of Dan 12:4, 9 appear to be the same time.

That's it, Brethren. Our end-time chronology is now in place. The Seven-Year Tribulation view is in error, and so is the pretribulation rapture theory. When we understand the *last* trumpet, it is obvious that both doctrines go directly against the Word of God! But no sense crying over our past miscalculations; let's just ask the Lord to show us what Revelation is really all about.

Rev 1:19 Write the things which thou hast seen, and the things which are, and the things which shall be hereafter.

Rev 1:19 is the key verse in the book. "Write the things which thou hast seen" -- *past tense* -- "the things which are" -- *present tense* -- "and the things which shall be hereafter" -- *future tense*. If we look at the book of Revelation from the Apostle John's time as we should, then Revelation is not just futuristic. Instead, it contains accounts of the past, present, and future *from John's own time*. That is really important. Revelation was written in a first century setting and that is where we must stand if we are going to have any idea of what that book is all about.

It is now apparent that the Lord designed Revelation to summarize His dealings with fallen man of all eras, and the book does touch on events that took place before and during John's lifetime. However, we can now also see that Revelation is primarily about what would happen after John's time -- about the monumetal happenings that were about to take place during the great 2000 year spiritual battle of the Christian Era.

Have You Heard?

CHAPTER 12

But refuse profane and old wives' fables,
and exercise thyself rather unto godliness.

For we have not followed
cunningly devised fables,
when we made known unto you
the power and coming
of our Lord Jesus Christ.

1TI 4:7 & 2PE 1:16

Out of the Seven-Year Tribulation position came a host of other doctrines. Some views were contrived whole-cloth, while others were add-ons from prior beliefs. Among those ideas is the doctrine of a coming end-time antichrist who is supposed to do a lot of wicked things at the end of the Christian Era. Believe it or not, we are looking for a mythical end-time ruler who has been the subject of fanciful conjecture for centuries.

Mythical? Impossible. We all *know* that antichrist is coming, don't we? No, we really don't know it. Most of what we hear about antichrist is one theologian's theory built upon another's supposition, and that goes all the way back to the 1st Century. Who and where is he? Isn't this how we will know that the second coming of Jesus is near, when some fiendish creature in human form takes control of the world?

Maybe, but what does Scripture state, and what is mere speculation? To find out, let's think about all we have heard about antichrist. All the things he is supposed to be and do, those things we think we know about THE antichrist. Among other assumptions, antichrist is supposed to . . .

1. Appear at the end of the age;
2. Rule the world for
    3½ years as a good leader,
    3½ years as an evil leader;
3. Have the temple rebuilt;
4. Reinstate temple sacrifices for the first 3½ years;
5. Turn against the Jews for the second 3½ years;
6. Stop temple sacrifices in the middle of the 7 years;
7. Cause all to worship him;
8. Start the battle of Armageddon;
9. Persecute the "Seven-Year Great Tribulation" saints, and anyone else he can get his hands on;
10. Misc. other legends (depending on school of thought) including that as 666, he is Satan incarnate.

If you can believe it, not one of those ideas can be directly supported from Scripture. Not a single one! Some come from interpreting the 70th week as a Seven-Year Great Tribulation, while others are just wild-eyed fabrications.

The word "antichrist" does appear in the Bible, so really, who, where, and when is he? Let's look at every verse in the Bible that mentions antichrist by name, and don't worry, you aren't going to have to do a lot of reading. It's a very short list. If you think there are other verses, please get your concordance out and find them. Though the author has searched the Scripture diligently for thirty years, he has yet to find another single verse. To get the literal sense of these verses, the quotations are from Green's word-for-word translation of the Greek manuscripts, the Textus Receptus:[1]

> 1Jo 2:18 (Green's Interlinear) Young ones, a last hour it is, and as you heard that the antichrist is coming, even now antichrists many have arisen; from which you know that a last hour it is.

> 1Jo 2:22 (Green's Interlinear) Who is the liar except the *one* denying that Jesus not is the Christ? This is the antichrist the *one* denying the Father and the Son.

---

[1] The Textus Receptus (the received text) is the Greek manuscript from which the King James Version was translated.

1Jo 4:3 (Green's Interlinear) And every spirit which not confesses Jesus Christ in *the* flesh having come, of God not is; and this is the antichrist which you heard that it is coming, and now in the world is already.

2J 1:7 (Green's Interlinear) Because many deceivers went out into the world, those not confessing Jesus Christ coming in *the* flesh. This is the deceiver and the antichrist.[1]

Difficult as it may be to believe, that's every verse. There are only four verses in the whole Bible which mention antichrist by name. That doesn't agree at all with what we have heard about *the* antichrist, does it? Be that as it may, those are still all the direct references to him that there are in Scripture. Everything else we have heard about him is just interpretive guesswork. Read those verses again, paying particular attention to the last two. Do they say that a special personage, "the antichrist," is going to appear in the future? If they do, I fail to see it.

Who do these verses tell us the antichrist is going to be? They declare that antichrist is anyone who denies that Jesus Christ has come in the flesh, or that Jesus is the Christ. 1Jo 2:18 and 4:3 state, "You have heard . . . you have heard." The Holy Spirit, through the Apostle John, is not stating that a specific antichrist is coming. He only said that you "have heard" that one is coming.

To put that in today's language, you "have heard" that warts can come from toads. Your having "heard" it doesn't make it so, nor does your saying that you have heard it mean that you believe it. You are not declaring that "warts come from toads" as a fact. You are saying only that you heard people say that they do.

Neither is the Lord declaring in 1st and 2nd John that antichrist is coming at some time in the future. He only said that you have heard that he is. It really appears that the Holy

---

[1] The definite article *τη*, "the," appears in the Greek text before antichrist, and it is so translated in the NASB. All who deny Jesus are identified not just as "an" antichrist, but as THE antichrist. Some students of Greek believe that *τη* is an indefinite article, but the translators of the KJV, NASB, and NIV, with a full knowledge of the English language, have all translated *τη* as definite, so this is a reasonable assertion.

Spirit is using that figure of speech to deny a coming anti-christ and to straighten out a false 1st Century church belief. The Holy Spirit appears to be saying something along this order: "Listen to Scripture, Church. You are sitting there with a false doctrine. You have heard that antichrist is coming. I am telling you that he that denies that Jesus is the Christ, or that denies that Jesus Christ has come in the flesh is the antichrist, and that he is already in the world."

Brethren, since "you have heard" is what the Bible states, we can accept that as an article of faith. Everyone who denies the basic truths about the Lord Jesus is THE antichrist, and the Christian Era has been full of them. For centuries, one pseudo-prophet after another (using the numerology of the Greek or Roman calendar) has "decoded" the 666 of Rev. 13:18 and announced which special conqueror, potentate, pope, or guru was the one and only, genuine, bona fide, authentic, and real life antichrist:

> Rev 13:18 Here is wisdom. Let him that hath understanding count the number of the beast: for it is the number of a man; and his number is Six hundred threescore and six.

On the basis of numerical dexterity applied to that verse, and that verse alone, literally hundreds of world leaders have been identified as THE final antichrist. Throughout this era, Christians not grounded in the Word have followed false prophets disguised as godly seers. Do you suppose we will ever learn? It doesn't seem so. Instead of turning away from our false teachers, we wait around for some new numerologist to point us to his latest antichrist prediction.[1]

> Isa 8:19-20 And when they shall say unto you, Seek unto them that have familiar spirits, and unto wizards that peep, and that mutter: should not a people seek unto their God? . . . To the law and to the testimony: if they speak not according to this word, *it is* because *there is* no light in them.

---

[1] Not understanding the intent of prophecy, some attempt to predict to the day when Jesus shall return. They lead many astray. Families have sold businesses and homes, and their faith has been disturbed. When the predicted day passes, the unsaved can't help but mock with, "Where is the day of His coming" (2PE 3:4). Thus, the way of truth is held open to ridicule.

God is truth, and the real battle is for the truth. Serving the truth is inseparable from serving God. Satan's generals are not planning some massive military campaign. They are not driving around in staff cars, or directing battles from front line bunkers. Through his lies, Satan is battling for our hearts and minds. Satan is a spirit, and he is fighting for the souls of men (Rev 18:8-13).

His real generals and high priests are in our high schools and on our college campuses, even in so-called Christian ones. Since we are not tuned in to the kind of battle we are supposed to be fighting, we don't even know who Satan's real generals are: Kant, Spinose, Freud, Jung, Spengler, Hume, Voltaire, Sagan, Moon, Hari Krishna and the New Age, the liberals, the ACLU and the National Education Association. It is an endless roll call. Included are the names of every single person who holds or teaches a doctrine which rejects Jesus as the Savior of the world (1Jo 2:22).

God sees the terrible rebellion of each fallen man's heart. Every single person who turns from His Son is THE person who rejected Jesus. Every soul that turns away from God's Son rebels against our Heavenly Father, and, in so doing, he becomes a "man of sin."

THE MAN OF SIN

In his second letter to the Thessalonian church, Paul addresses several doctrinal issues of importance to the believers in that city. It appears that they were just sitting around on a mountain, waiting for Jesus to return. Paul affirmed their doctrine of the imminent return[1] of the Lord (doing away with the premillennial view in the process), but he also warned them that a few things had to take place

---

[1] The "imminent return" is a term used in theological circles to say that Jesus could return at any moment. The Lord so wrote His Word that every generation could believe that Jesus would return in their lifetime. This concept has been misused by many to predict the time and date of the Lord's return.

before the second coming. Then, as now, this passage of Scripture has been woefully misunderstood.[1]

For instance, have we not heard that there will be a great revival before Jesus returns? Guess what? That is exactly the opposite of what 2Th 2:3 teaches. In that verse, quoted below, we find that a great falling away precedes the Lord's return. Unfortunately, that is not the only derived doctrine from this passage that is opposed to Scripture. Since a coming antichrist is a dubious doctrine at best, maybe we should look at the verses about this "man of sin" again, to see if they might mean something else entirely:

2Th 2:2-3 That ye be not soon shaken in mind, or be troubled, neither by spirit, nor by word, nor by letter as from us, as that the day of Christ is at hand. Let no man deceive you by any means: for *that day shall not come,* except there come a falling away first, and that man of sin be revealed, the son of perdition;

2:4 Who opposeth and exalteth himself above all that is called God, or that is worshipped; so that he as God sitteth in the temple of God, showing himself that he is God.

2:5-7 Remember ye not, that, when I was yet with you, I told you these things? And now ye know what withholdeth that he might be revealed in his time. For the mystery of iniquity doth already work: only he who now letteth *will let,* [*more accurately rendered as restrains*] until he be taken out of the way.

2:8-10 And then shall that Wicked be revealed, whom the Lord shall consume with the spirit of his mouth, and shall destroy with the brightness of his coming: *Even him,* whose coming is after the working of Satan with all power and signs and lying wonders, And with all deceivableness of unrighteousness in them that perish; because they received not the love of the truth, that they might be saved.

2:11-12 And for this cause God shall send them strong delusion, that they should believe a lie: That they all might be damned who believed not the truth, but had pleasure in unrighteousness.

What temple do you suppose the Lord would be speaking of in 2Th 2:4? In the Old Testament, God's temple was in

---

[1] Premillennialists believe that Jesus comes for the saints at one time, and that the wicked are judged at the Great White Throne 1000 years later . 2Th 1:9-10 shows that Jesus comes for the saints and judges the wicked on the same day!

Jerusalem, but this epistle to the Thessalonian church is in the New Testament. And where is the temple of God in the New Testament? "Our bodies are the temple of the Holy Spirit." Think it through, Brethren. Because of the location of 2Th in the Bible, it is sound theology to conclude that the temple spoken of in this passage of Scripture is the human heart. As a matter of fact, it is poor theology to think otherwise. The same Paul who wrote 2Th 2 was also inspired of the Holy Spirit to write the following:

> 1Co 3:16 Know ye not that ye are the temple of God, and that the Spirit of God dwelleth in you?

> 2Co 6:16 And what agreement hath the temple of God with idols? for ye are the temple of the living God.

> Eph 2:22 In whom all the building fitly framed together groweth unto an holy temple in the Lord: In whom ye also are builded together for an habitation of God.

A physical temple in Jerusalem might be applicable for an unenlightened Jew, but it is heresy for the Church to think of its temple as a building on Mount Moriah, and Paul was no heretic. Furthermore, 1Th 2:16 implies that the books to this church were written after the temple was destroyed in 70AD, and Paul makes no mention of building a new one.[1] If Paul in 2Th 2 is speaking of a physical temple in Jerusalem, then he departed from the Holy Spirit's revelation to him of where God's temple is now located. That is most unlikely.

v.3: *"a falling away first"*: It is almost impossible to believe how different the Church is today from what it was just 40 years ago. In that short time, there has been worldwide a falling away from the Lord unprecedented in church history. Europe was the cradle of the Reformation, yet less than 3% of today's Europeans still cling solidly to the faith. In our own land, it is estimated that at best, the true followers of the Lord do not exceed 10% of the total population; some

---

[1] 1Th 2:16 "Forbidding us to speak to the Gentiles that they might be saved, to fill up their sins alway: for the wrath is come upon them to the uttermost." Some scholars would like to early-date this epistle, but the "wrath" Paul speaks of here is probably in reference to the 70AD destruction of Jerusalem and the 2nd temple.

conservative groups even hold that no more than 5% of Americans are really Christians.

Many so-called evangelical pastors and evangelists deny the whole purpose of the cross. Ignoring the balance of Scripture, they preach only a positive gospel, which is no gospel at all. Forgotten are, "For all have sinned and come short of the glory of God" (Rom 3:23), and, "For the wages of sin is death, but the gift of God is eternal life through Jesus Christ our Lord" (Rom 6:23). Neglected are the very precepts that lead us to kneel at the foot of the cross in broken-hearted repentance. The word Gospel means good news, and the good news is that Jesus died to save us from our sins. The shed blood of Jesus is the very essence of the gospel. Promised persecution is forgotten, and we have adopted a materialistic and self-serving theology.[1]

Despite a population explosion in the third world, there are fewer missionaries in foreign lands than there were just a generation ago. Thousands of retiring missionaries are returning home with only a handful being sent out to replace them. Furthermore, access to many foreign fields is being restricted by their local leaders.

In New Testament churches here at home, the Bible is treated with a carelessness that would have horrified our forefathers. Scripture is ignored or culturally interpreted to fit the lifestyle of the congregation. TV ministries, many of them openly heretical, have corrupted the Word of God with false doctrine, but are still looked up to by many as trustworthy servants of the Lord.

> 1 Ti 4:1-2 Now the Spirit speaketh expressly, that in the latter times some shall depart from the faith, giving heed to seducing spirits, and doctrines of devils; Speaking lies in hypocrisy; having their conscience seared with a hot iron.

As was true in the Dark Ages, the established churches have again taken the Bible away from the people, but this time the theft is more subtle. The individual believer is

---

[1] Here are three of many verses which invalidate today's prosperity doctrines: Joh 16:2 "the time cometh, that whosoever killeth you will think that he doeth God service;" Joh 16:33 "In the world ye shall have tribulation: but be of good cheer; I have overcome the world;" 2TI 3:12 "Yea, and all that will live godly in Christ Jesus shall suffer persecution."

strongly advised that he isn't qualified to understand Scripture without extensive formal training (translate that as boning up on our traditions and the commentaries, and plenty of secular studies). This puts to nought the Scripture which states, the Holy Spirit "will guide you into all truth" (Joh 16:13). The everyday Christian has been programmed to accept denominational dogma, regardless of whether or not that dogma is in line with the Bible.

As a result, modernistic seminaries now have a death grip on most of the local evangelical churches. Churches cannot last long if their leaders do not believe the very Bible they have been commissioned to defend. Our crucified Jesus is the life of the Church. If His life is not in it, all that is left is a pile of bricks. Current events are showing this to be true. Major denominations are on the verge of collapse.

Some of the more radical churches are experiencing explosive growth. In them, occult phenomena, cleverly disguised as a charismatic interaction with the Holy Spirit of God, are trapping many of the spiritually unwary. Few are in sufficient obedience to the Scripture to recognize the demonic origin of some of the blasphemous doctrines now being openly taught. Along with the great apostasy, from the above we can see that the man of sin is in the Church already. Please come quickly, Lord Jesus, or just as You asked, "Will faith be on the earth" when You return? (Luk 18:8).

v.3 *"the man of sin be revealed, the son of perdition"*: Since the second world war, out in the world there are an ever-increasing number of atheists, agnostics, and other cultists who are in the lawless state of total defiance against God. 1Jo 3:4 tells us that sin is lawlessness. The rebellious unredeemed, still in their sins, are men of lawlessness, and doomed to destruction. At no other time in the Christian Era has there been such an open disregard for God's revealed Truth. Compare with Joh 17:12, Heb 10:3-9.

v.4 *"who opposes and exalts himself above every so-called god or object of worship"*: Secular humanists state that man is a god, their manifesto declaring (and I hate to write it): "Man made God in His own image." By these declarations they exalt themselves above every god. They replace God in their hearts with scientific formula, trading a knowledge of the Giver of Life for a limited understanding of what He has made.

v.4 (cont.) *"so that he takes his seat in the temple of God, displaying himself as being God"*: That phrase, by itself, shows us that the "man of sin" is not a human being, but a spirit. Our bodies are the temple of the Holy Spirit. Only a spirit being could take his seat in the human heart. In some of the charismatic churches, demons are invading people, giving false gifts and claiming to be the Holy Spirit.[1] Hindu guru or charismatic, the doctrines are sometimes the same. The wrappings have been changed to trap the simple.

Leaders of numberless cults declare: "Look to the god within yourself," or "Get in touch with your inner self" or "Channel with a master." This is supposed to be your inner god-like voice communicating with an ascended spirit (translate that as a demon). All these suggest that the power of a god is within man himself. This places man's ego in the temple of the Holy Spirit, claiming an authority there, which is God's alone, by sovereign right.

v.7 *"only He who now restrains will do so until He is taken out of the way"*: Throughout the Christian Era, the Holy Spirit has quickened the heart of man to his need for a Savior. However, in Gen 6:3, the Lord tells us that sometime in the future He would restrain His Spirit from doing so. Though the Holy Spirit will never leave the heart of the believer, the Lord makes no such promise to those who remain in rebellion to Him. One godly old pastor said, "I don't see the Holy Spirit working in the hearts of the unsaved like I used to." When the Holy Spirit stops restraining the evil in men's hearts, we Christians face a terrifying future.

v.9 *"with all power and signs and lying wonders"*: Now we have guided missiles and hydrogen bombs bringing fire down

---

[1] The enemy's intellect should not be underestimated. This satanic attack is brilliant. Satan has brought false doctrine and false spiritual manifestations into the Church under the guise of being the Holy Spirit of God. Many are afraid to speak against these sins for fear of blasphemy against the Holy Spirit. If we don't know our Bibles, we get caught in this trap. This is the subject of *Demons in the Church*, Ellis Skolfield (Fort Myers, FL, Fish House Publishing) 1993.

out of Heaven, nuclear submarines and interstellar probes, movie special effects, and TV wizards. TV is a wonder, indeed, showing an "image" of the world system, and many people worship it several hours a day (Rev 13:15). It shows mostly ungodliness and lies. If these are not false wonders, what does it take to qualify?

Our medical science can keep empty bodies alive long after the Lord may have taken the soul. Paleontologists deny the existence of God with their billion-year calendars. Psychologists try to deal with guilt without leading people to Jesus, ignoring the truth that Jesus' blood is the only thing in Heaven or on earth which can wash away sins. Psychology is a "rational" interaction with the occult, which keeps man's eyes averted from the cross.

So the man of sin is all around us. That malicious spirit of antichrist is in the worldly, the disbelieving, the liberal scholar who tries to disprove the Bible. Malignant and unrepentant men, some even "disguising themselves as servants of righteousness" (2Co 11:15). The man of sin isn't some superhuman tyrant just waiting for the right time to take over the world. The spirit of antichrist is in the unmerciful landlord, the drug pusher, the dishonest businessman, the occultist, the Satan worshiper with his hidden rites, and the crooked judge who steals from widows for a price. Today, he is everyone's neighbor, from the racketeer in our own home town, to the Islamic terrorist in some hidden safe-house.

About now you are saying to yourself, "But wait a minute, if there isn't going to be any antichrist in our future, what about the mark of the beast? Aren't the beasts of Rev 13 and 17 the antichrist, and isn't he supposed to give the unsaved a mark in their hands or on their foreheads?"

Well, before we can determine what that mark is, we need to identify the beast who gives it, so we should probably cover one of the beasts of Revelation next.

Leopard-Bear-Lion

CHAPTER 13

I will bring the worst of the heathen,
and they shall possess their houses:
I will also make the pomp of the strong to cease;
and their holy places shall be defiled.

EZE 7:24

As the Lord's Word continues to open, it appears that more of Daniel and Revelation is about Jerusalem and the Holy Land during the Christian Era than the Gentile church has to date believed. The historic setting for the next verse is mount Nebo, in 1406BC. It is from Moses' final oration to the Children of Israel before they entered the land of Canaan.

> Deu 11:11-12 But the land, whither ye go to possess it, *is* a land of hills and valleys, *and* drinketh water of the rain of heaven: A land which the LORD thy God careth for: the eyes of the LORD thy God *are* always upon it, from the beginning of the year even unto the end of the year.

The Lord's eyes continue to be upon the Holy Land. He never stopped, and His covenant with Israel for that land is everlasting.[1] Do you think the Lord has forgotten His promises about the land where Abraham offered up Isaac, where His temple was to be built, "a house of prayer for all people"? That land where His Son was to die, "not only for our sins, but for the sins of the whole world"? (1Jo 2:2). Of course not.

---

[1] Please also read 2Ch 7:12-16 and Eze 43:7. These verses do not stand alone; Gen 16:18-21, 17:8, Num 34:1-15, Jos 21:43, Exo 23:31, Act 7:5 affirm that the land of Canaan is always a land Holy unto the Lord.

Throughout the Christian Era, we in the Church have somehow gotten it backwards. We think we should make Gentiles out of Jews. But we have been grafted into Israel, not the other way around. The Bible directly states that the Gentile church has been grafted into Israel (Rom 11:17). If the land of Canaan is Holy unto the Jews, then it is holy unto us. If Jerusalem is a Holy City to the Jews, then it is a Holy City to the Church. Most of Bible prophecy should be viewed from that perspective.

> Gal 6:15-16 For in Christ Jesus neither circumcision availeth any thing, nor uncircumcision, but a new creature. And as many as walk according to this rule, peace *be* on them, and mercy, and upon the Israel of God.

In Daniel and Revelation, the Lord revealed the future of all the "Israel of God," both Jew and Gentile, and the future of His Holy Land. That future, of course, begins at the times of the prophets themselves. Daniel was positioned from 606BC to 533BC (at the beginning of Gentile domination of the Holy Land), so he is a prophet to "the time of the Gentiles." With the exception of those few verses which relate to the ultimate time of the end (Dan 8:19-25), his book was fulfilled in 1967AD.[1] John, however, was strategically positioned in 95AD, at the beginning of the Christian Era. He is apparently the prophet to our era. As we have already seen, Revelation's time-times and day-years have been fulfilled in new Israel. So we should look at the possibility that even more of Revelation might be fulfilled by 1967, including its beasts. Let's examine this possibility in more detail.

TIMES AND FOUR EMPIRES

Revelation is an allegorical book. It is full of figurative language such as *beasts* and *horns*, *seals* and *trumpets*, *candlesticks* and *bowls*, and figurative expressions must be figuratively interpreted.

For instance, nobody believes for a minute that in the final days, the Lord is going to have His holy angels up in Heaven pouring out a literal alphabet soup of trials from huge

---

[1] Please again compare Luk 21:24 with Dan 12:4,9.

gold-rimmed alabaster "bowls" upon the Earth. Many severe trials are indeed going to come upon us, but enormous bowls full? Not likely. It is more rational to accept that the Lord is using the "bowl" figure to show the vast quantity and the great severity of the coming trials rather than His method of delivering them to the Earth.

Neither does anyone believe that we are going to have a flaming red, ten-horned, seven-headed dinosaur roaring about with an all-decked-out, blood-drinking "lady of the night" riding on its back. Nor are we likely to see a real, live creature that looks like a leopard-bear-lion beast, all rolled up into one, with blasphemous names tattooed all over seven heads. Nor are we likely to hear a spirited oration from a stone idol that looks like that Leopard-Bear-Lion. However, if we are going to interpret Revelation literally, that is what we have to believe because that is what Revelation says. Since none of the above is even remotely sensible, then Revelation, for the most part, must be figurative. It must be God's eternal plan given to us in pictorial language.

Pictorial language is as different from English as Akkadian. If the only language you spoke was Akkadian, and I wished to tell you something, I would have to speak to you in Akkadian. If I addressed you in English, you would not understand me. Some of my English words might sound familiar, and you might even try to make sense out of what was said, but you would just be guessing, and you would probably be guessing wrong. That is what Revelation is like. It was written in pictorial language. Revelation cannot be understood unless we "speak" the pictorial language in which it was written. Throughout the Christian Era, this pictorial language has been sovereignly hidden from us, reserved for the last days.

As we have already seen, understanding Bible prophecy is cumulative. We needed to understand day=years before we could identify the Abomination that maketh Desolate. Then we needed to recognize the Dome of the Rock for what it is before we could understand the 70th Week, and so on. In the same way, we need to know who the Beasts of Daniel 7 represent before we can understand what the Leopard-Bear-Lion Beast of Revelation 13 is all about.

Let's begin with a little review of Daniel 7. This is a rather lengthy quote and commentary, but I know of no better way to explain these verses. Comments are set within the Bible text itself, in *italics*. Please study this passage carefully because your ability to identify the beasts in Revelation will depend upon your understanding of these principles:

Dan 7:3-4 And four great beasts came up from the sea [*the sea is the peoples and nations of the world, Rev 17:15*], diverse one from another. The first *was* like a lion [*The national emblem of Babylon was th winged lion -- The Ishtar gate of that city has bass reliefs of winged lions upon it*], and had eagle's wings: I beheld till the wings thereof were plucked, and it was lifted up from the earth, and made stand upon the feet as a man [*The Neo-Babylonian Empire, begun under Nebopolasser, was brought to the peak of its power in 606BC by his son Nebuchadnezzar. Nebuchadnezzar was the most absolute monarch in all human history*], and a man's heart was given to it [*Also a reference to Nebuchadnezzar, who came to the Lord late in life, Dan 4:37*].

Dan 7:5 And behold another beast, a second, like to a bear [*After Babylon fell, 536BC, Medo-Persia came into power -- The Persians were "raised up" over and ruled the Medean half of the empire*], and it raised up itself on one side, and *it had* three ribs in the mouth of it between the teeth of it [*The Medo-Persian Empire conquered three other empires: Lydia, Babylon, and Egypt*]: and they said thus unto it, Arise, devour much flesh.

Dan 7:6 After this I beheld, and lo another, like a leopard, which had upon the back of it four wings of a fowl [*Alexander the Great defeated the Medo-Persian Empire at the Battle of Isseis, in 332BC*]; the beast had also four heads [*Alexander had four great generals under him*]; and dominion was given to it [*After Alexander died in Babylon, 323BC, his empire was divided between his four generals: Ptolemy, Selucius, Lycimicus, and Cassander*].

Dan 7:7 After this I saw in the night visions, and behold a fourth beast, dreadful and terrible, and strong exceedingly; and it had great iron teeth: it devoured and brake in pieces, and stamped the residue with the feet of it [*Rome destroyed the remnants of the divided Grecian Empire and began to control the Holy Land in 65BC -- The Roman Empire continued until 476AD*]: and it *was* diverse from all the beasts that *were* before it; and it had ten horns [*After Rome fell, it was divided into roughly ten Eastern and western nations which have continued down to this day.*].

Dan 7:8 I considered the horns, and, behold, there came up among them another little horn, before whom there were three of the first horns plucked up by the roots [*Probably Adolf Hitler -- The Nazi regime covered almost all of the old Roman Empire. Which three nations the Lord is talking about here is in question: however Nazi Germany did pull Austria, Poland, and France up by the roots*]: and, behold, in this horn *were* eyes like the eyes of man [*Same expression as is used to describe Nebuchadnezzar, so the Lord is telling us of a single king here*], and a mouth speaking great things [*Dan 7:11 continues on to tell us of the fall of Nazi Germany, which was the death-knell of the Roman Empire*].

Dan 7:12 As concerning the rest of the beasts [*Lion, Bear, and Leopard -- Babylon, Medo-Persia and Greece*] they had their dominion taken away: yet their lives were prolonged for a season and time [*After Rome fell, the Holy Land again came under the dominion of the descendants of the three first beasts, Babylon, Medo-Persia, and Greece. They came back into power as the 1st Islamic Jihad of 634AD. They conquered Jerusalem in 639AD, and ruled that city for most of the Christian Era. A time of 1000 years, plus a season of 250 years=1250 years. The Mohammedans ruled in the Holy Land for 1260 years, from 688AD to 1948AD*].

Dan 7:16-20 I came near unto one of them that stood by [*an angel*], and asked him the truth of all this. So he told me, and made me know the interpretation of the things. These great beasts, which are four, *are* four kings [*or kingdoms, compare with Dan 7:23*], which shall arise out of the earth. But the saints of the most High shall take the kingdom, and possess the kingdom for ever, even for ever and ever. Then I would know the truth of the fourth beast [*Rome*], which was diverse from all the others, exceeding dreadful, whose teeth *were of* iron, and his nails *of* brass; *which* devoured, brake in pieces, and stamped the residue with his feet [*Rome dominated the whole known world for about 400 years*]; And of the ten horns that *were* in his head [*the Roman Empire divided into many smaller states including the major European nations we know of today*], and *of* the other which came up, and before whom three fell; even *of* that horn that had eyes, and a mouth that spake very great things [*Adolf Hitler*], whose look *was* more stout than his fellows [*The Hitler regime. That regime was the last gasp of the old militaristic Roman Empire*].

Dan 7:21-22 I beheld, and the same horn made war with the saints, and prevailed against them [*the Jews were the saints when the Lord gave Daniel this prophecy, and 6,000,000 Jews were killed by the Nazis*]; Until the Ancient of days came, and judgment was given to the saints of the most High; and the time came that the saints possessed the kingdom [*and in 1948AD the Jews had a nation again*].

Dan 7:23-24 Thus he said, The fourth beast shall be the fourth kingdom upon earth [*This is how we know that this passage is not about just individual kings, but really about kingdoms or empires*], which shall be diverse from all kingdoms, and shall devour the whole earth, and shall tread it down, and break it in pieces. And the ten horns out of this kingdom *are* ten kings *that* shall arise: and another shall rise after them; and he shall be diverse from the first, and he shall subdue three kings [*Austria, France and Italy were indeed subdued by Hitler during WW2*].

Dan 7:25 And he shall speak *great* words against the most High [*Satan speaks out against the Most High*], and shall wear out the saints of the most High [*When this was written, in 552BC, the Jews were all the saints there were*], and think to change times and laws: and they shall be given into his hand until a time and times and the dividing of time [*Recognizing time as 1000 years, 1Pe 3:8; and the Hebrew idiom of time, times and half a time as 2½ times -- The Jews were given into the enemy's hand from 552BC, when this prophecy was given, until the new nation of Israel, 1948AD. That is 2½ x 1000 or 2500 years*].

Since it is evident that this "time, times and half a time" was fulfilled in 1948AD, regardless of who we wish to claim as the "Little Horn" of Dan 7, that person would have to be placed before 1948. Looking at history, it appears that Adolf Hitler and the German Third Reich accurately fulfill this prophecy.[1]

Now the most important understanding from the above extensive quote is that the "beasts" in Daniel were not conquerors or kings. In fact, they were not men at all. Those "beasts" were empires. Nowhere in the Bible does the Lord change that definition, and that is the key that unlocks the hidden mystery of the identity of the beasts in Revelation. It is really a pretty obvious key once you see it:

The Biblical definition for beasts is Empires!

---

[1] The little horn out of the Fourth Beast of Dan 7 (Rome) is not an end-time ruler. Dan 8:17-19 identifies the little-horn out of the He-Goat (Greece) as the end-time enemy of new Israel and the Church. Since Syria-Lebanon was recognized as Grecian during John's time, the final enemy leader to come against Israel will be a Mohammedan, probably out of the Syria-Lebanon area.

Now the main purpose of the above exercise was to firmly establish the allegorical identity of the first three Middle Eastern empires that dominated the Holy Land after the fall of the Kingdom of Judah:

Lion = BABYLON.
Bear = MEDO-PERSIA
Leopard = GREECE

The modern counterparts of those beasts are:

Lion = IRAQ
Bear = IRAN
Leopard = SYRIA-LEBANON

Nowhere in the Bible have these allegorical identities been changed. Lion remains Babylon or Iraq, Bear remains Medo-Persia or Iran, and Leopard remains Greece or Syria-Lebanon throughout Scripture. So when we read of a beast in Revelation with those same names, we have every reason to believe that the Lord is telling us of the offspring of those empires:

> Rev 13:1-2 And I stood upon the sand of the sea, and saw a beast rise up out of the sea, having seven heads and ten horns, and upon his horns ten crowns, and upon his heads the name of blasphemy. **And the beast which I saw was like unto a leopard, and his feet were as *the feet* of a bear, and his mouth as the mouth of a lion**: and the dragon gave him his power, and his seat, and great authority.

The Leopard-Bear-Lion Beast (LBL). Note that this one beast looks like all three of those old empires rolled into one. So what has tied these three separate Middle Eastern states (Iraq, Iran, and Syria) together during the last two thirds of the Christian Era? The false prophet, Mohammed. Though they have sometimes battled each other, for 13 centuries Iraq, Iran, and Syria have been the home of the Shiite Moslems, the lair of assassins, a haven for terrorists and the supporters of all who hate Israel and the Christian nations. That is not just a guess, Brethren; read your history. The Islamic states have always been the enemies of the Church; they are now, and these descendants of Ishmael will continue to be enemies until the very day that Jesus returns. Why? Well, notice who

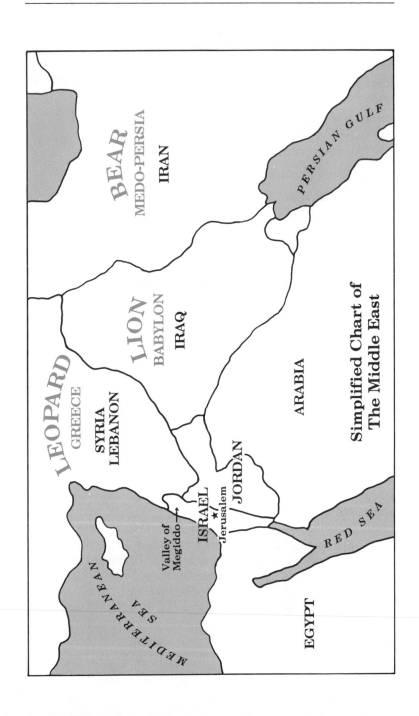

empowers these countries, the dragon, and the dragon (Satan) has always been the relentless enemy of God's people.

So the Leopard-Bear-Lion is Syria-Iraq-Iran, and their Islamic friends. But now we need to know when he will be in power, and to establish that we need to do a little review:

> Rev 11:2 But the court which is without the temple leave out, and measure it not; for it is given unto the Gentiles: and the holy city shall they tread under foot forty *and* two months.

The 42 months of Rev 11:2 were explained at length in Chapter 5. They are 1278.34 days=years, and it was exactly 1278.34 years from the construction of the Dome of the Rock in 688, until Jerusalem was again under Jewish control in 1967. So we already have historic pins for interpreting 42 months as years. Now in the LBL prophecy, Rev 13:5, we see 42 months again. LBL was granted authority over Jerusalem for 42 months:

> Rev 13:5 And there was given unto him a mouth speaking great things and blasphemies; and power was given unto him to continue forty *and* two months.

Since "the holy the city was tread underfoot for forty and two months" (Rev 11:2), and the Leopard-Bear-Lion was given dominion to "blaspheme God's tabernacle" for forty and two months (Rev 13:5-6), these prophecies are obviously parallel. They are about the same 688 to 1967AD Mohammedan rule of Jerusalem. From these verses we can now positively identify the LBL of Revelation 13 as the Islamic states of the Middle East. The Leopard-Bear-Lion is not some antichrist at all, but the same Islamic nations that now stand against Israel and the West. It is now apparent that the account of LBL was fulfilled between 688 and 1967.

Let's look at Rev 13:3-10 in detail. Explanatory notes are again set within the text, in *italics*:

> Rev 13:3-4 And I saw one of his heads as it were wounded to death [*The battles of Vienna, and Tours struck a blow against the Moslems which destroyed their hope of world conquest*]; and his deadly wound was healed [*After WW2, the western nations sent a major portion of their capital into the Middle East which enabled the Mohammedan states to rebuild*]: and all the world [*Remember that Bible prophecy is ethnographic -- The "whole world" seemingly refers to the part of the planet John knew about, John's*

known world. The Lord is not telling us of the Far East, Australia, or the Americas here] wondered after the beast. And they worshipped the dragon [*This verse shows that Islam is not another route to heaven -- The Dragon=Satan, ergo, The Mohammedans worship Satan*] which gave power unto the beast: and they [*the Moslems*] worshipped the beast, saying, Who *is* like unto the beast? who is able to make war with him? [*During the 1st Jihad they were totally victorious over the weak Christian mid-eastern states and the Eastern Roman Empire*].

Rev 13:5-6 And there was given unto him a mouth speaking great things and blasphemies; and power was given unto him to continue forty *and* two months. [*the Mohammedan domination of Jerusalem from 688 to 1967 is 42 months of day=years*] And he [*LBL, the Mohammedan states*] opened his mouth in blasphemy against God, to blaspheme his name, and his tabernacle [*The Mohammedans built a shrine on the footstool of God's feet*], and them that dwell in heaven [*we dwell in the heavenlies, right now, with Christ, Eph 2:6 "and raised us up with Him, and seated us with Him in the heavenly places, in Christ Jesus"*].

Rev 13:7-9 And it was given unto him [*LBL*] to make war with the saints, and to overcome them [*The 1st Jihad overwhelmed the idolatrous Coptic Church*]: and power was given him over all kindreds, and tongues, and nations [*remember that Bible prophecy is ethnographic, that it primarily addresses the countries that surround the Holy land*]. And all that dwell upon the earth shall worship him, whose names are not written in the book of life of the Lamb slain from the foundation of the world [*again a reference to show that Islam is not another road to Heaven*]. If any man have an ear, let him hear.

Rev 13:9-10 He that leadeth into captivity shall go into captivity [*during the 1st Jihad, the whole area of the Coptic church went into captivity, including the Holy land*]: he that killeth with the sword must be killed with the sword [*those aggressive Mohammedan armies of the Middle Ages were defeated at Tours and Vienna, with great loss of life*]. Here is the patience and the faith of the saints.

The beasts of Revelation appear to be figurative representations of Satan's total kingdoms on Earth, both physical and spiritual. The Leopard-Bear-Lion appears to be a VISIBLE aspect of Satan's unseen spiritual kingdom in the Middle East. The Mohammadans who controlled the Holy Land were held together by a common religion, a spiritual unity, rather than by a common ethnicity. In Rev 13:2, the prophet also declares that the Middle East is the seat of Satan's power, and his throne does appear to be there.

THE TEN HORNS OF THE LEOPARD-BEAR-LION

There is probably one more aspect of the Leopard-Bear-Lion we ought to look at. When God gave the land of Canaan to Abraham, He set the boundaries thereof: From the "River of Egypt" at the southern border of the Gaza Strip, to the River Euphrates near Damascus in Syria. That area has always been the land the Lord gave to Isaac and Jacob. The Jews know it, and the Arabs know it, but the Arabs have been trying to steal the land God gave to Israel ever since:[1]

> Gen 15:18-21 In the same day the LORD made a covenant with Abram, saying, Unto thy seed have I given this land, from the river of Egypt unto the great river, the river Euphrates: The Kenites, and the Kenizzites, and the Kadmonites, And the Hittites, and the Perizzites, and the Rephaims, And the Amorites, and the Canaanites, and the Girgashites, and the Jebusites.

Those peoples were the original inhabitants of the land. When Joshua and the Children of Israel entered Canaan in 1406BC, God commanded them to drive every one of those people out. They didn't do so. Instead, Israel enslaved them and put them to forced labor.

When Nebuchadnezzar took the Jews captive to Babylon, he left the "poorer people in the land." That would have included the descendants of those Canaanite slaves, and the descendants of those slaves have been a thorn in the side of Israel ever since. They are a thorn in the side of Israel today. They are the Palestinians![2] Did you count the number of the different original inhabitants? There were ten, and they are probably the "ten horns" of the Leopard-Bear-Lion. That is so important, I am going to say it again:

---

[1] Though the Arabs are also children of Abraham through Hagar, God gave the Holy Land to the people born through Sarah's son Isaac: "Neither, because they are the seed of Abraham, *are they* all children: but, In Isaac shall thy seed be called" (Rom 9:7).

[2] The name Palestinian is derived from Philistine. Those people were the worst of David's enemies. Goliath of Gath was a Philistine.

*The ten horns of the Leopard-Bear-Lion are probably
the militant Palestinians led by Yasser Arafat and their
murderous terrorist arm, the Hamas.*

If you question the validity of that conclusion, just read
the *Jerusalem Post* sometime. In Israel, Jews are daily being
tortured and killed by Palestinians. Terrorists are trying to
destroy God's people, one soul at a time, and take their land,
one square inch at a time. May Y'shua defend them, for no
one else will. If an Israeli kills a terrorist in self-defense, it is
front-page news in the world's newspapers as a murderous
act. But if a Palestinian bombs a bus full of women and
children, you may read about it in a 2" filler, on page 10, as
almost justifiable homicide. Supposedly, these terrorists are
just "misunderstood" people who are being oppressed by the
Jews. Should we be surprised? No. That is what we should
expect the news media to say, considering the influence that
OPEC money and Mohammedan extremists now have on the
economies and news agencies of the western world.

THE TWO-HORNED BEAST

Following the LBL beast is another beast: the beast with
"Two Horns like a Lamb." Since the 42 months of LBL's
dominion take us from 688 to 1967, this later beast should
give us information on events that take place AFTER 1967AD.

Rev 13:11 And I beheld another beast coming up out of the earth;
and he had two horns like a lamb, and he spake as a dragon.

Note how this beast is described: He is "like a lamb." The
Greek word used here for lamb is *arnion*,[1] accurately defined
as "a little lamb." *Arnion* appears 26 times in Revelation, and
in every time but this one, *arnion* refers to the little "*lamb* of
God, which taketh away the sins of the world" (Joh 1:29). So
why use a lamb to describe this new beast? Because this
beast would appear to be Christ-like, it would appear to be
Christian. But Two-Horns would speak like the dragon. In
other words, this beast would appear to be a Christian empire, but would be influenced by Satan.

---

[1] ἀρνίον, Strong's No. G721. arnion, ar-nee'-on; diminutive from G704;
a lambkin: lamb.

Now, this beast has two horns. In other words, this empire would have two major kings or kingdoms, or it would rule in the Holy Land at two different times. These kingdoms might exist at the same time, or from examples like Dan 8:3 and 8:8, these horns could appear at different times. So how can we know who these kingdoms are? While the Bible doesn't directly state who they are, it does tell us when they will rule:

> Rev 13:12 And he exerciseth all the power of the first beast before him [*i.e., in his sight or presence*], and causeth the earth and them which dwell therein to worship the first beast, whose deadly wound was healed.

The Elizabethan English is a little confusing here, but that "before him" in Greek is *enopion,* or "in the sight of."[1] The two-horned beast will rule *in the sight of,* or in the presence of, the Leopard-Bear-Lion beast. Now read Rev 13:5 again. From that verse we recognize that the LBL beast was given authority from 688 to 1967AD. For this lamb-like beast rule "in the sight" of LBL, he would have to rule during the same time. His two horns would have to come up between 688 and 1967! That is the key to the identity of this Two Horned Beast, so I'm going to say it again:

> *For the beast with Two Horns like a Lamb to be in the presence of the Leopard-Bear-Lion Beast, he would have to exist while LBL was in power, and his two horns would have to come up between 688 and 1967!*

"In his presence" also means something else. Two Horns and LBL would coexist. Two Horns would not destroy LBL, but would be given authority while LBL remained in the Holy Land. So let's look at the history of the Holy Land, and see if any so-called Christian nations ruled there sometime between 688 and 1967AD.

The Mohammedans conquered Jerusalem in 639AD. Forty-nine years later, Abd el Malik began construction of the Dome of the Rock on God's holy mountain. Construction was completed in 705AD, and Islam ruled victorious in Jerusalem

---

[1] ἐνώπιον, Strong's No. G1799. enopion, en-o'-pee-on; neut. of a comp. of G1722 and a der. of G3700; in the face of (lit. or fig.):--before, in the presence (sight) of, to.

for the next 400 years. Satan must thought have it was all over in the Holy Land for the Jews and the Church. The Mohammedans rejoiced over defeating God's Two Witnesses, a fact which was predicted in the prophecy about them:

> Rev 11:10 (NASB) And those who dwell on the earth will rejoice over them and make merry; and they will send gifts to one another, because these two prophets tormented those who dwell on the earth.

Then in the 11th Century, Pope Urban II called for the Crusades to begin. Christian knights came from all over Europe, captured Jerusalem, and ruled various parts of the Holy Land. For the next 200 years, control of the land was by no means certain. But by the end of the 13th Century, the Crusaders were driven out, and Islam again ruled Jerusalem. They continued to rule there through several Islamic regimes, the final one being the Ottoman Empire.

Though we don't read a lot about it in western history books, the Crusaders raped, murdered, and pillaged the Jews and Arabs who were living in the Holy Land. They indeed "spoke like the dragon!" They didn't destroy the Dome of the Rock, nor drive the Mohammedans from the land. The Crusaders were "in his sight." They were the first horn, and they were in the presence of the Leopard-Bear-Lion!

Seven Centuries later, during World War I, a later group of "Christian knights" again fought against an Islamic empire and entered the Holy Land. Lawrence of Arabia and General Allenby, with the blessing of the League of Nations, took what was to become known as the *British Mandate*. Again the western nations, appearing "like a lamb," ruled in Jerusalem, and from 1917 to 1948AD, Great Britain controlled the Holy land. They did not destroy the Dome of the Rock, nor drive the Mohammedans out, and they were the second horn "in the sight" of the Leopard-Bear-Lion.

In 1948, the new nation of Israel was established, which ended Gentile domination of the Holy Land. But twice, during the 42 months, "Christian nations" did rule in the presence of the Leopard-Bear-Lion Beast, so the western "Christian" nations (so-called) are the beast with Two Horns like a Lamb!

THE HEALED BEAST

That takes us to 1948AD, but that is not the end of the Two Horned beast (2H) nor of the Leopard-Bear-Lion (LBL):

> Rev 13:12-14   And he [*2H*] exerciseth all the power of the first beast [*LBL*] before him, and causeth the earth and them which dwell therein to worship the first beast [*LBL*], whose deadly wound was healed. And he [*2H*] doeth great wonders, so that he maketh fire come down from heaven on the earth in the sight of men, And deceiveth them that dwell on the earth by *the means of* those miracles which he had power to do in the sight of the [*LBL*] beast.

After the World War II, the beast with Two Horns experienced an accelerated growth in its economies and industry. With western oil fields insufficient for its needs, Two Horns turned to the Middle East. Over the next four decades, a major portion of western hard currency flowed into the coffers of the Leopard-Bear-Lion. Those Middle Eastern nations then used those funds to buy modern weaponry from the West. So the Beast with Two Horns "healed" the beast who had a wound of the sword, and Leopard-Bear-Lion came back to life! For the first time in 13 Centuries, Islamic states again threaten the peace of Israel and of the West.

Indeed, the Beast with Two-Horns "performs great signs" which deceive men and turn their eyes from the Lord. The western nations are the most scientifically advanced on earth. If one had been standing on the streets of Baghdad in 1991, the phrase, "and he even makes fire come down out of Heaven to the earth in the presence of men," would have been no mystery. American guided missiles and smart-bombs were indeed a "fire from Heaven" that was visible to all.

We have dived to the bottom of the bottomless sea, harnessed the atom, sent probes beyond our solar system, and placed men on the Moon. These are great signs which deceive us into thinking that man is God (2Th 2:4).

IMAGE OF THE BEAST

There has probably been as much written about the image and mark of the beast (Rev 14:14-18) as there has about any other passage in the Bible. It has always been assumed that this "image of the beast" was something physical, a statue that was carved, cast, or sculpted out if stone, wood, or metal. But that is not all the dictionary says that an image can be.[1]

An image is a likeness of any kind. A photograph is an "image" of the original scene, and a book is an "image" of the thoughts of a writer. If we use that definition for "image," and a biblical beast is a figurative picture of an empire, then an "image" of that beast would be a later empire that is like one that came before it.

> Rev 13:14 And he [*the Two Horned Beast*] deceiveth them that dwell on the earth by *the means of* those miracles which he had power to do in the sight of the beast [*LBL*]; saying to them that dwell on the earth, that they should make an image to the [*LBL*] beast [*a likeness of, or a new Islamic power*], which had the wound by a sword, and did live.

An image is a likeness, and now a likeness of the first Mohammedan beast is springing up all over the western world. The fastest growing religion in Europe is Islam, and as of this writing, the largest mosque in the western world is in Rome. The largest place of worship in Toronto, Canada, is a mosque, and there are more people attending mosques in England than there are going into the Church of England. In Holland, state-owned Christian churches are being turned over to the Mohammedans, and 14% of the immigrants into the United States are Islamic. Now we can understand some verses which appear within the Seven Bowls of Wrath:

> Rev 16:12-14 And the sixth angel poured out his vial upon the great river Euphrates [*which flows through the LBL*]; and the water thereof was dried up [*as the waters that separated them were figuratively dried up, they figuratively became one land, and through Islam they have spiritually become one people*], that the way of the kings of the east [*LBL*] might be prepared. And I saw three unclean spirits [*Leopard-Bear-Lion is a three- part empire*] like frogs *come* out of the mouth of the dragon, and out of the mouth of the beast, and out of the mouth of the false prophet [*Mohammed*]. For they are the spirits of devils, working miracles, *which* go forth unto the kings of the earth and of the whole world [*for the first time in history, Islam is now spreading into the*

---

[1] **Im·age**:. A duplicate, counterpart, or other representative reproduction of an object. One that closely or exactly resembles another, a double. A mental picture of something that is not real or present.

western world], to gather them to the battle of that great day of God Almighty.

Note the location of this prophecy: the River Euphrates. That's the Middle East, the lair of the Leopard-Bear-Lion. The LBL beast is a three-part beast. Notice how many evil spirits like frogs there are: THREE. It is the release of these three demons into the world which will trigger Armageddon, and we see how Mohammedanism is spreading. In the United States today, radical Shiite groups are meeting in secret to plot our destruction while 60% of the funding for the terrorist Hamas comes from radical Mohammedans right here in this country. To its own harm, the Two-Horned Beast helps the Leopard-Bear-Lion to gain strength again:

> Rev 13:15-16 And he [*2H*] had power to give life unto the image of the [*LBL*] beast, that the image [*or likeness*] of the [*first LBL*] beast should both speak, and cause that as many as would not worship the image of the beast should be killed.

Now the western nations, including our own government, favor Arabic and Islamic interests over those of Israel. Our spiritually blind leaders support the interests of the Mohammedan states above those of our closest ally. Palestinians have access to the highest echelons in our administration, and Mohammedans are graciously granted all the air-time they need to subvert our people. We laugh at the faith our founding fathers died for and refuse to help our brethren in Israel to house their homeless returnees. The Leopard-Bear-Lion speaks, and we listen! And though it hasn't happened yet, our listening to him will probably lead to the destruction of the Church in the western world:

> Rev 11:7 And when they shall have finished their testimony, the beast that ascendeth out of the bottomless pit shall make war against them, and shall overcome them, and kill them.

That death may be physical, but surely it is spiritual, as the Church stumbles about in a self-induced doctrinal trance. Blinded by tradition, lethargy, and the cares of this world, we keep right on playing our little religious games. But at no time since the Reformation has the Church at large known less about the Lord Jesus Christ, or His sacred Word, than it does right now.

In Matthew 24:25 the Lord promised He would tell us about all this in advance, and He did. But Jesus will return like a thief, anyway, for few there be that can hear what "the Spirit sayeth to the churches."

GRAPH NUMBER 18

Allegorical Figures in Daniel			
Reference	Figure	Fulfillment	Date
Dan 2:38	Head	Babylon	606-536BC
Dan 2:39	Chest	Medo-Persia	536-332BC
Dan 2:39	Thighs	Greece	332-65BC
Dan 2:40	Legs	Rome	65BC-475AD
Dan 2:41	Ten Toes	One-World	1948AD-
Dan 7:4	Lion	Babylon	606-536BC
Dan 7:5	Bear	Medo-Persia	536-332BC
Dan 7:6	Leopard	Greece	332-65BC
Dan 7:7	Terrible	Rome	65BC-475AD
Dan 7:25	Little Horn	Adolf Hitler	1936-1945AD

The Leopard-Bear-Lion Beast of Rev 13:2-10

Rev 13:2-10	LBL	The Mohammedans	688-1967AD

The Seven Heads of the Scarlet Beast, Rev 17:10

"Five have fallen"

Rev 17:10	Head One	Canaanites	circa 2600-1406BC
	Head Two	Assyria	745-606BC
	Head Three	Babylon	606-536BC
	Head Four	Medo-Persia	536-332BC
	Head Five	Greece	332-65BC

"one is"

Rev 17:10	Head Six	Rome	65BC-475AD

"One has not yet come, and when he comes he must remain a short space."

Rev 17:10	Head Seven	The Mohammedans	688-1967AD

"and the beast which was and is not even he is the eighth"

Rev 17:10	The Beast Himself	???	1948AD-

Mark of the Beast

CHAPTER 14

And the smoke of their torment
ascendeth up for ever and ever:
and they have no rest day nor night,
who worship the beast and his image,
and whosoever receiveth
the mark of his name.

REV 14:11

As a matter of historic reality, the Jews took control of Jerusalem in 1967, and Luk 21:24 was then fulfilled. Luk 21:32 states that within one generation of that time, "all things" would be fulfilled. All things -- nothing left out. So unless a different way can be found to interpret those verses, within one generation of June 6th, 1967, it will all be over and we will be in the Eternal Kingdom of God!

This understanding led to finding that the day-years of Dan 12:11, Rev 11:2-4, and Rev 12:6 were already fulfilled in the new nation of Israel -- which led to understanding time, times, and half a time -- which led to the Two Witnesses -- which led to the salvation of a Jewish remnant -- which led to questioning an end-time antichrist -- which led to understanding beasts as empires -- which led to understanding the Two Horned Beast like a Lamb. Now, here is the question: Since that two-horned beast is already here, where is his mark? To find out, maybe we ought to look at biblical marks in general.

The beasts of Revelation are different aspects of the enemy's world-wide empire. In Rev 17, we see the satanic empire as a scarlet beast spanning world history. In Rev 13, we saw that same empire as the Leopard-Bear-Lion beast spanning much of the history of the Holy Land during the Christian Era. LBL is the Mohammedan world, and Mohammed appears to be THE "false prophet" of Rev 16:13. In our own time, we see the banking system of the Two-Horned Beast "like a lamb" controlling the world's economies "in the presence" of the Leopard-Bear-Lion. So which of these three beasts gives the mark? A careful study of context shows us:

> Rev 13:15-16 And he [*2H*] had power to give life unto the image [likeness] of the [*LBL*] beast, that the image [*likeness*] of the [*first LBL*] beast should both speak, and cause that as many as would not worship the image [*likeness*] of the [*LBL*] beast should be killed. And he [*2H*] causeth all, both small and great, rich and poor, free and bond, to receive a mark in their right hand, or in their foreheads.

The western nations give this mark, and how they do so and what that mark represents are important for this last generation to understand.

Did you know that the "mark of the beast" is not the only mark in the Bible? The Lord also uses a mark to seal His servants on their foreheads (Eze 9:4, Rev 7:3, Rev 14:1). From Scripture and history, it appears that the Lord's mark is only visible in the spiritual world. If God's mark is only visible in the spiritual world, is it possible that Satan's mark is also visible only in the spiritual world? Having already found the day-years and much of Bible prophecy already fulfilled, is it possible that the mark of the beast is also in the process of being fulfilled, and we haven't seen it?

God's message to us in the Bible is primarily spiritual, and He didn't want to make it difficult for us to grasp. So throughout Scripture, the Lord uses illustrations of natural things that everybody recognizes to explain spiritual principles. With the "mark of the beast," it appears that the Lord is using a common 1st Century "mark" figure to describe a condition that exists in the unseen spiritual world. So when we read about a biblical seal or mark, we need to place ourselves in the historic position of the writer and ask, "What did a seal or mark mean to someone who lived at the time John wrote about them?"

When a valuable letter or package was sent from one place to another, hot wax was melted onto the edge of the scroll or merchandise. Then before the wax hardened, an authorizing mark or signet was stamped into the hot wax. The wax seal prevented tampering while the mark identified the sealing personage, be it a king, or governor, or some other delegated authority. An official seal was considered untouchable, and no unauthorized person would dare break one, on pain of death. The seal and mark placed a parcel under the authority and protection of the person who sealed it.

Now, let's look at seals and marks from a biblical standpoint. In 586BC, just before Jerusalem fell to the Babylonians, the prophet Ezekiel saw a mark, placed by a holy angel, on the foreheads of the faithful Jews.

> Eze 9:4, 6 And the LORD said unto him [*an angel*], Go through the midst of the city, through the midst of Jerusalem, and set a mark upon the foreheads of the men that sigh and that cry for all the abominations that be done in the midst thereof . . . Slay utterly old *and* young, both maids, and little children, and women: but come not near any man upon whom *is* the mark.

There is ample biblical record of the fall of Jerusalem, but nowhere is there a record of that mark being seen by any ordinary witness. Just Ezekiel saw it, and he saw it only in a vision. Here is the parallel account of the fall of Jerusalem written by a historic chronicler who didn't see the mark:

> 2Ch 36:17 Therefore he brought upon them the king of the Chaldees, who slew their young men with the sword in the house of their sanctuary, and had no compassion upon young man or maiden, old man, or him that stooped for age: he gave *them* all into his hand.

Compare the two verses above. They are obviously two different accounts of the same identical scene, but the writer of II Chronicles didn't report seeing that mark, nor those angels. Why? Because he didn't see them. Those seals and angels that Ezekiel saw were visible only in the spiritual world. That mark was a spiritual mark. Eze 9:6 also tells us why this mark was given. It was given by a holy angel to identify and protect those faithful Jews from the angels of destruction who were about to slay the inhabitants of Jerusalem. Those faithful Jews were indeed sealed with a mark which showed them to be under the authority and protection of the Lord our God!

In Rev 7:4, we again have a spiritual sealing; here we see 144,000 of Israel sealed. But this time, they are sealed at the beginning of the Christian Era.[1] In Rev 14:1, the great eternal Name of that sealing authority is revealed:

> Rev 14:1 And I looked, and, lo, a Lamb stood on the mount Sion, and with him an hundred forty *and* four thousand, having his Father's name written in their foreheads.

Unless we wish to suggest that the 144,000 Israelites of Rev 7, and 144,000 people of Rev 14, are two different groups (each of which contains 144,000 people), then these are repetitive prophecies about the same Israelites, and this is the same sealing. There is no historic record of any such sealing being seen at any time during the Christian Era, so this would also appear to be an invisible spiritual sealing. Note what this mark is. It is the name of "God the Father." In other words, Israel was struck with a spiritual mark which showed to the destructive angelic beings of Rev 7:1-3 that they were under the protection and authority of the Sovereign God. We Christians are sealed in like manner.

As directly stated in Scripture, Christians are sealed with the Holy Spirit of promise (Eph 1:13). The Holy Spirit placed a mark on each of us when we were saved. Undoubtedly, it is the same seal that we read about in Rev 14:1, "the name of His Father." It is a very real seal, but we don't see it on anybody, do we? No, so our seal is also invisible in the natural world. The Holy Spirit's seal is invisible. However, His seal is indeed a real seal and glows bright and clean in the spiritual world! What a wonderful truth.

The mark of the beast appears to be either Satan's name, or his empire's name (or as 666, his system's name) in the spiritual hand or forehead of his servants. Since the Lord's seal is invisible, it is reasonable to believe that Satan's seal, "the mark of the beast," is also invisible in the natural world.

---

[1] Revelation's chiasmic form plus other internal evidence within the book shows each of its prophecies to be a repetitive picture of the Christian Era. From Rev 7:1-2 itself, we can historically position this sealing to be at the time of the Cross *(Please See Appendix III)*.

Could not Satan use this invisible mark to identify his servants to the rest of the unseen spiritual world? If he does, then it is very likely that evil men have been so marked by the enemy throughout human history.

Of course, there will be some who will accuse me of "spiritualizing" this passage, but examine the passage itself. In Rev 13, we read about "beasts" and "horns" and other obviously figurative expressions, so it is only sound theology to interpret the whole passage as figurative, including the mark of the beast.

WHAT DOES THE 666 MEAN?

Since Revelation is spiritual in nature, could 666 be God's way of describing an unseen spiritual seal in an understandable way? 666 could represent spiritual characteristics. If we can discover what 666 means spiritually, we should be able to find out who has the mark, and what it is. If a person displays the attributes of 666, maybe we could recognize which individuals belong to the beast. How can we confirm this? By looking at spiritual marks as described for us in Bible prophecy and by studying biblical examples of sixes. Besides Revelation, there are only three other places in Scripture where 666 is used:

> 1Ki 10:14 Now the weight of gold that came to Solomon in one year was six hundred threescore and six talents of gold.

> 2Ch 9:13 Now the weight of gold that came to Solomon in one year was six hundred and threescore and six talents of gold.

> Ezra 2:13 The children of Adonikam, six hundred sixty and six.[1]

In the 1Ki and 2Ch quotes above, gold, the medium of exchange, is shown as 666. The nations surrounding Israel

---

[1] Solomon's tax collector (who gathered those 666 talents of gold) was Adoniram (Hebrew for "lord of the heights"). In Ezr 2:13, we find an Adonikam (Hebrew for "lord of rising") that had 666 children. It is possible that this is the same man and that a scribal transliteration altered the name by one letter during the captivity. If so, we have a biblical personage in finance that had 666 descendants. That leads to the possibility that the descendants of Adoniram are behind world banking and tax-gathering today and could be the tools the enemy will be using to bring in the mark of the beast.

were in economic bondage to Solomon and had to give him gold. Looking at Rev 13:17, we note "no man might buy or sell" unless he has the mark. Neither can a man "buy or sell" if he does not have gold or some other acceptable medium of exchange. So this mark is related to a person's economic bondage. Let's say it again. Having the mark of the beast shows a person to be in economic bondage.

Daniel is a marvelous book; it has so many prophetic guidelines hidden away in it. In Dan 3, Nebuchadnezzar built an image of what? Gold! He decreed that all should bow before his image or be thrown into a fiery furnace. That image was 6 cubits wide by 60 cubits high. That is 66666666666 which, from a symbolic standpoint, is a lot of 666's. This concept would be guesswork if we didn't have the following verses from the same chapter:

> Dan 3:5 That at what time ye hear the sound of the cornet, flute, harp, sackbut, psaltery, dulcimer, and all kinds of musick, ye fall down and worship the golden image that Nebuchadnezzar the king hath set up:

> Dan 3:10 Thou, O king, hast made a decree, that every man that shall hear the sound of the cornet, flute, harp, sackbut, psaltery, and dulcimer, and all kinds of musick, shall fall down and worship the golden image:

> Dan 3:15 Now if ye be ready that at what time ye hear the sound of the cornet, flute, harp, sackbut, psaltery, and dulcimer, and all kinds of musick, ye fall down and worship the image which I have made; well: but if ye worship not, ye shall be cast the same hour into the midst of a burning fiery furnace; and who is that God that shall deliver you out of my hands?

Well, our God is certainly able, and He surely did deliver Shadrach, Meshach, and Abednego, but did you count the number of musical instruments in each verse? There are six in each, and there are three such verses.[1] The Lord did not have Daniel repeat six musical instruments three times as an exercise in High Syriac grammar and sentence structure. If a six is repeated three times, we have 666.

---

[1] There is another listing of musical instruments in v.7, but it records only five instruments. What that five means is open to question.

Sixty years pass -- or ten sixes, now there is a strange coincidence -- and on the night Babylon fell, Belshazzar the king held a great feast for a thousand or so of the empire's dignitaries. He invited all the Babylonian court nobles and their ladies to attend. After they had partied a bit, in a supreme act of defiance, he had the vessels of the temple of the Lord brought before him, so he and his friends could drink a little wine from them:

> Dan 5:2-4 Belshazzar, whiles he tasted the wine, commanded to bring the golden and silver vessels which his father Nebuchadnezzar had taken out of the temple which was in Jerusalem; that the king, and his princes, his wives, and his concubines, might drink therein. Then they brought the golden vessels that were taken out of the temple of the house of God which was at Jerusalem; and the king, and his princes, his wives, and his concubines, drank in them. They drank wine, and praised the gods of gold, and of silver, of brass, of iron, of wood, and of stone.

Did you count the number of gods? There are six. So we see another six, this time six false gods. These gods are made of the major building blocks of all manufactured goods: gold, silver, brass, iron, wood, and stone. Music is a call to worship them. Throughout the Old Testament, gold, music, and revelry are associated with the worship of idols. Aaron's calf was made of gold, and after sacrificing to it, "the people sat down to eat and to drink, and rose up to play" (Exo 32:6). God hated these idols, and the idolatry of the Israelites was the major reason the Lord permitted them to go into captivity. These multiple sixes in the Old Testament are not there by accident, are they? Let's see if we can put them together with other Scriptures to uncover what they might mean.

Since God's real mark is invisible in the natural world, Satan's mark of Rev 13:16 is probably also invisible unless we can find Scripture which leads us to believe differently. The author can find no such Scriptures, so from a biblical standpoint, Satan's mark is probably an invisible spiritual mark. Let's put it all together:

> Rev 13:16-18 And he causeth all, both small and great, rich and poor, free and bond, to receive a mark in their right hand, or in their foreheads: And that no man might buy or sell, save he that had the mark, or the name of the beast, or the number of his name. Here is wisdom. Let him that hath understanding count the number

of the beast: for it is the number of a man; and his number is Six
hundred threescore and six [*i.e.*, *666*].

We need to go back to Daniel for a moment. Babylon was
the center of world commerce, worshiping the almighty gold
daric.[1] The seat of governmental authority in Babylon was
Nebuchadnezzar the king. He was an absolute monarch. At
the sound of 6x6x6 kinds of music, he commanded everyone
in his empire to bow down and worship his 6 x 6666666666
image of gold. The king was in essence saying: "I order you to
worship this gold. I have made gold my god. I worship it; you
must make it your god, too. I support it with my authority,
and I will make it sound enticing for you." Governments today
bow down before their economic systems and order their
citizens to support them.

Ever since God marked Cain, who slew his brother Abel,
there have been marks: one for God's servants and one for
those belonging to the enemy. Through the ages, Satan has
tried to turn man away from God. He has used false gods,
disguised as materialism of every kind. Gods of gold, silver,
brass, iron, wood and stone.

We have them with us today. They are wrapped in
packages that appeal to our western minds and have more
interesting labels. We are too sophisticated to bow down to
some stone idol, so we call our idols automobiles, jewelry,
furniture, televisions, computers, and boats. We bow down to
these present-day gods without any problem at all. Same
gods, 20th century names. We worship them, so they are also
a stumbling block to us. Using music, Satan makes them
sound pretty for us. Advertising jingles and spotlights on the
rich and famous market the world's goods in abundance. Ah,
and there can also be financial success, power, and sexual
prowess. We are programmed to believe that in this life, that's
all there is of any worth. "O Lord, how has Satan been able to
deceive Thy people so?"

When someone turns himself totally over to the love of
this world and excludes the Living God from his life, he has a
mark on him that angelic beings see. It may be hidden in his
hand as a credit card or struck between his eyes as the

---

[1] The daric was an early gold coin used throughout the Middle East.

consuming thoughts of a depraved mind. He is under the authority of the ruler of this world and has become his blind slave. If he becomes openly evil, that mark even becomes visible to Christians. The greed and wanton pleasure-seeking, the drugs, the immorality, and egocentricity become a spiritual "mark of the beast" on him that won't wash off. You can see the sin in his face. It is a brand that sears his soul. Though you hope desperately that it isn't there, if you look carefully you can see it. He is without any hope, and his final end is eternal fire:

> Rev 14:9-11 And the third angel followed them, saying with a loud voice, If any man worship the beast and his image, and receive his mark in his forehead, or in his hand, The same shall drink of the wine of the wrath of God, which is poured out without mixture into the cup of his indignation; and he shall be tormented with fire and brimstone in the presence of the holy angels, and in the presence of the Lamb: And the smoke of their torment ascendeth up for ever and ever: and they have no rest day nor night, who worship the beast and his image, and whosoever receiveth the mark of his name.

DOES TWO-HORNS ALSO GIVE A PHYSICAL MARK?

When we look at the account of the Two-Horned Beast in Rev 13:12 and the verses following, we read, "and he causes . . . and he gives . . . and he performs . . . and he deceives" Since the "he" throughout the rest of Rev 13 is the Two-Horned Beast, then the Two-Horned Beast is the one who gives this final mark! It can no longer be argued that Two Horns is other than the western so-called "Christian" nations, and the western world controls world economies. Notice that "no one can buy or sell." Two-Horn's mark is an economic bondage.

People's indebtedness to the world system grows worse by the day, and many have almost sold their souls to keep their material possessions. Sooner or later, this global economic system will become so oppressive that the public will be forced to choose between Jesus and the world. Those who make a final decision to turn aside from the Lord Jesus and become enslaved to the worldly and material pleasures of this Beast will have Satan's mark upon their foreheads. They will be the bondservants of the enemy. They are doomed forever.

Throughout the Christian Era, saints without number have refused to submit to godless systems. This has resulted in terrible economic deprivation, and worse, for millions of the brethren. Many have been driven from their farms or lost their employment. Millions have been imprisoned and killed. They could neither "buy nor sell." Second and third-century Church records show that during the Roman persecutions, many Christians could not trade in local markets unless they sacrificed to Caesar and confessed his deity. From then on, all the way down through Adolf Hitler, like conditions have existed in various parts of the world.

Today, these conditions still exist in parts of Africa, some southeast Asian nations, and in all the lands under Mohammedan rule. Worldwide, over 30,000 Christians a week are dying for the name of Jesus. Besides getting shot, strangled, and crucified, many Christians can neither buy nor sell because they will not bow down to the New Age humanists, Lenin, or Allah, nor accept Mohammed as his prophet -- Somalia being a good example. In this country, we are so isolated from the suffering of the faithful brethren that we forget that the Nazis murdered 6,000,000 Jews and countless Christians, Pol Pot killed 1,500,000 or so Christians, and the Communists are estimated to have killed more than 8,000,000 in the Gulag. Praise God, those faithful brethren did not take the mark. They have joined the saints standing under the altar who cry, "How long, Oh Lord, how long?"

The enemy's mark is not a sign of the Antichrist, nor is it a sign that we are in the "Great Tribulation." Instead, biblical evidence would lead us to believe that the mark of the beast is Satan's mark, on his servants, which in one form or another has existed throughout time.

Conditions in this country will worsen soon. We too, may not be able to buy or sell unless we pledge allegiance to a system which would require that we deny the Lord. (Examples to date include the public school science teacher, who refused to teach evolution and lost her job as a consequence. Without a job, she lost her ability to buy or sell.)

COULD A COMPUTER CHIP BE THE MARK?

Western science has developed the technology that would enable it to implant a record-keeping and identifying microchip under a person's skin, and by law, world governments could soon require their citizens to accept such an implant. However, the implantation of some physical device under the skin (regardless of its function) would not in itself mean that someone had taken the "Mark of the Beast." For an electronic device to be that mark, some declaration of one's spiritual position would have to accompany its acceptance. It would have to be understood that the receiving of such a device was *prima facie* evidence that the person receiving it had rejected the Lord Jesus as his Savior. There are several ways to prove it. Here are two:

1. A device could be implanted in a person's body without his knowledge or approval (while under anesthesia) or it could be implanted by force, totally against his will. A person goes to Hell because he rejects the Lord Jesus as his Savior, not because of something that happens to him in the flesh. So merely having a physical device implanted within one's body would not send someone to Hell.

2. While Jesus was casting demons out of a blind and dumb man (Mat 12:22-24), He told the surrounding Pharisees about the unforgivable sin. Since worshiping the beast and receiving his mark are also unforgivable, identifying that sin is the key to understanding the mark of the beast:

> Mat 12:31-32 Wherefore I say unto you, All manner of sin and blasphemy shall be forgiven unto men: but the blasphemy *against* the *Holy* Ghost shall not be forgiven unto men. And whosoever speaketh a word against the Son of man, it shall be forgiven him: but whosoever speaketh against the Holy Ghost, it shall not be forgiven him, neither in this world, neither in the *world* to come.

Notice that EVERY sin except blasphemy against the Holy Spirit will be forgiven a man. That is absolutely the only sin that God will not forgive. John the Baptist, through the Holy Spirit, also told his disciples about an unforgivable sin:

> Joh 3:36 He that believeth on the Son hath everlasting life: and he that believeth not the Son shall not see life; but the wrath of God abideth on him.

Here we read that if someone rejects the Lord Jesus, he will NEVER be forgiven. But wait a second. Isn't blasphemy against the Holy Spirit the only unforgivable sin? Yes, indeed, so rejection of the Lord Jesus and blasphemy against the Holy

Spirit have to be one and the same sin, or there would be TWO sins that are unforgivable! Let me explain.

No one comes to Jesus through his own volition. God the Father, through His Spirit, draws us all to His Son (Joh 6:44, Joh 12:32). The Holy Spirit witnesses in our hearts that the Gospel is true, to the point that we KNOW it to be so down in our innermost being. If we stand against the Holy Spirit's irrefutable witness, we are turning against God with the sure and certain knowledge that we are turning against the truth. That is what happened to those Pharisees. The Lord of Glory was standing before them casting out demons. Meanwhile the Holy Spirit was witnessing in their hearts, saying:

> Mat 17:5 This is my beloved Son, in whom I am well pleased; hear ye him.

The Pharisees who hardened their hearts against that irrefutable witness committed blasphemy against the Holy Spirit. The unforgivable sin is rejection of the witness of the Holy Spirit in our hearts by which we know that Jesus is the Christ. Once we understand that doctrine, the implantation of an electronic credit device would have to be accompanied with some final rejection of the Lord Jesus for it to be the "Mark of the Beast." Man is looking on the computer chips; "the Lord looketh on the heart" (1Sa 16:7).

The Lord Jesus is now seated at the right hand of God the Father, far above all rule and authority and power (Eph 1:20-21), and He now spoils Satan's house ("the strong man's house" of Mat 12:29). As the unsaved are led to Jesus, He has been despoiling Satan's kingdom throughout the Christian Era. None of God's children can ever get Satan's seal upon them. God's children have been transferred out of the kingdom of darkness and into the kingdom of His dear Son, Col 1:14. In the mind of God, that was not a temporary transfer. The children of God are forever sealed with the name of God the Father on their foreheads (Rev 14:1).

The Scarlet Beast

CHAPTER 15

And the light of a candle shall shine
no more at all in thee;
and the voice of the bridegroom and of the bride
shall be heard no more at all in thee...
And in her was found the blood of prophets,
and of saints,
and of all that were slain upon the earth.

REV 18:23-24

Positioned at the fall of the Davidic kingdom in 606BC, Daniel looked into the future from his own time and saw the four great Gentile empires -- and their descendants -- who would rule the Holy Land for the next 2500 years. Through the Great Image and the Four Beasts, Daniel correctly identified the major Middle Eastern empires of the ancient world as Babylon, Medo-Persia, Greece, and Rome. The descendants of those empires have continued to control the Holy Land right on down until 1948-1967AD. Though the Lord told Daniel how long this Gentile domination would last (in the time, times, and a half), Daniel didn't understand *time* (Dan 12:8), so until this generation, nobody knew when the Time of the Gentiles would end. However, Daniel did fulfill his primary ministry of telling the Jews about their future during the time of the Gentiles. The "Great Image" of Dan 2, and the "Four Beasts" of Dan 7, are obviously repetitive prophecies about the "time of the Gentiles."

Six centuries years later, the Lord inspired another apocalyptic prophet, the Apostle John, to write the book of Revelation. John was positioned at the beginning of the Christian Era, and his book is primarily about this era.

Revelation is also a visionary work, and it is organized exactly like Daniel, as a series of repetitive prophecies.

The two beasts of Revelation 13 and 17 are repetitive pictures of world history, and they are repeated in an organized way.[1] These two beasts give us different pictures of similar times. The Leopard-Bear-Lion tells us of the beast from the Middle East, while the Scarlet Beast give us an overview of what is going on in the rest of the world.

> Rev 17:3 So he carried me away in the spirit into the wilderness: and I saw a woman sit upon a scarlet coloured beast, full of names of blasphemy, having seven heads and ten horns.

When world history is overlaid with the seven heads, these heads fit the world empires that have controlled the Holy Land down through the ages. But to understand who these heads are, we need to look at them from the historic position of the Apostle John, in about 100AD:

> Rev 17:10-11 And there are seven kings: five are fallen, and one is, and the other is not yet come; and when he cometh, he must continue a short space.

Rome existed during John's lifetime, so Rome was empire number six, the one that "is." The "five fallen" would then be five empires that ruled in the Holy Land before John's time.[2] Four of those empires can be solidly documented: Assyria, Babylon, Medo-Persia, and Greece. The first "king" is less certain, but he probably represents the Canaanites, and the

---

[1] Rev 17 equals Rev 13 as the B=B of Revelation's 2nd chiasm. Chiasms are one of the Hebrew poetic forms found throughout the Bible. Appendix III contains a complete explanation of how bifids and chiasms are key to understanding the apocalyptic books.

[2] Some teach that the seven kings of the Scarlet Beast are Roman emperors of the 1st and 2nd centuries and that Revelation was primarily written to the Church of John's time. However, we can now conclusively prove that the Two Witnesses, the Leopard-Bear-Lion, and the day=years are repetitive prophecies that span thousands of years, with fulfillments in our own time. Consequently, it is hermeneutically unsound to conclude that out of the whole book of Revelation, only Chapter 17 would be addressed to the Church of the 1st Century, and in so doing depart from the repetitive pattern the Lord revealed to the Church through the prophet Daniel. *See Appendix III.*

descendants of those Canaanite city states have again come to life, as the Palestinians.

A 7th empire would follow Rome and continue a little while. After Rome fell in 475AD, the next major empire to rule in the Holy Land was the Leopard-Bear-Lion, and in God's eternal eyes, the Mohammedans did remain a little while. 1260 years is a "short space" for the eternal I AM.[1]

Since the seven heads of Rev 18 are earthly empires that have existed through both the Old and New Testament eras, the Scarlet Beast out of which those heads came must also have existed for thousands of years. No human empire has lasted through millennia, so this beast must represent some unseen creature or kingdom that has existed in the spiritual world over thousands of years. And he has! This Scarlet Beast has been influencing the empires of men of every age, and those kingdoms were given into his hand long ago, just as the Bible told us at the temptation of Jesus:

> Luk 4:5-6 And the devil, taking him [*Jesus*] up into an high mountain, showed unto him all the kingdoms of the world in a moment of time. And the devil said unto him, All this power will I give thee, and the glory of them: for that is delivered unto me.

Since the Scarlet Beast transcends time, it would almost have to be a figurative representation of Satan's spiritual domain down through time. Satan was given dominion over all the kingdoms of the earth, so Satan himself is the Scarlet Beast.

> Rev 17:8 & 11 The beast that thou sawest was, and is not; and shall ascend out of the bottomless pit, and go into perdition: and they that dwell on the earth shall wonder, whose names were not written in the book of life from the foundation of the world, when they behold the

---

[1] Nazi Germany almost duplicated the old Roman Empire, and it lasted for a very "short space" (just 12 years), so I wrote in *Hidden Beast 2* that Nazi Germany was probably the 7th head. I was wrong. Since a "short space" is a rather vague term, I looked at it from man's perspective rather than God's. That "short space" may really mean something like, "I'm going to the store, and I am going to continue there for a little while," indicating that I am going to spend some time at the store. When the Lord declared that the 7th head would continue "for a short space," it appears He was stating that Leopard-Bear-Lion Beast would rule in the Holy Land for some time, just as the day=years and times have already shown us.

beast that was, and is not, and yet is. And the beast that was, and is not, even he is the eighth, and is of the seven, and goeth into perdition.

There is something else peculiar about this satanic beast. This wicked beast "was, and is not, and shall ascend out of the bottomless pit." What can that mean? It means that before Jesus went to the cross, Satan had direct control over the empires of the world, but by John's time "he is not." Satan somehow lost his dominion at some point in time, and was cast into the bottomless pit. So when and how was Satan cast into that pit, and by whom? Therein lies one of the most blessed truths in the New Testament.

In the sovereign plan of God, Jesus was not granted authority over all things, nor was He given a kingdom, until after He ascended to the right hand of God the Father. Before then, as a matter of biblical truth, the kingdoms of this earth were given into Satan's hand (Luk 4:6). But after the Lord was crucified, all things were given into Jesus' hands, and He now rules over a very real spiritual kingdom that exists today:

Eph 1:20-23 Which he wrought in Christ, when he raised him from the dead, and set *him* at his own right hand in the heavenly *places,* Far above all principality, and power, and might, and dominion, and every name that is named, not only in this world, but also in that which is to come: And hath put all *things* under his feet, and gave him *to be* the head over all *things* to the church.

That is reality. The kingdom of the Lord Jesus exists right now, today. Satan had it all his way until Jesus went to the cross. But after Jesus was crucified and rose from the dead, the enemy was finished, and he knew it. While Jesus was still on earth, He told his disciples about it several times:

Luk 10:18 & Joh 12:31 And he said unto them, I beheld Satan as lightning fall from heaven . . . . Now is the judgment of this world: now shall the prince of this world be cast out.

We find this same event recorded in Revelation but told to us in figurative language:

Rev 20:1-2 And I saw an angel [*Jesus*] come down from heaven, having the key of the bottomless pit and a great chain in his hand. And he laid hold on the dragon, that old serpent, which is the

Devil, and Satan, and bound him a thousand years [*and thus, the thousand years of Rev 20 is a figure of the whole Christian Era*].[1]

You know, Brethren, we have been looking for Jesus' kingdom through the wrong end of our spiritual telescopes, and the Church has been fed "doctrines of demons." Just as Scripture has declared three times, we Christians have been ruling with Christ ever since the cross.[2] We are even now "seated in the heavenlies with Him" (Eph 2:6). With all that has happened to the brethren during this era, it may not seem like we have been doing much ruling, but we have been ruling, just the same. Our kingdom has never been of this world. It is in the heavenlies, where Christ is seated at the right hand of God. Christians are here on earth, among the servants of Satan, for a specific purpose. Jesus bound the "strong man" at the cross and we are here to lead the lost to the Lord Jesus.

Mat 12:29 Or else how can one enter into a strong man's house, and spoil his goods, except he first bind the strong man? and then he will spoil his house.

Every time we lead a soul to Jesus, we are carting off Satan's property. So what do you think the enemy's response would be to the saints carting off his goods? Here is the truth:

2Ti 3:12 Yea, and all that will live godly in Christ Jesus shall suffer persecution.

If we do the job the Lord has us on Earth to do, we are going to be persecuted for it. It goes with the territory. The Lord did not promise us a life of ease when we came to Him and were transferred into His spiritual kingdom. From the above verse, it is apparent that He promised us persecution. If we are not suffering persecution for Jesus, it isn't the world's fault, nor the devil's; it is ours. Persecution shows that we are doing something right. Defeat comes when we allow the enemy to lead us into the activities of his world to the point where we become indistinguishable from the unsaved.

---

[1] For a full explanation of why Rev 20:1-7 should be viewed as a figurative picture of the Christian Era, please read Appendix II.

[2] 1Pe 2:9, Rev 1:6, Rev 5:10.

When he does so, we stop being witnesses, and in a very real sense we loose Satan to influence those who are about us.

We want our Christian lives to be quiet and sweet and free from trials, but that has never been the Lord's plan for us. Millions of precious, humble saints who stood for Jesus have been horribly murdered throughout this era. Is there some reason we should expect better? Persecution is the norm for believers. Being a Christian isn't some effortless fire-escape to keep us all out of Hell. It is a lifetime commitment to our Lord and Savior, Jesus Christ, even unto torture and death. When a saint dies for Jesus' sake, it isn't defeat; it is victory, for "a servant is not greater than his Master":

> Rev 12:11 And they overcame him by the blood of the Lamb, and by the word of their testimony; and they loved not their lives unto the death.

That is what it is supposed to be like. Christ is the rock upon which we stand, and sin does not have dominion over the saints in Jesus' kingdom. Dead or alive, we reign with Christ. Satan was totally defeated at the cross, cast down, and throughout this era he has been bound in the abyss that he might not deceive the nations. But then we read . . .

> Rev 17:8, 11 The beast that thou sawest was, and is not; and shall ascend out of the bottomless pit, and go into perdition . . . and they shall wonder . . . when they behold the beast that was, and is not, and yet is . . . And the beast that was, and is not, even he is the eighth, and is of the seven, and goeth into perdition.

Who was bound and cast into the bottomless pit? Satan himself, so Satan is the 8th Beast. He lost direct control of the nations at the cross, but he still "is," and he has been ordering his fallen angels about to tempt the hearts of men throughout this age. The enemy did not again gain direct control of the nations until after the time of the 7th head (the Leopard-Bear-Lion) was fulfilled, 1948-67. Jesus bound Satan at the cross and cast him into the abyss, and to whom did He give the keys? The Lord gave the Church the keys:

> Mat 16:19 And I will give unto thee the keys of the kingdom of heaven: and whatsoever thou shalt bind on earth shall be bound in heaven: and whatsoever thou shalt loose on earth shall be loosed in heaven.

In this generation of ease, the Church has gotten off its knees -- which again loosed Satan's chains -- and once again the enemy and his angels have been released upon the Earth. He is not a human antichrist, nor a statue on the old temple mount, and you are not going to visibly see him. But the enemy has been released from his prison, and he goes forth to deceive the nations:

> Rev 20:7-8 And when the thousand years are expired [*the Christian Era*], Satan shall be loosed out of his prison, And shall go out to deceive the nations which are in the four quarters of the earth, Gog and Magog, to gather them together to battle: the number of whom *is* as the sand of the sea.

As this era draws to a close, you see national boundaries collapsing and a one-world super economy developing. A one-world religion is in the making, a global ecumenism that is trying to embrace every faith. But that ecumenism is not the Gospel of Jesus Christ that is able to save men's souls from the wrath to come. It is the great religious whore, and it is inspired and run by the enemy.

THE TEN HORNS OF THE SCARLET BEAST

Within Israel's borders are the Palestinians, the Infitada, and the terrorist Hamas, while outside its borders lie a group of radical Islamic states. All are avowed enemies of Israel, and they fulfill the Leopard-Bear-Lion. But under the influence of the 8th beast (Satan), a godless council of ten will soon rule the rest of the world for one hour (two weeks).[1] With Satan loosed from his prison, he will be in direct control of ten political regions to further his plans for world dominion.

> Rev 17:12-13 And the ten horns which thou sawest are ten kings, which have received no kingdom as yet; but receive power as kings one hour with the beast. These have one mind, and shall give their power and strength unto the beast.

Historically, visible world empires have always been controlled by visible public figures, but these ten horns are different. First, they don't come out of one of the heads but from the beast itself, so they are not the descendants of one

---

[1] In day=year time, one hour is about two weeks (or 15.44 days).

of the seven previous empires. Second, they are not real kings or political leaders, but they receive power "as kings," so they are some kind of shadow empire, behind the scenes, and that exactly fits global conditions today.

Shortly after the World War II, a group of multinational financiers and politicians in the United States formed the Council on Foreign Relations (CFR), and out of it came the Trilateral Commission (TC). In 1954, the CFR hosted a meeting in the Bilderburg Hotel in Oosterbeek, Holland, with the express purpose of regionalizing Europe. Today's European Common Market is a product of that meeting. A further development of that meeting was the establishment of a European arm of the CFR named the Club of Rome. The Club was given one major task to perform. It was to divide the world into ten economic regions and plan for their unification under one economic head. The Club held its first meeting in 1968, and proposed that these ten trading areas be known as ten kingdoms.[1] These one-world organizations are all intertwined, with many members in common. There are other even less visible groups, like the Illuminati, but they all have the same goal: total economic and political control of the world.[2]

A few years later, the international bankers and politicos put their plan into action by forming a committee called the General Agreement on Tariff and Trade (GATT). It should come as no surprise that GATT views the world as the same ten kingdoms envisioned by the Club of Rome. In speaking of these international financiers, Barry Goldwater is quoted as saying:

> The Council of Foreign Relations is the American branch of a society which originated in England...(and)...believes national boundaries should be obliterated and one-world rule established. The Trilateral Commission is international ...(and)... intends to be the vehicle for multi-national consolidation of the commerce and banking interests by seizing control of the political government of the United States.

---

[1] Nicolo Nicolov, *The World Conspiracy* (Portland OR, Nicolov 1974) p220.

[2] Gary H. Kah, *En Route to Global Occupation* (Lafayette, LA, Huntington House Publishers, 1992) pp.23-50.

What (they) truly intend is the creation of a world-wide economic power superior to the political government of the nation states involved. As managers and creators of the system, they will rule the future.[1]

Goldwater's words were indeed prophetic. By 1987, the Trilateral Commission (TC) controlled 60% of the world's wealth through banks, presidents of multi-nationals, media moguls, politicians, and university authorities.[2]

The CFR and the Trilateralists see the world as ten king-doms, and almost every important appointed or elected official in Washington, *of either party*, is a member of one or both of those organizations. The United States, Canada, and Mexico are Region One of this Ten-Horned hegemony, and that is what NAFTA was really all about: the forming of Region One.

The CFR has been in control of US policy for some time now. At the suggestion of the chairman of the CFR, President Nixon initiated a special enforcement arm of the executive branch known as the Federal Emergency Management Agency (FEMA). Ignoring state boundaries, this agency sees the United States as ten management regions and recognizes the same ten global kingdoms established by the CFR, TC, and GATT.[3] Structurally, FEMA can behave as a federal police force that is answerable only to the executive branch. From a positional standpoint, FEMA and the BATF are not unlike the Gestapo and SS of Nazi Germany, and with the stroke of a pen, this country could now be placed under martial law.

In its own publication, a CFR spokesman declared that it intends to make an end run around national sovereignty to "get us to the new world order."[4] It will probably use contrived monetary emergencies resulting in local disturbances followed

[1] Barry Goldwater, *With No Apologies*, as cited by Nicolo Nicolov, *The World Conspiracy* (Portland OR, Nicolov 1974), pp161-164.

[2] Hillarie du Berrier, *Bulletin* (Ft Collins, Co, Committee to Restore the Constitution, Dec 1989), p4.

[3] Mihajlo Mesarovic, *Mankind at the Turning Point* (New York, NY, E. P. Dutton & Co, 1974), p143

[4] Richard N. Gardner, Member of CFR, and former deputy Assistant Secretary of State for International Organizations under both Johnson and Kennedy. *Foreign Affairs,* the quarterly periodical of the Council on Foreign Relations (New York, NY April 1974), p52.

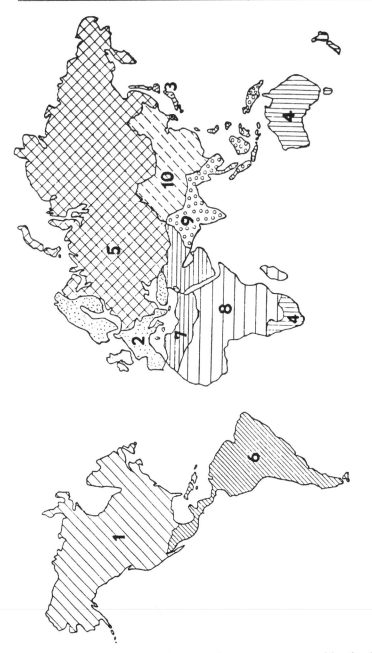

Map of the regionalization of the world system as proposed by the Club of Rome. This same map appears in many multi-national publications. However, Region 1 has now been modified to include Mexico, and that is what the implementation of NAFTA was really all about.

by "crisis management" controlled by its enforcement agencies. If this scenario is correct, then the autonomous nature of FEMA and the BATF make some sense. Since the United States is now the single most powerful nation on the globe, the subjugation of this country is central to one-world plans, and the agencies are now in place that would enable those plans to be put into effect.

Do not be deluded by what you read or hear in the news media, Brethren. Major heads of our communications network are members of the CFR and TC. The propaganda we hear from media sources is distorted to further one-world agendas. The long range goal of all agencies covertly controlled by international financiers is to destroy all national sovereignty and bring in a world financial government ruled by them.

> Rev 13:17 that no man might buy or sell, save he that had the mark, or the name of the beast, or the number of his name.

It all begins to fit together, doesn't it? But it would be of little importance to Christians who are walking in the Lord were it not for one cataclysmic problem. According to their plans, these ten "kingdoms" are to be governed by a council of ten so-called "wise men." These "wise" financial and political world leaders are not Christians. They are New-Agers, and many are outright occultists who are channeling with demons.[1] Most of them overtly hate fundamental Christians (no big surprise, considering it is Satan who controls them), so when they come into power, severe persecution, imprisonment, and death will again be the lot of the saints.

> Rev 11:7 And when they [*the Two Witnesses*] shall have finished their testimony, the beast that ascendeth out of the bottomless pit shall make war against them, and shall overcome them, and kill them.

---

[1] There is a "meditation room" in the UN. In its center is a large block of black stone. Behind the stone is an abstract of what might be the sun or the all-seeing eye of Osiris. William Jasper writes in *Global Tyranny, Step by Step* (Appelton, WI, Westren Islands): "New Age Guru Shri Chinmoy who leads meditations there says: 'The UN is a chosen messenger of God ...a divine messenger...One day the world will treasure the soul of the UN as its very own.'" Many one-world leaders are New-Agers. Some are occultists while others are into demonic eastern mystery religions.

Here is that beast out of the bottomless pit again, and the Jews and the visible church -- the two Witnesses -- are right in his gun-sights. The spiritual condition of the Church has been discussed so thoroughly that it need be mentioned no more, but now that we know who the ten horns are, the above verse exactly parallels the final prophecy about the harlot that sits on the Scarlet Beast:

> Rev 17:16 And the ten horns which thou sawest upon the beast, these shall hate the whore, and shall make her desolate and naked, and shall eat her flesh, and burn her with fire.[1]

That fate is still in the future for the visible church, Brethren. It will be destroyed, so it is of inestimable importance for the Remnant Church to know what we are supposed to do. It isn't going to be life as usual: going to church, raising our children and grandchildren, and saving for a retirement to some quiet nook in the country.

As so-called Christians play the harlot with the toys of the enemy, that woman decked in royal apparel who sits astride the beast can be none other than the visible church. She includes the Protestants, with their $5,000,000 sanctuaries, the Roman Catholics, with their so-called papal authority, and all who have departed from the Word of God. Changing a few people in the Senate or Congress isn't going to make any difference. Getting a new President isn't going to change anything. Most of our revered political, industrial, and media leaders and many well known religious names are members of the CFR, TC, COR, Illuminati, or all four.[2]

A new, so-called "laughing revival" or some kind of super-whammy charismatic experience won't change the outcome, either, because it won't change the hearts of people. Being washed in the blood of the Lord Jesus and being given a new heart are what change people. The magic show you see in the Church today is just part of the enemy's grand deception --

---

[1] The term "whore" or "harlot" was used throughout the Old Testament to describe Israel when it turned away from the Lord: Isa 1:21, Jer 2:20, 3:1-8, Eze 16:1-41, Hos 2:5, etc. God hates it, and that same term is applicable to the Laodicean church of today.

[2] For additional information on one-world multinational agencies and their connection with the Masonic order: Garry H. Kah, *En Route to Global Occupation* (Lafayette LA, Huntington House, 1992).

geared to lull Laodicean believers to sleep -- and it has done just that. The truth is this: We are in the final generation, and Satan has been loosed upon the Earth:

> Rev 17:12-13 And the ten horns which thou sawest are ten kings, which have received no kingdom as yet; but receive power as kings one hour with the beast. These have one mind, and shall give their power and strength unto the beast.

Since Scripture declares that a ten-horned entity will exist at the end of this age, fighting against it with sword and lance won't be the answer. The appearance of the Ten-Horns is one of the last signs that "our redemption draweth nigh" (Luk 21:28). What we need now is to find from scripture how the Lord intends for us to escape from Ten-Horn's clutches.

Remembering the day=year calendar, an hour equals about two weeks. Those "hours" appear in Revelation seven times. The "hour of trial" of Rev 3:10 equals two weeks. "In that same hour" of Rev 11:13 equals two weeks. "The hour of judgment" of Rev 14:7 equals two weeks. "In one hour" is recorded three times in the destruction of Babylon (Rev 18:10, 17, 19). All of these are parallel prophecies about the same time, and because of these "hours," Armageddon will probably last about two weeks.[1] The carnage could continue on, but to save the few elect who are still hanging on by their fingernails, Jesus will put a stop to it.

> Rev 17:14 These shall make war with the Lamb, and the Lamb shall overcome them: for he is Lord of lords, and King of kings: and they that are with him *are* called, and chosen, and faithful.

With today's weaponry, two weeks is probably long enough. If it were to last much longer, there might not be a Mount Zion upon which the Lord could stand when He returns. God will bring "all nations forth for war" in this final battle, so the Ten-Horns of the Scarlet Beast will also be involved. Seven times in Revelation we read of the "hour of trial," and that hour is almost upon us. With the exception of that hour, the emergence of Ten-Horns, and the battle of Armageddon itself, there is little prophecy left to be fulfilled.

---

[1] Pray that this hour is not a multiple because if it is, we could be looking at fifteen years of unimaginable trials.

European nations are fast sliding into the Middle-Eastern camp, and Mohammedanism is the fastest-growing religion in Europe. In many church congregations in Holland, not one single born-again believer remains. Islam is taking over many state-owned churches there and turning them into mosques.[1] About now, we would probably just as soon not read the prophecy of the earth's destruction as recorded in Isaiah 24. The Lord commanded us to be sober and vigilant for a reason. Our God is a consuming fire:

> Isa 24:17-20 (*excerpts*) Fear, and the pit, and the snare, *are* upon thee, O inhabitant of the earth. And it shall come to pass, *that* he who fleeth from the noise of the fear shall fall into the pit; and he that cometh up out of the midst of the pit shall be taken in the snare: for the windows from on high are open, and the foundations of the earth do shake. The earth is utterly broken down . . . it shall fall, and not rise again.

That is a sobering passage of Scripture. Since the Church is going to be on Earth until all prophecy is fulfilled (1Co 15:52), "we who are alive and remain" will see every bit of that. Our flesh cringes from these things and makes us wish that "happy, happy, happy, we're all going to be raptured out" had some credibility, but that won't happen. We are going to be here until there is "time no more" (Rev 10:6-7).

> Amo 5:18-20 Woe unto you that desire the day of the LORD! to what end *is* it for you? the day of the LORD *is* darkness, and not light. As if a man did flee from a lion, and a bear met him; or went into the house, and leaned his hand on the wall, and a serpent bit him. *Shall* not the day of the LORD *be* darkness, and not light? even very dark, and no brightness in it?

Woe to us, indeed. What are we to do? Well, fear not, Brethren. The Lord had our future planned long ago. Our God is on the throne, and we can place our trust in Him. In times as ruthless as these are going to get, there will be nowhere else to turn, and that is exactly how it should be:

> Luk 21:36 Watch ye therefore, and pray always, that ye may be accounted worthy to escape all these things that shall come to pass, and to stand before the Son of man.

---

[1] This is the assessment of a fellow Christian writer presently living in Holland, Franz Zigers of den Helder. His letter is in the author's files.

The Iron Gate

Wherefore come out from among them,
and be ye separate, saith the Lord,
and touch not the unclean thing;
and I will receive you,
And will be a Father unto you
and ye shall be my sons and daughters,
saith the Lord Almighty.

2Co 6:17-18

Though written ten years ago, the following allegory was never more appropriate than it is right now. It may be what the remnant church will be like when the Lord returns. *Hidden Beast 1,* (Fort Myers, FL, Fish House, 1989)

There was a wicked city. In the middle of the city was a lofty church. That church had the tallest steeple that ever was built. In that steeple was the grandest bell that ever was made. When the bell was struck, it pealed forth with such a mighty knell that every building in the city rattled. Some even shook to their foundations. At first, it was all very frightening because here and there a building would collapse. But nothing had fallen in a long, long time, so the townsfolk had gone back to playing and dancing in the streets.

Seeing the church, Christian tried to go inside. But in the middle of the doorway was a big iron gate. It had strong iron bars. Looking through the bars he saw lots of people inside. They were marching around in lock-step and chanting the same words to each other over and over and over again. They nodded approval to each other and kept telling each other how great they all were. They were God's elect, weren't they, and that was that.

Christian tried with all his might to open the gate, but it wouldn't budge. Then he noticed a heavy bronze plaque. It was bolted to the gate with big bronze bolts. The headline engraved on the plaque read:

Church Doctrines and Traditions

Imposing and well-dressed men rode up in fancy cars. They mounted pedestals and stood guard over the plaque. The pedestals were very tall, and had signs on them which read, *Pastors and Evangelists Only*. These elevated men held out collection plates and cried, "Give, give. Oh, give more! We need to build a bigger church, and get a louder bell." Other men with arm-bands that read *Theologian* stood behind them as reinforcements.

People came up and bowed to the men; then the people turned and breathed on the plaque and polished it with their handkerchiefs, as one would a pair of glasses. Some folks even knelt down before the plaque and kissed it. For all of them, the iron gate swung open by itself. There wasn't any light on the plaque, the print was very small, and there was an awful lot of it. So Christian held up his Bible, which shines in the dark, so that he could see.

Squinting and adjusting his bifocals, he started reading the fine print. As he read, he muttered and groaned and became more and more agitated. Finally, Christian could stand it no longer.

"These doctrines do not agree with Scripture," he cried in a troubled voice.

Christian opened his Bible and began to read it aloud. As each verse of Scripture was read, a crack appeared in the plaque, then another, and another, until the plaque shattered into a million pieces. As it splintered and fell, it made a little rattling sound, but at that sound, the buildings of the wicked city quaked and fell, until none were left.

The people in the church clapped their hands and cackled with glee, "The wicked city has fallen, the wicked city has fallen!"

They puffed out their chests and ran around shaking hands and congratulating each other. They never realized that it was not their bell, nor their lofty church, but the reading of the Bible, which made the buildings fall. After the commotion had died down some, most of them went back to their marching, while others started working on a new plaque. They were so busy making sure that everyone was keeping in step that they forgot to take down their iron gate.

Christian didn't want to chant or march in lock-step behind an iron gate, so with Bible in hand, he turned and walked away. A few people with Bibles in their hands came out from the church and went with him. As they strolled along, they were all joyously singing, reading their Bibles, and sharing what they read with any passerby who would listen.

Soon there was a huge crowd around them singing and reading their Bibles. Then someone said, "Let's build a church and make a plaque . . ."[1]

The above is not to suggest that every church is apostate nor that every pastor has departed from the truth. There are still a few good churches and a few good pastors out there. The Lord always has a remnant, and He never leaves Himself without a witness. There just aren't very many now, and the above allegory fairly well describes the trends within all the churches today, regardless of denomination. Here is how you know. In the following verse, the Lord gave us three important commands about His Word:

> Deu 12:32 What thing soever I command you, [1] observe to do it: [2] thou shalt not add thereto, [3] nor diminish from it.

Satan found out long ago that there were three easy ways to weaken the Church: (1) tempt the assembly to neglect the Word, (2) weaken it through adding false doctrines, or (3) lead people to reject part of Scripture. He is well on the way to accomplishing all three, for "in vain they do worship me, teaching for doctrines the commandments of men" (Mat 15:9).

Is this what your church is like? You go to services three times a week, seeking a little spiritual reality for your life, but in Sunday school they rehash last week's TV programs and talk about the string of bass that George caught. The pastor drones out some soothing Charles Haddon Spurgeon sermon

---

[1] The *Iron Gate* allegory does not appear in John Bunyan's *Pilgrim's Progress*, but I give that elder brother credit for the idea.

you heard twenty years ago, and you remember the last pastor, who ran off with that sexy young organist. You also think about Tom, who lost his job, and about how his family didn't have enough to eat and remember how that didn't stop the elders from giving the pastor a raise, nor from using the rest of the tithe to expand the sanctuary. And you've been seriously asking yourself, "Is this what church is really supposed to be like, and can this be where God really wants me to worship?" [1]

You do indeed "sigh and groan" over the abominations committed in your midst, but what can you do? Your mother and father were life members of your church, you were baptized in it, and the church down the street isn't any better. Could you even find a church that is truly concerned about your family's spiritual growth or that really has a heart to help you raise up your children in the nurture and admonition of the Lord?

If you are asking those questions of yourself and see no answers, welcome to the Remnant Church. The answer is the same as it has always been: It is in the person of Jesus Christ, and the Lord didn't intend to make following Him difficult. Sooner or later, the Lord will call you out from that apostate church, and He will show you through the Bible how easy it is to worship Him the way He intended for His children to do it all along, "in spirit and in truth." It is all in God's Word, and we had better learn how, for very soon, the only refuge that will be left to us will be the Lord our God:

> 2Co 6:17-18 Wherefore come out from among them, and be ye separate, saith the Lord, and touch not the unclean *thing;* and I will receive you, And will be a Father unto you, and ye shall be my sons and daughters, saith the Lord Almighty.

Brothers and Sisters, it may not have happened to you yet, but if you are troubled by what is happening to your church, or by what is being taught there, sooner or later the Holy Spirit is going to lead you out of that church.

---

[1] 2Th 2:3 Let no man deceive you by any means: for *that day shall not come,* except there come a falling away first. 2Ti 4:4 And they shall turn away *their* ears from the truth, and shall be turned unto fables.

With a heavy heart, many sound, Bible-believing Christians are now leaving established denominational churches and attending no formal church at all. In many cities, hungry brethren spend Sunday after Sunday in a futile search for Bible-teaching churches, and can't find one. Some Christians are falling away, but a remnant -- Ah, the remnant -- are forming little home-church groups. They are meeting in living rooms and cellars and garages, in any room large enough to hold a dozen brethren or so.

It's a scary thought, being on your own with just the Lord Jesus to sustain you. But don't worry -- Jesus can handle it. He planned this whole thing long ago, you are part of His plan, and He loves you. Just obey Him, and don't look upon what is happening in your heart as if it were a bad thing. It is the Lord's protection unto you. As we discussed in the last chapter, the visible church will soon be destroyed, and the Lord is leading you out of it . . . *to hide you:*

> Isa 26:20-27:1 Come, my people, enter thou into thy chambers, and shut thy doors about thee: hide thyself as it were for a little moment, until the indignation be overpast. For, behold, the LORD cometh out of his place to punish the inhabitants of the earth for their iniquity: the earth also shall disclose her blood, and shall no more cover her slain.

Five times in the New Testament we read about where the Church was located. In each case, the Church was in the home of an individual believer, and nowhere in the New Testament are we told that we should meet anywhere else.[1] In fact, the Greek word for church, *ekklesia,* could probably be better translated as "the called out ones," rather than "the assembly."[2] The first century "called out ones" were unsung

---

[1] Act 8:3, Rom 16:5, 1Co 16:19, Col 4:15, Phil 1:2.

[2] Strong's No.G1577. ekklesia, ek-klay-see'-ah; from G1537 and G2564. *ek* meaning "out of," and *kaleho* meaning "to call" or "called." The word "church" itself comes from the old English/Germanic word *kirke,* which meant a ritualistic pagan circle. Meeting in a *kirke* was rooted in the pagan concept that people could stand in a "circle of agreement," holding hands, and call upon demonic forces. (from *Church,* Smith's Bible Dictionary, Flemming-Ravell). Unaware of its true spiritual significance, many evangelical churches have now adopted this demonic ritual and have included it in their worship service.

little groups of believers, meeting in homes where they were hidden by the Lord from the swords of their enemies. Very soon, we, too, will have to assemble in the same way. The enemy hates the Church, and since he has now been loosed, he will soon physically attack it here in the United States, just like he has almost everywhere else on the planet.

Most of us have been programmed to believe that we can't worship the Lord, serve communion, baptize, or even have elders unless some sectarian seminary sends an "ordained" pastor to do the job in an "approved" manner: building a building complete with pipe organ, stained glass windows, a choir, a music minister, and so on. It just isn't so:

> Psa 51:17 The sacrifices of God *are* a broken spirit: a broken and a contrite heart, O God, thou wilt not despise.

> Joh 4:23 But the hour cometh, and now is, when the true worshippers shall worship the Father in spirit and in truth: for the Father seeketh such to worship him.

As church doors close, or as assemblies depart from the truth, the very survival of the true Church will depend upon the little godly sheep who are willing to walk before the Lord with a broken and contrite heart. Its survival always has. The true saints will need to learn from the Bible for themselves and gather with other like-minded brethren who are seeking the Lord's face. And it's all right to do that, you know. After all, the Lord ordained each of us to be a king and a priest:

> Rev 1:6 And hath made us kings and priests unto God and his Father; to him *be* glory and dominion for ever and ever. Amen.

We have a thousand pages of guidance on just how to gather together. It is called the Bible. Throughout the Christian Era various men and organizations have told us exactly what each verse is supposed to mean, or exactly how each church ordinance should be observed. But if we just trust the Word, The Spirit of Truth, will teach you, Himself (Joh 16:13).

In this chapter, I considered writing the usual "rules" on how to hold a meeting, serve communion, baptize, and so on. But then I realized that I would be doing exactly what got the Church in trouble in the first place: giving dictums of behavior beyond what Scripture has already stated.

It's all in the Bible, Brethren. Everything the Lord wants a believer to do is in the Word of God. We simply need to follow His orders. Suffice to say that the qualifications for eldership are found in 1Ti 3:1-7 and Tit 1:5-9, and how communion should be served is recorded in Mat 26:26-28 and 1Co 11:23-26. There is no scripturally specified method for baptism, but we do have early church history to guide us.[1]

If you are in one of the few good churches that remain in the land, stay there until you feel that nudge of the Holy Spirit to leave it. But when you do, get out of it in a hurry because you won't have a lot of time to play around:

> Mar 13:15 let him that is on the housetop not go down into the house, neither enter *therein*, to take any thing out of his house: And let him that is in the field not turn back again for . . . his garment.

Brethren, Christians and Jews will again be tortured and killed, so we need to get ready. For instance, it would be wise to get your name off church records as soon as possible. Not everyone in the church is saved. Many servants of the enemy are lurking there as wolves in sheep's clothing. They smile and sound sanctified, but they would betray you in a minute.[2]

---

[1] Many brethren in home churches now follow a first century church mode of baptism. First, they ask the new convert to renounce his past sinful life. Then they ask the convert to make a firm declaration of his new position in Christ Jesus. Though the words below are not struck in stone, the confession of faith goes something like this:

"I turn away from, reject, and totally renounce Satan and all his works, and his kingdom, and his angels. I repent of and renounce all my sins, and ask God to forgive me for them. I accept the Lord Jesus Christ as my personal Savior and I ask Him to become Lord of my life."

Then, observing the command of Jesus in Matthew 28:19, the new brother or sister is baptized "In the name of the Father . . . in the name of Jesus Christ His Son . . . and in the Holy Spirit . . . Amen." If the new believer is being immersed, he is immersed only once. But if he is being poured over, as was a first century practice (see *The Didache*), the convert is asked to kneel, and he is poured over three times: once as each name of God is spoken. The mode of baptism is not nearly as important as getting it done. Don't dawdle around. Baptism is not just for show; it was given to believers for a sound spiritual reason (1Pe 3:21).

[2] If you think all this to be an over dramatization: I personally know a Christian sister who, as a child, suffered years of unbelievable satanic ritual abuse at the hands of the elders of her "evangelical" church. This happened years ago, but she is still in hiding and fears for her life. In another case, a church elder and his wife were a young man's satanic godfather and godmother. This young man has since come to the Lord.

Jesus sets the membership of His church in the "Book of Life," and that is the only place your name needs to be recorded. Your name being on some visible church's roll has nothing to do with serving the Lord, and it will eventually risk you and your family's safety for no good purpose. You can't lead anybody to Jesus if you are lying face-down in some gutter with a bullet in the back of your head. Sound far-fetched? Well, it's reality. That is the fate of our brethren in many other parts of the world, even as we write.

If you believe none of this could happen in your town or think that your friends and neighbors would never betray you, that is what the Protestant brethren in Ireland thought before 125,000 were tortured and killed by their neighbors. That is what 1,000,000 brethren in Cambodia thought before the Khmer Rouge wiped them out. That is what the Jews in Nazi Germany thought before they were herded into cattle cars that took them to the gas chambers of Buchenwald, Treblinka, and Auschwitz.

Every true Christian is willing to die for the Lord Jesus. But it is wrong to endanger your loved ones through some foolish inaction that has nothing at all to do with serving God. In Isaiah 26:20-27:1, the Lord directs us to hide at the end of time, and Jesus said, "Night cometh, when no man can work," Joh 9:4. Surely that time is upon us. In accordance with those verses, it would be fitting to make preparations for a coming holocaust while we still have the freedom to do so.

To give you an idea of how persecution has already begun in Europe, the media in Holland are beginning to publicly call our Christian brethren "dogs." Through this kind of overt anti-Christian propaganda, the Dutch people are now being programmed to look favorably upon the grievous havoc that will soon befall their little Christian community.

Once we grasp the reality of where we fit into Bible prophecy today, then we can understand why so many brethren around the country are being led of the Holy Spirit to do what they are doing: the hidden underground houses, the mountain hideaways, the cabins built in secluded forests, the stored food, and the ships being built or outfitted to move large numbers of brethren to places far away. There isn't any organization, denomination, or charismatic leader motivating these believers. The Lord is burdening the hearts of individual saints to do His will in preparation for the end. They believe God meant it when He said:

> Rev 18:4   And I heard another voice from heaven, saying, Come out of her, my people, that ye be not partakers of her sins, and that ye receive not of her plagues.

DEAR FELLOW PASTOR OR ELDER:

Because of what you learned in seminary, you may have concluded that I am just some sort of doomsday alarmist, and if you have, I understand. But consider this: Most of the prophetic fulfillments written about in this book can be proven biblically and historically, and if we remain consistent with our interpretation of Bible prophecy, the foregoing conclusions about our future are all but inescapable. Forget your denominational position and favorite end-time commentator for a while. Get out your Bible, and see for yourself if what is written here is true. These events could begin to be fulfilled in five days or in five years; only the Lord knows. But a terrible time of trouble is surely going to come upon us all, and the Lord has graciously given us a little time to get ready.

Prepare the brethren to hide from the coming fury of the enemy. Prepare to destroy every vestige of your church membership rolls. If you have them on computer, put a good Wipe-Disk program on your hard-drive that you can activate in a hurry, and learn how to use it. Don't wait until the last minute to make preparations. You could be too late.

Meanwhile, warn the brethren to get free from debt, for debt is the trap that will bind them in slavery to the Ten-Horns. Stand with them in their fight against the worldly sins that do so easily beset us all. Many will not listen, and many will be killed, anyway, but if you let the brethren remain in darkness about the fire-storm to come, you could find yourself responsible for their many deaths.

Satan won't be loosed for long, just a short space, but if you do not warn the flock the Lord has put into your care . . Oh my, look at the blood of the saints that will be upon your hands when you stand before Jesus.

> Eze 33:6 . . . if the watchman see the sword come, and blow not the trumpet, and the people be not warned; if the sword come, and take *any* person from among them, he is taken away in his iniquity; but his blood will I require at the watchman's hand.

Coming Tempest

CHAPTER 17

Put ye in the sickle, for the harvest is ripe:
come, get you down; for the press is full,
for their wickedness is great.
Multitudes, multitudes in the valley of decision:
for the day of the LORD is near
in the valley of decision.

JOE 3:13-14

So that's it? We just save a little food and water, read the Bible some, pray a lot, and huddle in our homes until the Lord returns? No, of course not. We know the Lord must have a more significant end-time role for the Remnant Church to play than that.

The Lord never puts His major witness on the sidelines, and because He doesn't, I hated writing this chapter. There is no pleasure in writing about adversity. As John stated when he ate the little book of Revelation, "It was in my mouth sweet as honey: and as soon as I had eaten it, my belly was bitter."

Eze 2:10 And he spread it before me; and it *was* written within and without: and *there was* written therein lamentations, and mourning, and woe.

As we have already discussed, Scripture shows that a terrible upheaval is coming upon all the Earth's peoples. We can face it prepared or unprepared -- that choice is ours -- but one way or another, we are going to face it. We Christians will be here until the end of time (Rev 10:6-7).

Everything may not take place as outlined in the next two chapters, but there is sufficient historic evidence to show that what follows is a credible projection of what the next three to five years may be like. Some of what is recorded here is happening to brethren in other parts of the world right now, and Scripture leads me to believe that these same trials will befall us all before the Lord returns. The broad picture of future events is clear enough, but the factors involved in their coming to pass are so complex that the timing and order of their happening are all but impossible to foresee.

THE MILLSTONE

There are five major groups influencing what is to come: the ten trading kingdoms coming together as the Ten-Horns, the Moslems as the Leopard-Bear-Lion, the apostate church, the true Church, and Israel. The part each shall play at the end is not totally clear. But make no mistake -- since 1967, Jerusalem and the new nation of Israel are central in God's plan. The Lord first tells us of Israel's end-time role in Zechariah, a role which He confirms in Revelation:

> Zec 12:3 And it will come about in that day that I will make Jerusalem a heavy stone for all the peoples; all who lift it will be severely injured. And all the nations of the earth will be gathered against it.

And so it has come to pass. Despite the virulent animosity of her Arab neighbors, Israel controls Jerusalem, and Israel remains a sovereign nation among the Arab states even to this day. As the above verse predicts, Israel was forced to fight several wars, but those who have come against her have been severely injured. We find a confirming verse about a great stone in Revelation's lament over Babylon.

> Rev 18:21 And a mighty angel took up a stone like a great millstone, and cast *it* into the sea, saying, Thus with violence shall that great city Babylon be thrown down, and shall be found no more at all.

In both Old Testament and New we read about this stone. So let me ask you, how many great stones is the Lord going to cast to the earth during the end-times? We know of only one -- Jerusalem -- so Rev 18:21 must also be about Israel.[1]

---

[1] Elsewhere in Scripture, Jesus is referred to as a rock or stone, but not in Revelation. In that book Jesus is called a Lamb slain, the Alpha and Omega, the Son of man, a Bridegroom, an Angel, and King of kings and Lord of lords. He was never a rock "cast." He is the Son of God.

Remembering that the sea is all the people of the Earth (Rev 17:15), in the above verse we read that Israel is cast in among the nations to the nation's great dismay. In accordance with Zec 12:3, all will eventually turn against her. Then it will be the Remnant Church and only the Remnant that will be standing as Israel's ally. Even now, not one nation remains her committed friend, not even our own.

We also read that this "great stone" will cause the fall of the "great city," Babylon. So Israel will at least be partly responsible for the fall of Babylon. As to Babylon's identity, it can now be shown with some certainty that Babylon is an allegorical picture of all the unsaved people who have ever lived on this earth. We should talk about Babylon for a bit because our end-time enemies are her children.

As the New Jerusalem is the sum of all the saints in God's kingdom,[1] so Babylon is the sum of all of the servants of the enemy. Babylon isn't a place; it is all the people within a spiritual kingdom, and there are only two: God's and Satan's:

> Rev 18:24 And in her was found the blood of prophets, and of saints, and of **all that were slain upon the earth**.[2]

Notice the "all," with nobody left out. According to this verse, the blood of every servant of God *throughout time* stains the hands of the people of Babylon, so Babylon can't be just

---

[1] If Rev 21:2 and Rev 21:9-10 are carefully studied, it becomes apparent that the new Jerusalem is not a material place of buildings and streets. It is a pictorial representation of the OT saints and the Church: "I will show you the bride of Christ . . . and he showed me the new Jerusalem." Ergo, the Bride = New Jerusalem. Since the saints are scripturally defined as the bride of Christ, the Holy City has to be the total body of believers, both OT and NT (Rev 21:12-14). The church has been looking at this city from a human viewpoint. God is not building a gold and tinsel city in which man may dwell. For 6000 years, He has been building for Himself, a city out of people in which He will dwell. Rev 21:3 states: "And I heard a loud voice from the throne, saying, 'Behold, the tabernacle of God is among men, and He shall dwell among them, and they shall be His people, and God Himself shall be among them.' " When the New Jerusalem is seen in that light, we can then understand that mystery Babylon is the other side of the coin. Mystery Babylon is the sum total of all the unbelievers who have ever lived.

[2] The "prophets" are Old Testament believers; the "saints" are the New Testament church. That "all" is pretty inclusive, so it includes every single servant of the Lord, regardless of the era in which he lived.

some physical city that exists at a specific time. Babylon is not New York, Rome, Hong Kong, or some other geographic center of wickedness. The Lord doesn't care about this city's buildings or walls. God cares about its people, and Babylon is people. The Lord is using Babylon as an allegorical picture of the spiritual condition of those who have chosen to follow the enemy. Babylon is all the wicked souls who have ever lived and walked on this earth, and she is shown as a city of trade, even trading in "the souls of men" (Rev 18:13).

Ah, "trading" in the souls of men. There is the key word: *trade*. How do we see the Ten-Horns today? As ten regions or kingdoms of *trade*, so it all begins to fit together, doesn't it?

Rev 17:12 And the ten horns which thou sawest are ten kings, which have received no kingdom as yet; but receive power as kings one hour with the beast.

THE TEN HORNS

There are many Christians who discount any one-world conspiracy as errant nonsense, but the activities of today's political and economic leaders fit the Ten Horns of the Scarlet Beast far too well to be coincidental. Could the ten global trading kingdoms now emerging on the world scene be just another numerical fluke that by some wild quirk of chance just happens to fit Scripture? That would be hard for any thinking person to swallow.

In Rev 17:12, these horns appear "as kings," with no crowns, so these hidden economic rulers may never become visible to us on the world scene. But visible or in the shadows, they are really there. It is Satan, the 8th Beast whom they follow, and it is Satan who is making the decisions for them. Under Satan's guidance, the Ten-Horns will have the same goals the enemy has always had: to set up a satanic kingdom on Earth and to annihilate God's people.

So the enemy is going to initiate wars and disturbances only in wicked third world countries, correct? Oh, Satan will cause wars among them all right, but these Ten-Horns encompass the world, so Satan will cause societal break-downs in every country, and he will not miss the chance to attack you and me. Scripturally, there is only one nation that will stand against Ten-Horns, and that is why all nations will come against her. Despite all the troubles inside and outside

Israel's borders, that nation will stand because the Lord has decreed it so:

> Eze 38:8 you will be summoned; in the latter years you will come into the land that is restored from the sword, *whose inhabitants* have been gathered from many nations to the mountains of Israel which had been a continual waste; but its people were brought out from the nations, and they are living securely, all of them.

In the rest of the world, Ten-Horns will receive complete authority with Satan for "one hour." That is still two weeks in day=year language, so their kingdom will probably be in total control of world economies for about two weeks, at the end of which Jesus will stand on Zion.

Two weeks doesn't sound so scary, does it? Initially, we think we can live through that without any great problem. But those two weeks are only the time of Ten-Horn's total control. The setting up of Satan's covert empire is in progress as we write, and subverting all the world's systems is taking some time. The enemy isn't gaining control of everything all at once. He is using the domino principle: one nation or region at a time, one freedom at a time, one church, and one praying saint on his knees at a time, and he is masking what he is doing in three ways:

1. Through false end-time doctrines that keep the brethren from understanding what the Bible states about the events to come.

2. By distracting Christians from today's realities through a false sense of security.

3. By disguising his emerging kingdom as multinational "free trading zones" like Common Europe, South America, and on this continent, NAFTA.

Though they may not know it, the international financial consortiums are under Satan's control, and they are playing a pivotal role in the implementation of his plans. For instance, the International Monetary Fund (IMF) is not usually viewed as a molder of global political policy, but it is. Their hard assets are so vast that they exceed the GNP of most world powers. As directed by one-world organizations like the CFR, the TC, or the Illuminati, the IMF can cause major governments to rise or fall as they will. By granting or withholding a loan, or by manipulating a target country's currency exchange rate, the IMF can control the monetary policies of any nation on the planet, including the policies of the United States. The IMF can indeed decree "that no man [*or nation*] might buy or sell."

Rev 13:17 that no man might buy or sell, save he that had the mark, or the name of the beast, or the number of his name. Here is wisdom. Let him that hath understanding count the number of the beast: for it is the number of a man; and his number *is* Six hundred threescore *and* six.[1]

Right now, the enemy is having it all his way. His plans for the takeover of world economies are proceeding quite nicely. But at the end, his Babylon will fall, and the gold, silver, and jewels his Ten-Horned servants have schemed and murdered to get will be worth nothing at all:

Jam 5:1-4 Come now *ye* Rich men, weep and howl for your miseries that shall come upon you . . . Your gold and silver is cankered; and the rust of them shall be a witness against you, and shall eat your flesh as it were fire. Ye have heaped treasure together for the last days. Behold, the hire of the labourers who have reaped down your fields, which is of you kept back by fraud, crieth: and the cries of them which have reaped are entered into the ears of the Lord of sabaoth.

THE PEOPLE

Now is a time of sifting for the Church. In the great winds of change that are blowing upon the Earth, the Lord is winnowing His beloved wheat out from the chaff. The true brethren are not some vast, uncountable herd anymore, grazing peacefully on the Lord's thousand hills. When compared to the world's total population, the Remnant is just a little flock, but through His Spirit we are beginning to find each other. Many of us feel pretty isolated right now, with just a couple of close Christian friends in our church or town, but that's all right. The Lord is still in control, and somehow He is networking a faithful remnant all over the world. We need to be in prayer for each other and help each other whenever

[1] Adonikam's descendants were 666 in number (Ezr 2:13) and many of the controlling families in world finance are of Jewish extraction. This could be just a numerical coincidence, but it is one of only four places in Scripture where the number 666 appears.

we can because the true saints are all the real family we will ever know before the Lord Jesus returns.

> 2Ti 3:2-5 For men shall be lovers of their own selves, covetous, boasters, proud, blasphemers, disobedient to parents, unthankful, unholy, Without natural affection, truce breakers, false accusers, incontinent, fierce, despisers of those that are good, Traitors, heady, highminded, lovers of pleasures more than lovers of God.

Television and Nintendo-trained, the children of our own households are strangers to us. Among them are an ever-increasing number of New-Agers, occultists, and satanists, involved in depravities of every kind. They believe in a four-billion year calendar, evolution, rock music, and the new world order, and to them we appear as nothing but fools:

> Mat 10:36 & Mar 13:12 And a man's foes *shall be* they of his own household . . . brother shall betray the brother to death, and the father the son; and children shall rise up against *their* parents, and shall cause them to be put to death.

THE FACE OF THE ENEMY

How has all this happened in just one generation? Well, Satan and his angels -- with the willing aid of his college educated liberals -- knew all along that an ungodly curriculum in our public schools could destroy us. All Satan needed to do to wreck our Christian culture and destroy our land was to rob our children of their moral principles and isolate them from their Christian heritage.[1] He knew it all too well.

So right on cue, along came a few educational left-wingers. They knew full well the effect their plans would have on our Christian society. They they broke our culture intentionally. As an example of one such educator, John Dewey believed in no God, no soul, no immutable truths, and no absolutes, and taught that man could do whatever he wished without religious or moral restraint. As a professor at Columbia University Teachers College, Dewey was probably the most

---

[1] Despite strident rhetoric to the effect that our forefathers were all Deists, our founding fathers were predominately conservative and Bible believing Christians, a fact that can easily be supported from their many extant writings. Catherine Millard, *The Rewriting of American History* (Camp Hill, PA, Horizon House Publishers, 1991)

important single influence in the shaping our modern anti-Christian educational system.

Do you ever wonder where the American-born leaders of the CFR, the New-Age, and other anti-god and one-world groups got their immoral views? Though there were other influences, in great part their thoughts and actions are based upon the anti-Christian values of John Dewey. If you are looking for an antichrist, you would be hard pressed to find a more appropriate candidate for the office.[1]

In the 50s, a Dewey-trained, American-born financier and CFR executive funded the Kinsey Report, which began the so-called "sexual revolution." That report has since been found to be a biased fabrication, but it accomplished what it was funded to do. The concept of family unity was attacked, divorce rates rose, and promiscuity increased.[2] Ask yourself why sex education is now being taught in grammar schools, and why, as a part of that sex education, homosexuality is promoted as normal and acceptable. If a Christian child is forced to attend a public school today, his parents take the very real risk of seeing that child's morals destroyed and of seeing him totally lose his faith in God.[3]

Under the influence of those same satanically controlled groups, our school history books were revised to play down the achievements of this country. A so-called "multicultural" agenda became the watch-word for the leftist educational elite. Few realize the true goals of that program, but it is designed to divide rather than to unify, to pit one ethnic

---

[1] As a close friend of the Rockefeller family, John Dewey taught his views to David Rockefeller and his brothers, and they are leaders in the CFR. According to John Dewey: "There is no God and no soul. Hence, there are no needs for the props of traditional religion. With dogma and creed excluded, then immutable truth is also dead and buried. There is no room for fixed, natural law or permanent moral absolutes." Ralph Epperson, *The Unseen Hand*, p.298, as cited by Gary Kah, *En Route to Global Occupation* (Lafayette LA, Huntington House, 1992) p.60.

[2] Dr. Judith Reisman, *Kinsey, Sex and Fraud* (Lafayette LA, Huntington House Publishers, 1991).

[3] Winkie Pratney, *Devil Take the Youngest* (Lafayette, LA, Huntington House, 1992)

group or color against another, and thus destroy the cohesion of Americans as one people.[1]

We should be on our knees, crying out to God because of the educated heathen, the white-collared barbarians, who, through the public education system, have almost total control over the minds of our children. As our young people are indoctrinated with false teachings that are contrary to our predominately Christian past, all that our founding fathers planned for our people is passing into the night, and we are again entering a time of the long-knives. Violence is on the increase everywhere, and Americans are becoming a people given to violence. Eight hundred years before Christ, the prophet Joel saw this time coming clearly:

> Joe 3:10 Beat your plowshares into swords, And your pruning hooks into spears; Let the weak say, "I am a mighty man."

If the above were the whole story, it would be bad enough, but look at what is happening on the federal level. Most of our important elected or appointed officials support a one-world government and the termination of the United States as a sovereign nation. Our handsome officials don't look like the betrayers of our Constitution because they wear coats and ties and sound oh so "compassionate" on TV, but many are covertly maneuvering our country away from our traditional democratic form of government.

A small handful of honest legislators do try to defeat the unconstitutional mandates being issued by the one-world leaders through the executive branch and other authorities, but their efforts are not reported in the media (why am I not surprised), so the American people have no idea of what is really going on. Those who try to investigate the conspiracy, like Senator John Tower or Congressman Larry McDonald, are first discredited and then, by some fluke of fate, manage to get themselves killed in fatal airplane accidents.

---

[1] Our school campuses are bastions of liberal thinking, with faculties composed of atheistic teachers who are corrupting the minds of our young people. "Outcome Based Education" was designed to change the mores and cultural values of a Christian America. Peg Luksik, *Outcome Based Education, The States Assault on Our Children's Values* (Lafayette, LA, Huntington House Publishers, 1995)

Eze 22:27-28 Her princes in the midst thereof *are* like wolves ravening the prey, to shed blood, *and* to destroy souls, to get dishonest gain. And her prophets have daubed [*i.e., whitewashed over*] them with untempered mortar, seeing vanity, and divining lies unto them, saying, "Thus saith the Lord GOD, when the LORD hath not spoken."

As a tool of Satan, Ten-Horns has no reservations about starting wars, destroying our land, or killing our people. In fact, in their own publications, the multinationals declare that they intend to break down law and order and cause disturbances as necessary to bring in the "new world order." Any atrocity is acceptable if would help their agenda. Their plans include the deaths of many millions.[1] That should come as no surprise. Satan has no problem with anarchy. Satan is the author of confusion, and strife is one of his favorite tools.

THE MOHAMMEDANS

If Leopard-Bear-Lion sees the West in sufficient turmoil, the Moslems will probably use that as a window to attack Israel or the United States. Undoubtedly, Ten-Horns would like to use the general unrest brought on by a Mohammedan terrorist attack or natural disaster as an excuse to place this country under martial law and take it over.

But ten-horned authorities may not find the Mohammedans that easy to control, and they may never submit to the Ten-Horns. Those two satanically empowered governments appear to be scripturally concurrent and could remain so to the very end. The Moslems are even now fighting a jihad, a so-called "holy war" against us, and they fanatically hate everything Christian, Jewish, and Western.

Radical Shiites are in this country in increasing numbers, and they are laying plans to kill our people and disrupt our cities. We have forgotten what they think of us, but they haven't forgotten it for a minute. We are "the great Satan," if

---

[1] The Biological Diversity Convention, signed by the United States in 1993 (103rd Congress, Treaty Doc.103-20) may be the most heinous and subversive document to have been sent down by any administration to the U. S. Senate for ratification. If implemented and enforced, it could end our Constitutional freedoms forever, and cause the death of millions. It needs to be read to be believed.

you'll recall. The bombing of the World Trade Center in New York was just a taste of their intent. When so ordered by their radical mullahs, you may expect highly disruptive attacks from that fanatical quarter: bombings, robberies, reservoir poisonings, assassinations, or the like.

On the world political scene, the breakup of the USSR has been grossly overstated, and many eastern bloc watchers believe that Russia has now surpassed us militarily. In the view of those observers, the Russian "breakup" was really part of their long range military strategy to lull the United States into disarming unilaterally. If that is the case, they have in great part succeeded. Russia, or at least her southern break-away Moslem states, is arming the Leopard-Bear-Lion. If Russia joins LBL, as Eze 38-39 may indicate, we should expect a nuclear attack to fall upon us fairly soon. That attack would, no doubt, include air-bursts that would disrupt all communications and inactivate every electronic device containing a solid-state chip. Your automobile, radio, TV, refrigerator, computer, and even your battery-powered wristwatch would stop working.

SIGNS IN NATURE

Man is making changes to his environment that he may not be able to correct. As rain forests are cut down, viruses far deadlier than any we have ever known are being released into the environment. Bacteria that man thought conquered long ago are again appearing in new and deadlier drug-resistant strains. Viruses which used to attack only animals are now being transferred to human hosts with lethal results, the mouse-borne Hanta virus being only one example. If any of these new diseases become pandemic, they could result in deaths on a scale not unlike the Black Death of the Middle Ages. Whole populations could disappear overnight, and Scripture does appear to predict such a scenario.[1]

But what's even more disturbing is genetic engineering that has progressed to the point where the genetic code from

---

[1] A new horse morbilli virus kills both horses and humans by creating holes in the blood vessels that leak into the lungs until the victim drowns in his own blood. There is a similar new hemorrhagic fever in Kewait that is transmitted from sheep to humans by ticks, and another similar one in Africa. *Fort Myers News Press* (Ft. Myers, FL, April 7, 1995) p. A12.

one species can be grafted into the genetic code of another. Seeds from one species of plants are being hybridized with seeds from other species, and not one soul cries out against the appalling nature of the sin we are committing. We have ignored creation law. We have broken part of the everlasting covenant:

> Gen 1:12 And the earth brought forth grass, *and* herb yielding seed after his kind, and the tree yielding fruit, whose seed *was* in itself, after his kind: and God saw that *it was* good.

Every living thing that God has made, He made after his own kind. "After his kind -- after his kind -- after his kind" and seven times God told us so (Gen 1:11, 1:12, 1:21, 1:24-25, 6:20, 7:14). The Lord even commanded us not to plant seeds of various kinds in the same field.

> Deu 22:9 Thou shalt not sow thy vineyard with divers seeds: lest the fruit of thy seed which thou hast sown, and the fruit of thy vineyard, be defiled.

But have we obeyed His voice? No, we are even now manipulating the basic genetic makeup of man himself. As the result of this one sin, another unexpected calamity may be about to befall us:

> Isa 24:5-6 The earth also is defiled under the inhabitants thereof; because they have transgressed the laws, changed the ordinance, **broken the everlasting covenant**. Therefore hath the curse devoured the earth, and they that dwell therein are desolate: therefore the inhabitants of the earth are burned, and few men left.

The new diseases being loosed upon us could be the result of our breaking that everlasting covenant. Insignificant as what we have done may appear, because of one broken covenant, few men will be left when Jesus returns.

Is the Lord going to again rain destruction down upon the earth with His great and mighty hand (like He did on Sodom and Gomorrah)? Or is He going to let man bring destruction upon himself? Scripture doesn't say, but what is happening in the natural world is part of the prophetic picture so it is worthy of being reported here.

THE WARRIORS

In spite of disturbances, disease, and anarchy, an overt world takeover by Ten-Horns may not be all that easy. There is a hornet in his shirt that could sting him to the very end. Unlikely as it may sound, many ordinary people in the United States may trouble him, and here is why. As Israel was scattered over the whole world, so this nation has been gathered from the whole world. Black people being brought here as slaves was even a part of God's master plan. That was no accident, and they are now an integral part of this people. Recognizing that God is in control of all things, you just have to ask why all this happened the way it did.

Stand back now, and look at the Scriptures we have studied so far. Why did all these different peoples from every continent of the world come here? By coincidence? Of course not. In a very real sense, the different peoples of the United States may be a regathering of the dispersed tribes of Israel. We are the great melting pot, the bringing together of many peoples under one flag, as one sovereign nation under one God. We are probably Ephraim, the warrior tribe of Israel.

We were once a moral and godly people, and a remnant of that godly people remains. Even as we write, there is a mighty ground-swell of revulsion, like vomit rising out of the collective throats of Ephraim. Why? Because an oppressive and satanic enemy is among us. Like the early colonists who came before us, twenty-eight states have formed armed militia that are prepared to stand against all enemies "both foreign and domestic," and they are rapidly expanding. Many in the militia are Christian brethren not unlike the early settlers. They are just ordinary citizens, bound together by the same drives that motivated the early colonists: a love of God and country and an abiding hatred for tyranny of any sort.[1]

While many Christians are non-resistant, the Lord never took sword from David, so there is a difference of opinion on this issue. While many believe that we should allow ourselves to be killed for what is right, others believe that we should be willing to fight and even die for it. The Lord has always had

---

[1] Expect a major government and media effort to discredit citizen militia groups, even to having them falsely accused of illegal or terrorist acts. The Branch Davidians at Waco, TX are a prime example. This is not a statement for or against the activities of the Davidians or the militia, nor is it advocating violence against any duly elected official. This is merely a report on the attitudes of a growing segment of the American citizenry.

warriors who were willing to lay down their lives for God and country, and far be it from me to criticize them.

As He did for Daniel in the lion's den, the Lord can still miraculously deliver, but during this era, He has usually employed human armies to deliver His people. Consequently, it would be just as wrong to criticize a man for going to war when he believes that to be his godly duty, as it would be to criticize those who believe in non-resistance. I refuse to take issue with either position, but we should remember the lessons of history. Non-resistant Christians and Jews have suffered tortures beyond imagining in every country when Christian warriors did not rise up to defend them.[1]

The militant outlook of conservative Americans from every race and faith has not gone unnoticed by Washington, nor by the media, and both are reacting by calling some fundamental Christian groups "right-wing extremists" or "hate-mongers." Since conservative Christians are generally in opposition to anything left-wing or liberal, we can expect the government to become more oppressive against all Christians in an attempt to combat any resistance to their one-world agenda.[2] This could eventually lead to an open and possibly armed conflict between federal enforcement agencies and the American people, with an outcome that is by no means certain.

> Zec 12:8 and he that is feeble among them at that day shall be as David; and the house of David *shall be* as God, as the angel of the LORD before them.

---

[1] Most Jews blame Christians for the horrors that happened to them during this era, and not without reason. Jews suffered terribly at the hands of men who claimed to be Christians. However, that Jewish belief is for the most part an enemy deception designed to keep the true church and the Jews apart. Many Jews are alive today because the true Christians in Europe gave their lives to hide them during the Nazi holocaust, and Christians of many lands fought against Nazi Germany and her satanic "final solution."

[2] Major elected officials and bureaucrats of both parties support the one-world "new order" so it is improbable that electing a few different officials will alter the overall course of future events. The banking infrastructure that controls the ten trading "kingdoms" will still be in place. The present leaders of these organizations grow older and will soon retire from the scene, but the wicked spirit that controls them will influence others to take their place, so these malignant agencies will live on.

The Gathering

CHAPTER 18

But, The LORD liveth,
that brought up the children of Israel
from the land of the north,
and from all the lands
whither he had driven them:
and I will bring them again into their land
that I gave unto their fathers.

JER 16:15

Though similar political conditions exist elsewhere in the world, what follows now is primarily about what could happen in America if the internationalists continue on their present course. Ten-Horns will probably continue to nurture fractures in our society that will cause worsening conflicts between the federal government and the people.

Despite bad press, Americans are generally a peace-loving people, but given a cause, they can become quite aggressive. If the American people become aware of the covert international takeover of this land soon enough, it could provide just such a cause. Two hundred million or so guns are in the hands of average American citizens. That is why there is such a feverish media-blitz for "gun control." Gun control is not about the few drug dealers and other thugs who are killing each other in the inner city. The intent of anti-gun legislation is to disarm the people because a fully armed people is difficult to subdue.

National Guard units are not likely to fight against their own people, and it is doubtful if an informed American military would do so, either. That is why foreign troops are now based on our soil and why "internationalist" foreign-born generals are named as heads of our armed forces. Foreign troops under foreign generals would have few reservations about shooting American citizens. That is why we also hear that American troops should be placed under UN control and why it is alleged that some federal employees are receiving their paychecks directly from Interpol, the IMF, or other foreign interests.[1] That is also why inductees into our armed forces are asked on a written questionnaire if they would be willing to shoot American citizens if so ordered.

Lest you think all this just some whimsical pipe dream from an apocalyptic eccentric, just look at what you can prove for yourself. Look at the foreign-born members of the CFR and TC who have become Secretaries of State -- of both parties -- or military Chiefs of Staff. Is it possible that we don't have equally or better qualified American-born generals or diplomats? Ludicrous. So we have to ask, what is the enemy's hidden agenda here, and will his subversive plans of world dominion come to pass? Probably, and whatever does happen in this country will certainly have global impact.

Since the United States supplies food to many parts of the world, food everywhere could be difficult, if not impossible, to find. If the Lord so leads, you might want to lay in a few supplies soon. There could be armed pillagers roaming the streets, answerable to nobody but themselves, so prepare to either hide or to defend yourself.[2] Expect the dollar to be worthless, so have a little hard currency on hand. But don't bother to keep too much money of any kind. Food will be the only real currency during this final time of trial.

Remember, the goal of Ten-Horns is to destroy the cohesion of Americans as one sovereign nation under God, so as to bring this country into their new one-world order. Instigating unrest or a bombing is not beyond them. Anarchy, an armed conflict, or some natural disaster would be exactly what Ten-Horns could be looking for. The country could then

---

[1] *Voice of Liberty*, 7pm, Mar 24, 1995, WWCR, 5065 KHz,. Nashville, TN.

[2] Anarchistic conditions now exist in many major metropolitan areas, and those conditions are rapidly spreading into outlying districts. For example, an anonymous Tacoma, WA, police source reports that in 1994 there were approximately 2700 drive-by shootings in his city alone.

what Ten-Horns could be looking for. The country could then be placed under martial law, and our liberties would be over. Anyone who appeared to be out of line could be shot on sight, and you would need a pass to go anywhere or even to buy a loaf of bread. Once again, you could "neither buy nor sell." Christians and Jews would no doubt be blamed for the unrest, and severe and overt persecution of the brethren would then be initiated with a vengeance:

> 1Pe 4:17 & Joh 16:2-3 The time *is come* that judgment must begin at the house of God . . . yea the time cometh, that whosoever killeth you will think that he doeth God service. And these things will they do unto you, because they have not known the Father, nor me.

THE MOUNTAINS OF ISRAEL

What follows now is reality for the brethren in many parts of the world -- right this instant! Many people are now fighting the enemy and are being killed or imprisoned behind barbed wire. Some of those prisoners are being drugged or tortured in an attempt to "reeducate" them away from their belief in God. We are not many years behind them and that will eventually happen here.[1] May the Lord of Hosts protect us with His mighty hand. Some are not equipped to defend themselves (the old, the infirm, the children), and some are non-resistant as a matter of conscience. At the very end, Scripture commands us all to hide (Isa 26:20). And we will have to hide. The Bible warns us that a time of anarchy is coming: a total breakdown of civilized law and order:

> Zec 14:13 And it shall come to pass in that day, *that* a great tumult from the LORD shall be among them; and they shall lay hold every one on the hand of his neighbour, and his hand shall rise up against the hand of his neighbour.

That tumult is *from the Lord,* so there will be confusion everywhere. But the Lord can use that confusion to move, and then to hide, vast numbers of His flock. There is no better way to hear where the Lord intends to hide us than to let the Lord

---

[1] You think that farfetched? This fate has already befallen many Christians in Russia, and as reported by to me by a USMC officer, it has also befallen some of our own servicemen. You see, many psychiatrists now believe that just being a Christian is evidence of mental illness.

tell you about it Himself. Now that you know who the dispersed of Israel are, you should be able to understand His voice . . . .

> Jer 3:14 Turn, O backsliding children, saith the LORD; for I am married unto you: and I will take you one of a city, and two of a family, and I will bring you to Zion:

> Zec 10:7-10 (excerpt) And Ephraim will . . . remember Me in far countries, And they with their children will live and come back. I will bring them back from the land of Egypt, And gather them from Assyria; And I will bring them into the land of Gilead and Lebanon, Until no *room* can be found for them.

Many now believe that every descendant of Jacob, the whole "Israel of God," both physical and spiritual, will be literally returned to the Holy Land. If so, then this new Exodus from the nations will be so much greater than the Exodus from Egypt that the former Exodus will be remembered no more:

> Jer 16:14-15 Therefore, behold, the days come, saith the LORD, that it shall no more be said, The LORD liveth, that brought up the children of Israel out of the land of Egypt; But, The LORD liveth, that brought up the children of Israel from the land of the north, and from all the lands whither he had driven them: and I will bring them again into their land that I gave unto their fathers.

> Jer 31:8-9 Behold, I will bring them from the north country, and gather them from the coasts of the earth, *and* with them the blind and the lame, the woman with child and her that travaileth with child together: a great company shall return thither. They shall come with weeping, and with supplications will I lead them: I will cause them to walk by the rivers of waters in a straight way, wherein they shall not stumble: for I am a father to Israel, and Ephraim *is* my firstborn.

As I read those touching words, I realize there is little more to be said. The doors of Israel are closed to believers in Y'shua now, but they won't always be. Somehow, the Lord is going to open them for a remnant. How that will happen is unclear, but it is going to happen because the Bible tells us so:

> Eze 34:11-15 For thus saith the Lord GOD; Behold, I, *even* I, will both search my sheep, and seek them out. As a shepherd seeketh out his flock in the day that he is among his sheep *that are* scattered; so will I seek out my sheep, and will deliver them out of all places where they have been scattered in the cloudy and dark day. And I will bring them out from the people, and gather them from the countries, and will bring them to their own land, and feed

them upon the mountains of Israel. I will feed my flock, and I will
cause them to lie down, saith the Lord GOD.

AMERICA, A COMFORT-ZONE NO LONGER

We have been living in safety for so many years that we
have developed an "it can never happen here" mind-set.
Affliction not only *can* come upon us, but it will, as a matter
of scriptural reality. The only question is how soon:

Rev 3:10 . . . the hour of temptation [*testing or trial*], which shall
come upon all the world, to try them that dwell upon the earth.

"Upon all the world" includes us, wherever we are. Today
we are sitting happily in our homes, living off the fat of the
land, but it won't always be so. The Children of Israel didn't
flee Egypt because they liked it there. They fled because they
were in such servile bondage and hard labor that even the
dangers of an unknown desert seemed preferable to them.
The same will be true for us. We're not going to leave our good
jobs, comfortable homes, and casual lifestyle until it gets bad
enough. It isn't in human nature to choose adversity, so the
Lord may use this time of trouble to make us willing to defend
our land, or to drive us back to Israel.

Dan 11:35 And *some* of them of understanding shall fall, to try
them, and to purge, and to make *them* white, *even* to the time of the
end: because *it is* yet for a time appointed.

As you have read this book, you may have been quickened
of the Holy Spirit to recognize that you are a member of the
Remnant Church. If so, you have known for some time that
the Lord has put an end-time calling on your life, but you
haven't known how to fulfill it. You've been wondering just
what the Lord has in store for you.

Well, to begin with, find like-minded brethren, but very
carefully. Ask the Lord to lead you to the right people.
Network with them, but make sure they are true believers.
The enemy will attempt to place Judases among us, so pick
your Christian friends prudently. You would not want the
brethren to be betrayed by someone you thoughtlessly
included in your circle of friends. Who knows what the Lord
might have you doing. Here is one possibility:

Jer 16:16 Behold, I will send for many fishers, saith the LORD,
and they shall fish them; and after will I send for many hunters, and

they shall hunt them from every mountain, and from every hill, and
out of the holes of the rocks.

You could be a hunter or fisher, a gatherer of the remnant. You might be out in the bushes gathering Christians
and Jews and hiding them, or taking them to Israel. Maybe
you are a defender of the wall, or a way-station provider for
the needs of others. Only God knows what He has planned for
you to do, so stay in prayer. Rest assured, the Lord has a
place and duty planned for every member of this body, and
His plans include you, no matter what your station in life
might be. Every one of us has a vital function to perform.

Continue to witness. Witness to what you now know
about the wrath to come, and of our Jesus who can carry us
through it all. Despite what may seem to be insurmountable
odds, those who are "called and chosen" will still come to the
Lord. Even in these last few seconds before a prophetic
midnight, there is an eleventh hour harvest. Even now we are
gleaning the last few sheaves from the corners of the fields
(Joh 12:25). Ask the Lord to open the doors before you, for if
the Lord does not go before us, we labor in vain (Psa 127:1).

We are in our dear Heavenly Father's hands, so fear not.
No matter how terrible times may get, He has not forgotten
how to protect the righteous. But even if the Lord permits a
fiery trial to come upon us, He can still give us the steadfast
hearts of Shadrach, Meshach, and Abednego:

Dan 3:17-18 our God whom we serve is able to deliver us from
the burning fiery furnace, and he will deliver *us* out of thine hand,
O king. But if not, be it known unto thee . . . that we will not serve
thy gods, nor worship the golden image which thou hast set up.

As the Lord our God strengthens us, we will bow the knee to
Him alone. But a fiery furnace isn't pleasant, so here is a
promise the Lord put in His Word for Ephraim's sake:

Hos 11:9 I will not execute My fierce anger; I will not destroy
Ephraim again. For I am God and not man, the Holy One in your
midst, And I will not come in wrath.

"Oh Lord, like the prodigals we are, we have sinned
against You. We have worshiped our modern gods of gold and
silver and iron and wood. We have departed far from You, not
in words so much as in our hearts. Please forgive us, Oh Lord
our God, and make it all right again. Please take us home."

And He will. In His own perfect time, the Lord Himself will do so with a mighty hand.

> Isa 43:5-6 Fear not: for I *am* with thee: I will bring thy seed from the east, and gather thee from the west; I will say to the north, Give up; and to the south, Keep not back: bring my sons from far, and my daughters from the ends of the earth; *Even* every one that is called by my name.

And thus, in the fullness of time, a remnant of Ephraim shall stand on the mountains of Israel. And we shall be standing there, shoulder to shoulder, with our long-estranged Jewish brethren, looking for Him whom we all have pierced.

> Mar 13:25 And the stars of heaven shall fall, and the powers that are in heaven shall be shaken. And then shall they see the Son of man coming in the clouds with great power and glory. And then shall he send his angels, and shall gather together his elect from the four winds, from the uttermost part of the earth to the uttermost part of heaven.

And the Lamb whose robe is dipped in blood will stretch out those pierced hands and say, "Welcome home, my dear children, welcome home."

> Rev 21:4-7 And God shall wipe away all tears from their eyes; and there shall be no more death, neither sorrow, nor crying, neither shall there be any more pain: for the former things are passed away. And he that sat upon the throne said, Behold, I make all things new. And he said unto me, Write: for these words are true and faithful.
>
> And he said unto me, It is done. I am Alpha and Omega, the beginning and the end. I will give unto him that is athirst of the fountain of the water of life freely. He that overcometh shall inherit all things; and I will be his God, and he shall be my son.

⊰ FINIS ⊱

Appendix 1

In fairness to Dr. Lurie, we come to different conclusions about the 70th week. Dr. Lurie believes it was fulfilled in the Nazi holocaust. However, his study in Hebrew showing *shavuim* to be a multiple of sevens is the basis for considering that the 70th Week might represent hundreds of years, or even millennia. Below is an abbreviated quote from Appendix I of *The Covenant, The Holocaust & the 70th Week*, Dr. David Lurie (Coral Gables, FL, Messianic Century, 1988) pp.83-86, which also includes a short quote from p.195 of T. J. Young's, *The Prophecy of Daniel*.

Daniel's weeks are periods of an integer multiple of seven years. A week can, in principle, be 7 years or 14 years long. Or it can be 49 years or 140 years long. Any integer multiple of 7 years is a priori acceptable . . .

The Hebrew word which the King James Version translates as "weeks" and the NIV translates as "sevens" is *shavuim*. Now *shavuim* is the masculine plural form of *shavua*, and *shavua* is the word used in both biblical and modern Hebrew to denote an ordinary 7-day week. The King James translators rendered *shavuim* as "weeks" and let it go at that, but the NIV translators recognized that *shavuim* is a rather peculiar form and so they rendered it as "sevens." What is peculiar about *shavuim* is the fact that the usual plural form of *shavua* is shavuot. That's the feminine plural form and it's the form used throughout the entire Hebrew Bible whenever an ordinary 7-day week is intended. Obviously, then, the *shavuim* are not ordinary 7-day weeks. If 7-day weeks had been intended, the form *shavuot* would have been used, not *shavuim*.

In fact, the word *shavuim* appears only in the prophecy of the seventy weeks and in one other place, Daniel 10:2,3. It appears nowhere else in the Old Testament. In Daniel 10:2,3 we read that Daniel mourned for three *shavuim yamim* or literally for three "sevens" of days. Now in this context it's clear that *shavuim* means just ordinary weeks. But the point is that this is the only place in the entire Hebrew Bible where the word *shavuim* appears and in this one instance, because the word is intended to denote ordinary 7-day weeks, Daniel takes care to put the qualifier *yamim* (meaning "days") after it. There is more than a hint here that when the word *shavuim* appears without a qualifier, as it does in Daniel 9:24-27, it has a more general meaning . . .

Israel already had the concept of Sabbaths of years . . . seven-year periods . . . built into her Law. Therefore . . . what could be more natural than to conclude that it is to these Sabbaths of years that the *shavuim,* the "sevens" Daniel 9:24-27, are referring?

The only problem with this conclusion is that if the Hebrew Bible already has a recognized term - Sabbaths of years - to denote periods of seven years, then why wasn't this perfectly well understood term used in Daniel 9:24-27? Leviticus 25:8-9 uses the Hebrew term *shebatot shanim* for Sabbaths of years. Why wasn't this term used in the prophecy of the seventy weeks rather than the term *shavuim?*

. . . if Daniel 9:24-27 does refer to standard seven year periods, to Sabbaths of years, then why does it refer to them with the peculiar word *shavuim,* a word that has the "wrong" plural form and that appears almost nowhere else in the entire Hebrew Bible, when there already existed at the time of Daniel's prophecy a perfectly well known and understood term - *shebatot shanim* - whose use was consecrated by the Torah, the most sacred part of the Jewish Scriptures?

We said earlier that the singular form *shavua* is used in both biblical and modern Hebrew to denote an ordinary 7-day week. But there's more to it than that. Etymologically, *shavua* has the same root as sheva, the word for "seven," and as E. J. Young has pointed out, the word *shavuim* is really a participle form, denoting something which is "sevened" or "besevened:"

> "The form is really a participle meaning besevened, i.e. computed by sevens...and here gives evidence of the fact that the word was originally masculine. What led Daniel to employ the masculine instead of the feminine however, is not clear unless it was for the deliberate purpose of calling attention to the fact that the word "sevens" is employed in an unusual sense. The word means divided into sevens..."

In this key passage, E. J. Young has pointed us toward the answer to the puzzle. The *shavuim* or "sevens" are periods of time that are *computed by sevens* or, even more explicitly, *divided into sevens* . . . But seven what? Days? Months? Years?

As you now know, I see those "sevens" as a multiple of years that can be reckoned through the 360 Sabbaths of a Jubilee year.

Appendix 11

The pictorial nature of Revelation was not fully understood by the Church until the 2nd half of this century. But since the 20th Chapter of Revelation *appeared* to be literal, back in 1640AD, a Dutch Reformed theologian, Jean de Labadie, concluded that at the end of the Christian Era, Jesus would return and physically rule over the earthly kingdoms of men for 1000 years.[1] The church calls this 1000 year time theory the "millennium." Theoretically, this "millennium" would be followed by another mini-Armageddon, Rev 20:8, and then, after the great white throne and all, we would eventually enter into the Eternal Kingdom of God. Since de Labadie's theory fit in perfectly with the dispensational scheme of things, Dispensationalists added premillennialism to their body of doctrine. However, the Church of de Labadie's day believed his view to be heresy, so they expelled de Labadie from the Dutch Reformed church. Not without good reason, one might add, and this is why:

Rev 20:2 is the one and *only* source for the premillennial view, and it only works then if you interpret it their way! You must literally interpret one verse in a book which most serious eschatologists understand to be primarily allegorical. Even to arrive at that view, de Labadie had to ignore two universally accepted rules of Bible interpretation:

1. *No Scripture should be interpreted apart from its context.* As already stated, most of Revelation is allegorical, and there is no textual reason to believe that Rev 20 should be interpreted differently than its context. Rev 20 just *appears* to be literal.

2. *A word study should be done in the original language to be assured that the passage is understood*

---

[1] Though de Labadie brought it into the reformation church, the premillennial view did not originate with him. Tertullian tells of a similar view that existed in the 3th Century.

224 οώζω, Survival Guide for a Remnant Church

correctly. The Greek word translated "thousand" in Rev 20:2, and throughout rest of the chapter, is *chilioi* (Strong's No. 5507).[1] *Chilioi* is an indefinite plural, and does not mean just one thousand. It could mean one thousand, but it could also mean many thousands. It appears that the premillennialists are basing a very important definite doctrine on a very indefinite plural.

That is the point: *chilioi* is an indefinite plural. Even though the translation of *chilioi* as one thousand is technically correct, if we insist on it meaning exactly 1000 years, then the sense of the passage could be lost. It is very possible that the Lord is telling us of an *indefinitely* long span of time, even thousands of years.

THE CHRISTIAN ERA

If it could be a long period of time, then when would it take place? Well, since it is scripturally provable that the saints reign with Christ, right now, in His spiritual kingdom, and that the saints have done so throughout the Christian Era (Eph 1:3, 1Pe 2:9, Rev 1:6, Rev 5:10), then the "thousand" year reign of Christ could be a pictorial representation of the whole Christian Era.

A figurative interpretation of Rev 20 is not as wild as one might think. Most of the Church considered Rev 20 to be figurative until de Labadie came along. So on the off-chance that some of those earlier saints could have been right, let's look at the verses which bring the premillennial view into question and look at Rev 20 figuratively:

> 2Th 1:7-10 And to you who are troubled rest with us, when the Lord Jesus shall be revealed from heaven with his mighty angels, In flaming fire taking vengeance on them that know not God, and that obey not the gospel of our Lord Jesus Christ: Who shall be punished with everlasting destruction from the presence of the Lord, and from the glory of his power; When he shall come to be glorified in his saints, and to be admired in all them that believe (because our testimony among you was believed) **in that day).**

---

[1] Strong's No. 5507, G5507; χίλια, chilioi, khil'-ee-oy; plural, of uncertain affinity; a thousand:--thousand.

First: Note the "YOU" of the first line. The Lord is speaking to the 1st Century Thessalonian church, i.e. the Church as it was then, and on down through time He is speaking to us. From context, it is apparent that the Lord was not speaking to some future group of "great tribulation" saints, after the Church had been taken up.

Second: The Lord will be revealed from Heaven with His angels, to take vengeance on the ungodly with everlasting destruction, and be glorified in the saints IN THE SAME DAY!

By dispensational tradition, we are taken to be with the Lord at one time when we will "admire Him," at the marriage supper of the Lamb, and then AFTER a 1000 year millennium, the wicked will be punished with everlasting destruction. But the same verses state something totally different. 1Th 1:7-10 teaches that the Church is taken to be with the Lord on the SAME day that the wicked are judged. At best, the pre-mill folks have to bend the above Scripture to fit their position. But that is not all:

> 1Co 15:51-52 Behold, I shew you a mystery; We shall not all sleep, but we shall all be changed, In a moment, in the twinkling of an eye, at the last trump: for the trumpet shall sound, and the dead shall be raised incorruptible, and we shall be changed.

> Rev 10:6-7 ... there should be time no longer: But in the days of the voice of the seventh angel, when he shall begin to sound, the mystery of God should be finished, as he hath declared to his servants the prophets.

> Rev 11:15 And the seventh angel sounded; and there were great voices in heaven, saying, The kingdoms of this world are become the kingdoms of our Lord, and of his Christ; and he shall reign for ever and ever.

There are some verses in Scripture that can be interpreted in various ways, but the above quotes are not among them. These verses are direct declarations of spiritual truth. They are clear statements of fact. These Scriptures, 2Th 1:7-10, 1Co 15:52, Rev 10:6-7 and Rev 11:15, are either true as they stand, or they are lies. If any of the above verses stood alone, maybe the premillennial position could be supported, but these four quotes teach us exactly the same thing:

1. 1Co 15:52 states that the Church is taken to be with the Lord at the Last Trumpet, and not before.

2. Our trumpet is the LAST trumpet. As a result, it would have to include the seven trumpets in Revelation, or it would not be the Last Trumpet.

3. Rev 10:6 states that at the 7th trumpet, there is "no more time," KJV.

4. Rev 10:7, states that at the 7th trumpet, "the mystery of God is finished."

5. Rev 11:15, states that at the 7th trumpet (which is the last), God reigns "for ever and ever."

6. 2Th 1:7-10 says that the wicked have their final judgment on the same day that the Lord comes for the saints.

All the above verses show that the premillennial view is not a scripturally viable option. If we are taken to be with the Lord at the Last Trumpet, and there is no more time at the Last Trumpet, then there isn't time for a thousand-year reign of Jesus after He returns for the saints. If there is no more time, then when the last trumpet blows, we will instantly be in the eternal kingdom of God.

Some theologians declare that the Last Trumpet of 1Co 15:52 does not include the trumpets of Revelation. Not only is there no Scripture for that theory, but it goes directly against 1Co 15:52 itself. If there were any more trumpets after the Last Trumpet of 1Co 15:52, then the Last Trumpet of 1Co 15:52 couldn't be the Last Trumpet, could it?

So rather than clinging to a dubious line of reasoning, let's see if we can find out how the above verses can lead us to interpret Rev 20. The Old Testament shows us some guidelines.

RULING WITH CHRIST

David was king over the historic kingdom of Israel. David and his kingdom were types of Christ and the Church. The name David is used many times in the Old and New Testaments to refer to the coming Messiah. The Church itself has been grafted into Israel, and we are of the seed of Abraham by adoption. As David was king over a historic nation of Israel, so the Church (as spiritual Israel) is now in Jesus' kingdom, and reigns with Him today. This is not pie-in-the-sky theology. Here are the Scriptures:

> Act 15:14-17 Simeon hath declared how God at the first did visit the Gentiles, to take out of them a people for his name. And to this agree the words of the prophets; as it is written, After this I will return, and will build again the tabernacle of David, which is fallen down; and I will build again the ruins thereof, and I will set it up: That the residue of men might seek after the Lord, and all the Gentiles, upon whom my name is called, saith the Lord, who doeth all these things.

> 1Pe 2:5 Ye also, as lively stones, are built up a spiritual house, an holy priesthood, to offer up spiritual sacrifices, acceptable to God by Jesus Christ.

> 1Pe 2:9 But ye are a chosen generation, a royal priesthood, an holy nation, a peculiar people; that ye should shew forth the praises of him who hath called you out of darkness into his marvelous light;

> Rev 1:6 And hath made us kings and priests unto God and his Father; to him be glory and dominion for ever and ever. Amen.

> Rev 5:10 And hast made us unto our God kings and priests: and we shall reign on the earth.

In Acts 15 above, notice that David's (figuratively Jesus') kingdom was restored *in the Church!* Then look at the tense of the verbs in the verses which follow: "are, are, hath made us kings and priests; and hast made us unto our God kings and priests." In Acts, the kingdom is restored. In 1Pe the present tense, in Rev the past tense. So we are kings and priests right now and reign with Christ today. Pretty hard to be kings if we have no kingdom. So what kind of kingdom are we ruling in today?

> Eph 1:20-22 which He brought about in Christ, when He raised Him from the dead, and seated Him at His right hand, far above all rule and authority and dominion, and every name that is named, not only in this age, but also in the one to come. And He put all things in subjection under His feet, and gave Him as head over all things to the church.

That's the scripturally declared kingdom of our Lord and Savior Jesus Christ, and it exists today. According to all the above quotes, right now the Church itself is the real live kingdom of Jesus. Look at what the Apostle John also said about himself:

> Rev 1:9 I John, who also am your brother, and companion in tribulation, and in the kingdom and patience of Jesus Christ, was in the isle that is called Patmos, for the word of God, and for the testimony of Jesus Christ.[1]

John states that he is a companion in *the* kingdom of Jesus Christ. So the Kingdom of Jesus Christ was in force while John was on Patmos! In the Greek text of Rev 1:9, the article τη *(te)* appears before both tribulation and kingdom. This Greek particle is translated "the" in the three major English translations in common usage today.[2]

Now a definite article implies that there is no duplicate. When I say, "THE Statue of Liberty," or "THE Washington Monument," I am doing so because there is only one of each. In the same way, when John declares (through the Holy Spirit) that he is a partaker in THE kingdom of the Lord Jesus, Rev 1:9, it is linguistically unsound to think that there is a different kingdom of Jesus still to come. Couple that with the following verse:

> Mar 9:1 And he said unto them, Verily I say unto you, That there be some of them that stand here, which shall not taste of death, till they have seen the kingdom of God come with power.

Now, Brethren, we have one of two alternatives. Either the Kingdom of our Lord began during the natural lifetimes of some of those 1st Century men, or some of them are still alive. Take your pick.

---

[1] G2347, θλίψει, thlipsis, thlip'-sis; from G2346; pressure (lit. or fig.):--afflicted, anguish, burdened, persecution, tribulation, trouble. θλίψει is translated "tribulation" throughout the NT. In the Gr. text, definite article, τῇ, appears before both tribulation and kingdom, John stating that "the" kingdom of the Lord Jesus and "the" tribulation were concurrent, and in existence during his own time. These epochal times continued on down through the Christian Era.

[2] Some scholars believe that τη, the Greek article (Strong's No. G5037) is really indefinite. It is rendered elsewhere as "also" or "both;" so its translation here is not certain. However, ALL major translators, including Green render τη in Rev 1:9 as "the," and "the" is certainly the definite article in English. See footnote 1 on p. 138.

When we put all these verses together, we can conclude that the reign of Jesus Christ began just when the Bible tells us it did:

> Act 2:33-36 (*excerpts*) For David is not ascended into the heavens: but he saith himself, The Lord said unto my Lord, Sit thou on my right hand, Until I make thy foes thy footstool. Therefore let all the house of Israel know assuredly, that God hath made the same Jesus, whom ye have crucified, both Lord and Christ.

And one more time for emphasis . . .

> Eph 1:20-22 Which he wrought in Christ, when he raised him from the dead, and set him at his own right hand in the heavenly places, Far above all principality, and power, and might, and dominion, and every name that is named, not only in this world, but also in that which is to come: And hath put all things under his feet, and gave him to be the head over all things to the church.

Those verses either mean what they say or they don't. But with this many quotes which teach exactly the same doctrine, to hold a different view requires just too much tippee-toeing around Scripture for comfort. Since the Bible states, in so many places, that Jesus has a real live kingdom that exists today, lets just accept it as the truth. Jesus' kingdom will continue in force until:

> 1Co 15:24 Then cometh the end, [*i.e. the last trumpet, Rev 10:6-7*] when he [*Jesus*] shall have delivered up the kingdom to God, even the Father; when he shall have put down all rule and all authority and power.

> 1Co 15:28 And when all things shall be subdued unto him, then shall the Son also himself be subject unto him that put all things under him, that God may be all in all.

That last quote is too conclusive to leave unamplified. At the last trumpet, all things are brought to an end; "there is no more time, and the mystery of God is finished" (Rev 10:6-7). In Rev 11:15, at the sound of the 7th trumpet, we see God reigning forever. That IS the end! At the end of time, Jesus turns His kingdom over to God the Father (1Co 15:24-28). Now look at the above verses again. Where in them lies a post 7th trumpet millennial kingdom? Nowhere that I can find. So where do we go from here? If the above understanding is correct, what can Rev 20 mean?

IT'S A QUESTION OF DOMAIN

God gave the Earth to Adam. Adam was made the ruler of the Earth and all that it contained (Gen 1:28). When Adam fell, he delivered his God-given authority into Satan's hands (Luk 4:6). We legally became Satan's possession. When "we were bought with a price," that was not just some theoretical acquisition. We were purchased from Satan's kingdom by Jesus' precious blood. We were transferred "out of the domain (kingdom, NASB) of darkness into the kingdom of His dear Son" (Col 1:13). If you are looking for the kingdom age, there it is, right where the Bible has been telling us it was all along.

One or two of the points in the above might look inconclusive, but, overall, the evidence is quite compelling. One or two verses could be explained in other ways, but the weight of Scriptural evidence appears to support that the kingdom of the Lord Jesus has existed ever since Act 5:2.

THE STRONG MAN

At the end of this age, Jesus will indeed return to the Earth with all His "holy ones" with Him, all in glorified bodies. That's us, and the saints who have gone before us.

> Rev 11:15 And the seventh angel sounded [*1Co 15:52 states that we go to be with the Lord at the last trumpet*]; and there arose loud voices in heaven, saying, "The kingdom of the world has become the kingdom of our Lord, and of His Christ; and He will reign forever and ever."

But many don't believe that verse. According to some, we will only rule with Jesus for 1000 years (while He is enthroned in glory, in Jerusalem, as King of kings, and Lord of lords). Then after the supposed 1000 year millennium, Satan will be loosed again, supposedly to deceive Earth's millennial rulers. Since it is the saints who would be ruling during Christ's "millennial kingdom," those rulers would include all the great elders like Abraham, Moses, Elijah, Daniel, Paul, and those dear martyrs of the middle ages who were burned at the stake for Jesus' sake.

Now here is the question: If Satan is unable to pluck us from Jesus' hand now (while we are still in our sinful bodies), how will he ever be able to do so while we are beholding the Lord Jesus in all His glory, ruling on Mt. Zion? Can we, the redeemed (then in our glorified bodies, and clothed in the brilliant righteousness of Christ) again fall into sin? If Satan could again deceive us, that would be sin indeed, and that sin would separate us again from the Lord. That is directly against 1Th 4:17, which states that when we are taken to be with the Lord, we will "ever be with the Lord!"

In Mat 12:29 we read, "How can one enter into a strong man's house, and spoil his goods, except he first bind the strong man? and then he will spoil his house." Satan is the strong man "of this present world," and Jesus is spoiling his house through the Church. We, the redeemed, are seated in the heavenlies with Christ right now, as Eph 2:6 teaches us.

However, if there were to be a future millennial kingdom, Jesus would be the "Strong Man" of that future kingdom. That future millennium would be Jesus' "house." Now let's quote that "strong man" verse again:

> Mat 12:29 ". . . how can one enter into a strong man's house, and spoil his goods, except he first bind the strong man? and then he will spoil his house."

The only way Satan would be able to despoil a future millennial house of the Lord's is if he could again bind Jesus. Impossible. Jesus now sits at the right hand of Jehovah of Hosts, God Almighty. I would not want to hold a doctrine that implies that Satan could bind Jesus at the end of some future age. In fact, the very concept borders on blasphemy.

Since it is impossible for Satan to bind Jesus at the end of some future millennial age, it is impossible for Rev 20 to be in our future. If Rev 20 cannot be in our future, then it must be an allegorical picture of the Christian Era. Look at what Jesus has already done to Satan's spiritual domain:

> Col 2:15 And having spoiled principalities and powers, he made a shew of them openly, triumphing over them..

That was no halfway victory. Our Savior, Jesus, triumphed over all the enemy's forces openly, and forever. Jesus does not need to defeat the enemy again and again and again. His victory was not conditional. Jesus' work on the Cross was an eternal and finished work, after which God the Father set up Jesus' Kingdom, just like Col 1:13 says He did. When Jesus returns, He will draw this age to a close, according to the Father's eternal purposes, and usher in the eternal

Kingdom of God. Jesus permitted Himself to be bound ONCE, at the cross, but no more. He can never again be bound. He is God, the Lord. Praise His Name.

AVOIDING MUDDY THINKING

If we are to walk in truth, we must guard ourselves against interpreting Scripture to fit our own preconceived notions, for "The Lord takes no delight in fools" (Ecc 5:4). Insisting on a literal interpretation of an allegory may display our orthodoxy before men but rob us of what the Lord would like us to learn from Scripture. The premillennial interpretation of Isa 11:6-10 is a glaring example of the "literal hermeneutic" carried to the point of absurdity.

Isaiah 11:1-5 has many allegorical elements: "A *shoot* [or *branch*] springs from the *stem* of Jesse . . . a *branch* from his *root* will *bear fruit* . . . He will judge with the *rod* of His mouth . . . righteousness will be the *belt* about His loins and faithfulness the *belt* about his waist," etc., etc. All these expressions are obviously figurative, and all conservative Bible scholars recognize this passage of Scripture to be a pictorial description of Jesus, the Messiah, to be born some 700 years later. This prophecy was fulfilled during Jesus' life on Earth and takes us to 32-33AD.

The first time the Jews were driven from the land was during the Babylonian captivity. The restoration after the Babylonian captivity was the first restoration of the Jews to the Holy Land. By the time of the crucifixion, the Jews had been restored from the Babylonian captivity and had been living in the Holy Land for 568 years. Now lets skip from Isa 11:5 to 11:11. There we read that the Lord will restore his people to the Holy Land "a second time!"

> Isa 11:11 Then it will happen on that day that the Lord Will again recover the second time with His hand the remnant of His people...

Thirty-seven years after Jesus was crucified, in 70AD, the Jews were dispersed for a second time into the nations, so the second restoration would have to take place after that. And it did. The second restoration took place in the new nation of Israel, established in 1948AD. In that year, after almost 1900 years among the Gentiles, the Jews were restored to the Holy Land . . . *for a second time*. Well, if Isa 11, verses 1-5 are about Jesus' life on Earth, and verse 11 can be positively pinned to 1948, to what time do you suppose the verses in between refer? Why, verses 6-10 would refer to the time in between Jesus' life on Earth and 1948, of course! The only contextually sound way to look at Isa 11:6-10 is figuratively, as a picture of the Christian Era.

Now premillennialists recognize the allegorical elements in Isa 11:1-5: the branch, the root, the fruit, the belt, the breath, and so on. Those common allegories are understood by all. No one really expects a literal *branch*, with leaves and all, to spring out of the forehead of David's father. All dispensational theologians recognize this passage as teaching that one of Jesse's descendants will be the Messiah. It is allegorical, and they all know it.

But when they read on a couple of verses, and see *a lion eating straw*, they say: "Ah, that must be literal, and since it hasn't happened yet, it must be going to take place in the millennium. And look here, folks: here is more irrefutable support for our premillennial view." Heaven help us! They further declare that during the millennium, a "nursing child will *really* play by the hole of the cobra," and "the leopard will *really* lie down with the kid," etc. . . thus doing away with God's natural law. Anything is possible with the Lord, of course, but a literal interpretation is not the most probable meaning of those verses.

Many well-known Bible teachers are great for accepting allegorical interpretations for allegories they understand, while demanding literal interpretations for the allegories they don't. All the while, they herald their orthodoxy by broadcasting their faith in a "literal hermeneutic." But if the passage in question is figurative, a "literal hermeneutic" will not lead us to truth. The literal or allegorical nature of a Scripture is not determined by the reader, but by the author, and some Scriptures cannot be recognized as literal or figurative unless the principles of hermeneutics are applied without doctrinal bias.

Interestingly enough, many Evangelical groups, including major Evangelical Bible colleges, use the premillennial view as a litmus test for orthodoxy. One Christian publisher even trumpets proudly that all of its publications are premillennial, as if a differing view on the millennium were mortal sin. But despite its popularity, the weight of scriptural evidence

234 σώζω, Survival Guide for a Remnant Church

appears to be against the premillennial view. It will be interesting to see if the Holy Spirit can again quicken the Church to the possibility that it is standing dogmatically -- on heresy.

BUT IS THIS TRUTH IMPORTANT?

Some brethren ask: "Does it really matter what we believe about the millennium? Isn't soul-winning where it's at, and won't we all end up in Heaven together, regardless?" The idea that any truth is unimportant is of the devil. It ignores the spiritual nature of the Christian battle and the shrewdness of the enemy. Every truth is important. Spiritual warfare is a never-ending contest for truth. As the father of lies, Satan is the author of every heresy that gets into the Church. Every false doctrine we believe or teach, no matter how minor it may seem to us, helps the enemy and weakens our witness.

But how can premillennialism hurt anyone? In the same way that the pre-tribulation rapture myth can hurt us. By rocking the Church to sleep with the sweet lullaby of "Judgment deferred," with the siren song that "hard times may be coming, but they're coming for the lost during the Great Tribulation, while we, the Church, because of our great piety and holiness, will be at the marriage supper of the Lamb, and later, ruling with Jesus in His wonderful millennial kingdom."

Nothing could be further from the truth! We were appointed as Jesus' spiritual priests and kings for this present age to despoil the domain of the enemy. Every time a saint leads a sinner to the Lord, he is breaking into Satan's house, and carrying off his goods (Mat 12:29).

Through the Gospel of Jesus Christ as affirmed by the blood of the martyrs and by the prayers of the saints, the enemy was bound throughout this age, "that he might not deceive the nations." And he didn't. The whole western world recognized Jesus as the Christ. Throughout this era, the Church changed the world, but not any longer. Now the world is changing the Church.

How come? Sin has always been bad, hasn't it? Satan has always been the father of sin, hasn't he? Of course, but in this generation, the individual saint has forgotten his responsibility for the lost:

Eze 3:18 When I say unto the wicked, Thou shalt surely die; and thou givest him not warning, nor speakest to warn the wicked from his wicked way, to save his life; the same wicked *man* shall die in his iniquity; but his blood will I require at thine hand.

The world is in the condition it is today because we have not done our job. And just as Scripture warned, Satan has been loosed upon us:

Rev 20:7-8 And when the thousand years are completed, Satan will be released from his prison, and will come out to deceive the nations which are in the four corners of the earth, Gog and Magog, to gather them together for the war; the number of them is like the sand of the seashore.

Jesus bound the enemy at the cross (Joh 12:32). Then the Church kept Satan bound during the Christian Era, through the prayers of the saints and by standing in the Word, regardless of the consequences. Jesus bound him and then gave the Church the keys:

Mat 16:19 I will give you the keys of the kingdom of heaven; and whatever you shall bind on earth shall be bound in heaven, and whatever you shall loose on earth shall be loosed in heaven.

But the lukewarm Laodicean church of our own day has again set Satan free. Look at the disgraceful spiritual conditions which have enveloped America during the last two decades. We Christians are responsible -- we were Jesus' kings and priests -- and if we really understand that we are responsible, then we will get busy serving the Lord so we will "not be ashamed at His coming." If we really believe that "judgment begins at the household of God," then we "work out our own salvation in fear and trembling," in godly fear of those trials "which are coming upon the earth":

Rev 12:11-12 And they overcame him because of the blood of the Lamb and because of the word of their testimony, and they did not love their life even to death. For this reason, rejoice, O heavens and you who dwell in them. Woe to the earth and the sea, because the devil has come down to you, having great wrath, knowing that he has only a short time.

However, if we believe that judgment is for the other guy, while we've been raptured out, or believe that judgment is still a thousand years away, ah, that's a different story. Then we can dabble in the world for a while, repenting when we see the

Antichrist coming or when the Great Tribulation begins. Meanwhile, to show our prolife conservatism, we lie down in front of an abortion clinic or two, while our lost friends and neighbors go to Hell because we did not tell them that in God's pure eyes, we are all monsters of iniquity, in desperate need of the cleansing blood of His dear Son.

Oh, my God, how far we have fallen from the true faith. As You declared, judgment indeed begins at Your household, and it justly comes for us. Some think all this to be at least 1000 years away. That is what the Jews thought just weeks before the fall of Jerusalem:

> Ezek 12:27-28 Son of man, behold, *they of* the house of Israel say, The vision that he seeth *is* for many days *to come,* and he prophesieth of the times *that are* far off.
> Therefore say unto them, Thus saith the Lord GOD; There shall none of my words be prolonged any more, but the word which I have spoken shall be done, saith the Lord GOD.

Appendix III

In the chapter on *The Last Trumpet*, we saw that time as a natural phenomenon would end at the 7th trumpet of Rev 11:15. Right then, we go into the eternal kingdom of God. But there is a problem. Since time ends at Rev 11:15, what do we do with the rest of Revelation? The beasts of Rev 13 and 17 do relate to the Christian Era, so Revelation must be repetitive. The question is this: Is Revelation repetitive in an organized way so that we can be sure our end-time interpretations are correct? The answer is hidden in Hebrew poetry.

Many major prophets wrote in a poetic form. Hebrew poetry is parallel in nature. A Hebrew poet would say something and then repeat the concept in different words. Just as the four gospels give four views of the life of Jesus, duplicate prophecies give different views of the same event. Repetitive prophecies tell the same prophetic story in different words. The repeats could be just a sentence, a paragraph, or even several chapters long. But, how do we identify repetitive prophecies when we see them? By recognizing the Hebrew poetic style in which they were written.

Some of the most elegant Old Testament poetry is written in Isaiah. In that book we spot one specific poetic style very quickly. Isaiah divided his book into two almost equal parts, and these two parts are repetitive.[1] Isaiah 1 through 33 is parallel to Isaiah 34 through 66, not just in a general sense, but in actual content:[2] Textual scholars call this particular repetitive structure the *bifidic* form. The dictionary definition of bifid is "to be split or divided into two equal halves or hemispheres." Look at the graph below. The last half of Isaiah

---

[1] The liberals see this division and claim that the last half of Isaiah was not written by Isaiah at all. Missing no chance to discredit the Scripture, if possible, they disregard well-known Hebrew poetic forms and invent a shadow author they called deutero-Isaiah. There is no historic nor textual basis for their contention, and Jewish scholars have always attributed the whole book of Isaiah to Isaiah alone.

[2] Packer-Tenny-White, *The Bible Almanac*, 1980, p349.

contains a different description of the same subjects that are covered in the first half.

GRAPH 19 -- BIFIDS IN SCRIPTURE

1st Half of Isaiah		2nd Half of Isaiah
CHAPTERS	CONTENT	CHAPTERS
1-5	Ruin and Restoration	34-35
6-8	Biographical Information	36-40
9-12	Blessings and Judgments	41-45
13-23	About Gentile Nations	46-48
24-27	Redemption and Deliverance	49-55
28-31	Ethics and Sermons	56-59
32-33	Restoration of Israel	60-66

In the apocalyptic books, particularly in Daniel, the *bifid* is as obvious as it gets. Through Daniel's book, God is addressing two audiences, the Gentile nations and the Jewish people, and He shows us this by having the book written in their two languages. Dan 2:4 through Dan 7:28 is in High Syriac *(to the Gentiles)*, while Dan 8:1 through 12:13 is in Hebrew *(to the Jews)*. The first half of Daniel is to and about the Gentiles who will rule in the Holy Land, while the second half is to and about the Jews during that same time. Both halves of Daniel are about the time of the Gentiles, and thus the book is *bifidic*.

In the first half of Daniel, even the chapters themselves form a parallel, but this parallel is in three steps. Chapters 2 and 7 are parallel, chapters 3 and 6 are parallel, and chapters 4 and 5 are parallel -- a kind of poetic stepladder. This isn't a bifid but a different form, and once again Isaiah has a simple example of this new poetic form:

> Isa 55:8 For my thoughts are not your thoughts, neither are you ways my ways, saith the LORD.

If we were to say that in normal English, we would say something like, "Your ways and thoughts are not like my ways and thoughts." But in this Hebrew poetic form it is My-your=your-My, for a stepladder like this:

GRAPH 20 -- A SIMPLE CHIASM

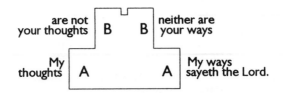

Isa 55:8   For my thoughts *are* not your thoughts,
neither *are* your ways my ways, saith the LORD.

This AB=BA stepladder is called a Chiasm,[1] pronounced *key-ah-zum*, Chiasms appear in Scripture from Genesis to Revelation. A chiasm can even have more than two steps. It can be ABC=CBA or even ABCD=DCBA. What the author declares in the steps going up, He repeats in the steps going down. Here are more examples. They have been shortened for clarity, but the full text is in your Bible:

GRAPH 21 -- TWO & THREE STEP CHIASMS

Psa 68:15-16	A.	The hill of God is as the hill of Bashan.
	B.	an high hill as the hill of Bashan.
	B.	Why leap ye, ye high hills?
	A.	this is the hill which God desireth to dwell...
MAR 5:3-5	A.	Who had his dwelling among the tombs
	B.	and no man could bind him,
	C.	no, not with chains:
	C.	he had been bound with chains,
	B.	neither could any man tame him.
	A.	And always he was in the tombs...

Now here is why it is important to understand chiasms: In the above AB=BA chiasm, there were not four concepts, but two concepts about the same subject that were repeated

---

[1] Packer-Tenny-White, *The Bible Almanac*, 1980, p364.

in different words. In the ABC=CBA chiasm, there were not six subjects. There were only three, about three conditions, and they, too, were repeated in different words.

If Daniel and Revelation are also chiasmic, they, too, would contain prophecies which are repetitive and parallel. Daniel would be 10 parallel prophecies about the time of the Gentiles, stated in different ways. Revelation would be 12 parallel prophecies, primarily about the Christian Era, stated in different ways. Let's first overlay Daniel, and then Revelation, with this little hypothesis, and see how it fits.

STEPLADDER IN DANIEL

In Dan 12:4, the Lord commanded Daniel to seal his book. Then just five verses later, God states that the book was sealed (Dan 12:9). Now, Daniel was a godly man who did what he was told, so somehow, Daniel did something to seal his prophecies between the time those two verses were written. The question is, what did he do? He could not modify the content of the visions he had seen, nor change the historic incidents, so he must have done something else.

Daniel scrambled his prophecies. He put them out of chronological order.[1] This is easy enough to prove because Daniel dated most of his chapters. When Daniel shuffled his prophecies, his book was sealed until the Lord wanted it opened. Now, let's see what that shuffling accomplished. Look at the graph of the chapters in the order in which they now appear in the Bible. The chapters with the (*) are the ones that are out of sequence.

---

[1] Both chs.6 and 9 were written in the 1st year of Darius. The dating of ch.6 after 9 can be determined by the address form Daniel used when a new king ascended the throne of Babylon. In ch.9 the correct introductory form for Darius is used, while it is omitted in ch.6. Daniel was a master of court protocol, so it is unlikely that he would have ignored it here. The dating of ch.5 after 8 is evident from within the text itself.

As an aside, the Lord has not permitted the author to fathom what the book means when it is put back into its correct chronological order. However, I sense there is a message there for someone.

DANIEL'S 1ST CHIASM

Chapter 5 was actually written after 8, and Chapter 6 was written after 9. Look at the subject column to the right. In the order the subjects now appear, a three-step chiasm has been formed. Isn't that grand?

GRAPH 22 -- DANIEL IS OUT OF CHRONOLOGICAL ORDER

		PROPHECY	SUBJECT
A.	ch.2	The Great Image	4 Gentile Nations
B.	ch.3	The Fiery Furnace	God's People in Tribulation
C.	ch.4	Nebuchadnezzar Insane	Gentile King Judged
C.	* ch.5	Belshazzar Killed	Gentile King Judged
B.	* ch.6	The Lion's Den	God's People in Tribulation
A.	ch.7	The Four Beasts	4 Gentile Nations
	ch.8		
	*	ch.5 was actually written here	
	ch.9		
	*	ch.6 was actually written here	
	ch.10		

If Daniel had not put his book out of order, there would be no ABC=CBA chiasm in his book. Something as complex as a chiasm doesn't happen by accident. It was deliberate, but what does it mean? Chiasms are repetitive! It appears that the Lord did this to give us a proof-positive clue that Daniel is a series of repetitive prophecies. When viewed in its entirety, the message of Daniel's 1st chiasm appears to be:

> *During the time of the Gentiles there will be four major empires -- and their descendants -- who will rule in the Holy Land. During that time, God's people will suffer great persecution. But at the end, God will judge those nations that have made His land a desolation and made captives of His people.*

Let's go into a little detail. There are two distinct types of messages in Daniel: prophecies and historic incidents. So what are historic incidents doing in an apocalyptic book? The prophe-

cies of the Gentile kingdoms in Dan 2 and 7 are straightforward
enough and easy to understand, but do the historic incidents
also have prophetic implications? Most of us don't think overly
long about the fiery furnace or the lion's den, but it appears that
they are prophecies of the time of the Gentiles, written in
symbolic language. With Daniel now open, we can walk up and
down his chiasmic step-ladder and see the hidden message of
both types of prophecy.

A. *Four Kingdoms: Dan 2, Dan 7.* Allegorical: the Great
Image, and the Four Beasts. During the time of the Gentiles
there would be four major empires who would rule in the Holy
Land. And so it has proved to be. After the fall of Judah in
606BC, Babylon, Medo-Persia, Greece, and then Rome, *and their
descendants,* were the only world empires to have ruled the Holy
Land. Since those four, there have been no other great world
empires there. Their descendants *(like LBL)* have controlled
Jerusalem all the way up to 1967.

B. *Tribulation: Dan 3, Dan 6.* Symbolic incidents: The Fiery
Furnace, and the Lion's Den.

Dan 3. Shadrach, Meshach, and Abednego are symbolic of
the whole Jewish people. The fiery furnace represents the trials
the Jews will go through during the time of the Gentiles. During
the time of the Gentiles, the Jews have suffered untold persecution, but as a people, the Lord brought them through it all. Does
anyone question the almost continuous persecution that world
Jewry has suffered during the time of the Gentiles, and can we
not see that God's protecting hand has been on them? Despite
impossible odds, the Children of Israel are still here.

Dan 6. In this incident, Daniel represents the godly Jew,
and the lion's den symbolizes his persecution. Daniel was in
captivity in Babylon for most of his life. God blessed him there,
and he became a chief satrap in the land. But other satraps
were jealous of Daniel's success, so they accused Daniel before
King Darius concerning his worship of the true God, which was
against the law. Because the Medes and Persians had unchangeable laws, Darius had to throw Daniel to the lions, even though
he didn't want to. The Lord protected Daniel and shut the
mouths of the lions. Next morning, the king took Daniel up out
of the lion's den and threw his accusers down into it.

Now the interpretation: Throughout the time of the Gentiles, God's people have been in a godless world. Like the laws of the Medes and Persians, God's laws are unchangeable. When we are in disobedience, Satan accuses the brethren before the Lord. Because of His unchangeable law, God has to allow tribulation to fall upon us; we go through a famine, or persecution, or war, or a holocaust. But if we rely on Him, the Lord saves us through it all. Exactly like Darius, at the end, the Lord will give the order for us to be "taken up" out of our trials, and the "accuser of the brethren is cast down."

That is exactly what has happened to all the brethren since the time of Daniel, but at the end, Jesus will cry, "Come out, and come up here, ye servants of the Most High God."

C. *Judgment: Dan 4, Dan 5.* Symbolic incidents: Nebuchadnezzar goes insane, and Belshazzar is slain. Nebuchadnezzar represents the kings and emperors of the world. Babylon symbolizes all the great economies of this world (Rev 18:11-19). Belshazzar ruled for a short time at the end of the Babylonian Empire, so he represents the final ruler of this world. At the end of the time of Gentile rule, God will judge those nations who have persecuted His people and made His land a desolation.

Dan 4. There were many great kingdoms before the Cross, but they rejected the witness of the Jewish people. That is symbolized by Nebuchadnezzar going insane. Nebuchadnezzar then repented, which is possibly a foreshadowing of the world recognition of the God of Heaven through His Son. Christianity became the faith of the whole known world, and "surpassing glory" was added to the western Christian nations.

Dan 5. The end of Babylon. Then the nations turned away from the Lord. The world has the Word of God *(the handwriting on the wall)* and the witness of the saints *(the candlestick, Rev 1:19)*, but the nations of the world still blaspheme God and turn away from all knowledge of Him. They drink wine from the holy vessels, but at the end of the party, Belshazzar dies. Thus, the kingdoms of this earth go to final judgment. This represents our own time, and the ungodly have no reprieve. Armageddon, the Great White Throne, and the second death are soon to come.

DANIEL'S 2ND CHIASM

The 1st chiasm was primarily to and about Gentile nations, while the second is about the future of the Jews during the 2500 years since the fall of Babylonian Empire. The second chiasm is an AB=BA, and its central message is:

After the Jews return from captivity, there will be two major empires, and their descendants, who will rule in the Holy Land into the far distant future. During that time Messiah will come to earth and be killed. The temple will also be desolated, but at the end of it all, the destroyer will go to final judgment.

Dan 8. The vision of a Ram and a He Goat. This vision tells us of Medo-Persia and Greece. The Ram and He Goat are primarily fulfilled before the cross, but this vision does contain information about the ultimate time of the end (Dan 8:17,19,23). A different vision about Medo-Persia and Greece is given in Dan 11 as the kings of the North and South. Let's look at a graph of this chiasm, and then we will discuss it:

Graph 23 -- Daniel's Second Chiasm

		SUBJECT
A.	ch.8	2 Gentile Powers
B.	ch.9:24-26	Messiah dies in Time of the Gentiles
B.	ch.9:26-27	The Time of the Gentiles
A.	ch.10-12	2 Gentile Powers

A. *Two Gentile Powers: Dan 8, Dan 11.* Except for the time of Roman rulership, Jerusalem and the Holy Land have been under the influence of the Medo-Persian and Greek Empires, their Moslem descendants (*LBL*), and the satanic princes of those countries. These princes have controlled the governments of the Holy Land from Daniel's time, right on down until 1967. Here is the supporting Scripture:

Dan 10:20 . . . now will I return to fight with the prince of Persia: and when I am gone forth, lo, the prince of Grecia shall come.

Dan 8:17,19 (*excerpts*) Understand, O son of man: for at the time of the end shall be the vision...Behold, I will make thee know what shall be in the last end of the indignation: for at the time appointed the end shall be.

Daniel 8:17-19 informs us that the latter half of the Ram and the He Goat is a vision of the very end, and Dan 10:20 tells us who is behind the scenes. The angelic being who was speaking to Daniel was not battling some mere mortal. These are satanic princes! At the end of time, out of the area controlled by those princes, a little horn -- a wicked ruler -- will arise who will lead the enemy's forces at Armageddon, but he will be brought to ultimate defeat when Messiah returns.[1]

"Finally," you say, "there is your Antichrist. I knew all along that one was coming." Not at all. This will undoubtedly be another political or military leader, but this one will be coming from the Middle East. The "little horn" of Dan 8 could be Hafez al Assad of Syria, Arafat the Palestinian, Hussein of Iraq, Libya's Maummwar Khadaffy, or one of those deranged mullahs from Iran. He could even be someone acting behind the scenes that we don't think is very important, like the hidden Ali Akbar Mohatashimi, a secret leader of the Iranian terrorists:[2]

DAN 8:9-11 And out of one of them came forth a little horn, which waxed exceeding great, toward the south, and toward the east, and toward the pleasant land. And it waxed great, even to the host of heaven; and it cast down some of the host and of the stars to the ground, and stamped upon them.

DAN 8:23-25 And in the latter time of their kingdom, when the transgressors come to the full, a king of fierce countenance, and understanding dark sentences, shall stand up. And his power shall be mighty, but not by his own power: and he shall destroy wonderfully, and shall prosper, and practice, and shall destroy the mighty and the holy people. And through his policy also he shall cause craft to prosper in his hand; and he shall magnify himself in his heart, and by peace

---

[1] Many try to identify the little horn of Dan 8:9-11 and 8:23-25 as Antiochus Epiphanies, the Greek king who desecrated the temple in 168BC. The problem with that interpretation is that 168BC was not "the time of the end" v.17, or "the appointed time of the end" v.19. Scripture declares this to be an end-time vision, and to date it remains unfulfilled.

[2] There is no reason to believe that we will be able to recognize the "little horn" of Dan 8 before he appears, any more than we were able to recognize Adolf Hitler as the "little horn" of Dan 7 until after Nazi Germany fell and Hitler was killed.

shall destroy many: he shall also stand up against the Prince of princes; but he shall be broken without hand.

This is the vision of the end (Dan 8:17 and 19), and this little horn does not come out of the Roman Empire, but out of the lands once ruled by Greece (Dan 8:21). The Grecian Empire of Alexander the Great covered the whole Middle East. Notice that this final ruler is going to use peace talks to put people off their guard. Sound familiar? Read the newspaper.

There is so much Scripture for the location and behavior of the final enemy of the Jews and the Church that it is difficult to avoid duplication. All end-time prophecy points to these countries. The final enemy of God's people will come from the Mohammedan world. However, from what we now know about Ten-Horns of the Scarlet Beast, the Mohammedan states won't be in that war by themselves. They will have help from the rest of the world. But at the very end, it won't be our weaponry but the Prince of princes who defeats them.[1]

B. *Messiah and Gentile Times: Dan 9:1-25, Dan 9:26-27.* Straight allegory. The 69 Weeks, and the 70th Week. Hear, Oh Israel: Messiah is coming. He is coming during the time of Gentile control of Jerusalem. Why? Because He is the Savior who died for the sins of the whole world, Jew and Gentile alike (1Jo 2:2). This is the cardinal message of the whole book of Daniel. In fact, the cross of Jesus at the end of the 69 Sevens is the central event of all creation. The cross is the primary message to God's elect throughout the whole world.

The 70th Week tells the history of the Jews from the 1st year of Darius to 1948AD. The land will be controlled by Gentiles for 2484 years. In the middle of that time, the temple mount will be desecrated, but in the fullness of time, the Lord will restore the Holy People to their precious land. Soon after the Jews are restored, the Lord will judge the satanic beings who caused that desecration. Daniel does not tell us how much time will pass between the restoration of the land and the destruction of the

---

[1] Included in the prophecy of the Ram and the He-Goat is a time period of 2300 *evenings and mornings* (Dan 8:14). From Scripture and history, we know that evenings and mornings are not days, and not times. The Lord has given us a day for a year, and a *time* has been identified, with some certainty, as 1000 years. The author confesses that he is not sure what *evenings and mornings* mean.

enemy. Luk 21:24-32 states that it will not be longer than a single generation.

Now that we understand the pattern, let's go to Revelation. The following summary is not intended as a full exegesis of that book. It is only an outline and study guide, but it is a foundation which will help students of prophecy understand almost every verse. Some of the allegories are still sealed. Maybe the Lord has left them for you to unravel.

CHIASMS IN REVELATION

In Rev 5:1, God the Father holds a scroll sealed with seven seals. It is written on both sides. This was very unusual in the time of John the prophet, 95AD. Most 1st Century scrolls were written only on one side, and there is a reason for this two-sided scroll.

> Rev 5:1 And I saw in the right hand of him that sat on the throne a book written within and on the backside, sealed with seven seals.

> Rev 5:5-6 (*excerpts*) . . . In the midst of the throne . . . and in the midst of the elders, stood a Lamb as it had been slain, And he came and took the book out of the right hand of him that sat upon the throne.

Careful study shows this "little book" to be the book of Revelation itself. It was given to the Lord Jesus after the cross, and it is a picture of the whole Christian Era. Jesus opens the Seven Seals, the Seven Trumpets, and the Two Witnesses. Before the seventh trumpet blows, the Lord tells us what He is going to do with the part of the book He has not read. In the verse quoted above, the book was sealed, but in the verse below it is opened:

> Rev 10:1-2 And I saw another mighty angel come down from heaven, clothed with a cloud: and a rainbow was upon his head, and his face was as it were the sun, and his feet as pillars of fire: And he had in his hand a little book open: and he set his right foot upon the sea, and his left foot on the earth.

As used in Revelation, "angel" can refer to several different kinds of beings. He can be one of God's angelic messengers, a fallen angel, Satan, a human messenger, the Holy Spirit, or the Lord Jesus Himself. Context is the key to his identity. A study of the description of the Lord Jesus in Rev 1 and elsewhere shows the angel of Rev 10:1-2 to be the Lord Jesus. The Lord then gives this little book to John.

> Rev 10:10-11 And I took the little book out of the angel's hand, and ate it up; and it was in my mouth sweet as honey: and as soon as I had

eaten it, my belly was bitter. And he said unto me, Thou must prophesy again before many peoples, and nations, and tongues, and kings.

Believe it or not, those verses explain it all. The little book is now open because the Lord has broken all the seals. Then He tells John, "you must prophesy again!" In other words: "Listen here John, turn this two-sided book over and read the other side. Repeat in different words what I have read in the Seven Seals and the Seven Trumpets." The little book was written on both sides because the Lord willed to read one side, and He wanted John to read the other. "Out of the mouth of two or three witnesses . . ." But prophesy to and about what? The above verses tell us exactly: the 2nd chiasm, Rev 12 - Rev 20, is about "peoples, nations, languages and kings."

The seventh and last trumpet blows in Rev 11:15, which begins the eternal kingdom of God. Since it is all over in Rev 11, plain as day, the Lord is telling John to go back to square one, and tell about the Christian Era again. Revelation 12 - 20 is a repeat of Rev 1 - 11. That is why the Lord told John, "You must prophesy again!" Revelation is bifidic!

If Revelation is like Daniel in other ways, it should also have a chiasm in both halves. It does, and here are the parallels: chs.2-3 are about churches, and now that we know who the Two Witnesses are, so is ch. 11. Ch. 6 is about Seven Seals, and chs.8-9 are about Seven Trumpets, both of which are symbolic pictures of conditions on earth during this era. The first half of ch.7 is the Jewish saints, the second half the Gentile saints. We again have a perfect ABC=CBA chiasm.

GRAPH 24 -- REVELATION'S FIRST CHIASM

		PROPHECY	SUBJECT
A.	ch.2-3	The Seven Churches	The Church
B.	ch.6	The Seven Seals	World Judged
C.	ch.7:4-8	The 144,000	Old Testament Saints
C.	ch.7:9-14	The Great Multitude	New Testament Saints
B.	ch.8-9	The Seven Trumpets	World Judged
A.	ch.11	The Two Witnesses	The Church

As was true in Daniel, Revelation has messages hidden within the chiasms. The 1st chiasm is about the spiritual world while the second is primarily about what is taking place in the visible material world. The 1st chiasm is primarily about the Church, and it details the role of God's people in a rebellious world. It is completely allegorical and can be understood only by extensive cross-referencing with other passages of Scripture which use like language. The central message of this chiasm is:

> *During the Christian Era there will be seven different church periods and seven different kinds of churches. The Jews and the Church will be God's Two Witnesses on Earth. Trials, plagues, famines, tribulation, and wars will take place. But the dead in Christ, both Jew and Gentile, will be with the Lord. In the fulness of time, God will set up His eternal kingdom.*

A. *The Seven Churches and the Two Witnesses: Rev 2-3, Rev 11.* In the seven churches of Rev 2-3, the Lord tells us what the Church will be like during the whole Christian Era, sometimes good, sometimes fair, and sometimes very bad. In Rev 11, God has placed His Two Witnesses on the Earth to stand against the enemy and preach the gospel. Throughout the Christian Era the Church and the Jews will be in great tribulation, but they will also be victorious. The record of the persecution of the brethren during the Christian Era is unassailable.

Though mighty empires have fallen around it, the true Church of Jesus still stands. The chart in Appendix IV shows how the seven churches of Rev 2-3 parallel church history in the Christian Era. At the end of the time of the Two Witnesses, 1948AD, the Church and the Jews were to lose their spiritual power, and so it has come to be. There will always be a faithful remnant, but in the last days Jesus will spit the lukewarm churches out of His mouth, and the enemy will destroy them (Rev 3:16 and Rev 11:7).

B. *The Seven Seals and the Seven Trumpets: Rev 6, Rev 8-9.* During the Christian Era, God will pour out His wrath upon unbelievers. It doesn't have to be that way, and because of His Two Witnesses, the world is without excuse. To bring the unsaved to repentance, many terrible things will happen. Anarchy, wars, famines, and natural disasters will abound (Rev 6:1-8). At the end there will be a mighty war with 200,000,000 horsemen fighting, Rev 9:16. Not until this generation could we field armies of that size. Man will hide in the caves in the ground and under mountains. But he will not repent of his rebellion and his sorcery and his idolatry (Rev 9:20-21).[1]

C. *The 144,000 and the Great Multitude:* Central to it all are the redeemed. They are those from this great tribulation whom the Lord Jesus has reconciled to the Father through His own shed blood. They are the physical seed of Israel (Rev 7:4-8) and the Gentile church (Rev 7:9). The seal on the heads of the 144,000 is the name of God the Father (Rev 14:1). The fifth seal (Rev 6:9) describes the brethren who have gone before us. They are clothed in white robes *(the righteousness of Christ)* and stand beneath the cross *(the altar in Heaven is a symbol of the cross)*. They do not cease to cry, "how long, Oh Lord, how long?"

> Rev 7:13-17 And one of the elders answered, saying unto me, What are these which are arrayed in white robes? and whence came they? And I said unto him, Sir, thou knowest. And he said to me, These are they which came out of great tribulation, and have washed their robes, and made them white in the blood of the Lamb. Therefore are they before the throne of God, and serve him day and night in his temple: and he that sitteth on the throne shall dwell among them. For the Lamb which is in the midst of the throne shall feed them, and shall lead them unto living fountains of waters: and God shall wipe away all tears from their eyes.

REVELATION'S 2ND CHIASM

Now that we understand the chiasmic pattern, the last half of Revelation is quite open. Most of these later visions can be related to world history. It is not the author's intent to belabor the chiasmic form, but it is one of the major tools to show that Revelation is repetitive in an organized way. It contains 12 concurrent prophecies about the history of Israel and the Christian Era. Remember in Daniel, how half of that book was to Gentile nations, while the other half was to the Jews? Though

---

[1] Throughout Scripture, angelic hosts are depicted as horsemen (2Ki 2:11, 2Ki 6:15-18, 2Ki 7:6; Zec 1:8, Zec 6:2-6; Rev 6:2-8, Rev 9:16, Rev 19:14). Consequently, a major portion of the 200,000,000 horsemen of Rev 9:16 may be unseen spiritual forces. If so, then we will not see vast human armies massed in the Middle East for this final battle.

the audiences are different, the pattern in Revelation is the same. The central message of this 2nd chiasm is this:

There will be seven major kingdoms throughout history. They will be ruled by Satan. Concurrent with those visible kingdoms, God will have a spiritual kingdom on Earth composed of the Jewish people and the Gentile church. In the fullness of time, Jesus will return to reward the saints and judge the wicked.

We have already seen that the first chiasm of Revelation is to and about the Church's spiritual role. This second chiasm is about kingdoms, both earthly and spiritual. The Jews and the Church are the Lord's spiritual kingdom on earth, while the beasts and Babylon are various aspects of the enemy's satanic kingdom, both seen and unseen. Babylon centers on the world socioeconomic system, while the beasts are governmental. In fact, the beasts are Satan himself, and he appears to us in two guises.

1. As the Scarlet beast he is the embodiment of the sin which is in the world, and he again goes forth to deceive the nations as the 8th beast who has been loosed.

2. Through Leopard-Bear-Lion he displays his control of the kingdoms of the Middle East, where lies the seat of his earthly throne.

Even Revelation's last two chapters are kingdom-oriented. They are about the new Heaven, the new Earth, and God's eternal kingdom.

Sometimes man's chapter breaks are in the wrong place, or don't belong in the passage at all because they interfere with the flow of Scripture. This last half of Revelation is an example. Rev 13 through 15 is all one prophecy, while Rev 17 through 19 is another. This 2nd Chiasm shows us both godly and satanic kingdoms and the final outcomes for both. The rejoicing of the saints is the subject of Ch 15, while God's wrath on the kingdoms that have rejected His Son is the subject of Rev 16. This ABC=CBA structure is a little complicated, and there are alternatives ways to view it, but careful study appears to support this version.

A. *Israel and the Church: Rev 12, Rev 20.* Straight allegory. The Woman with Twelve Stars, and the reign of Christ. Many take Rev 20 literally, the so-called millennium, because it appears to use literal language. The last trumpet, the chiasm, and the context make that view very difficult to support. More likely, this is the whole body of Christ, all the redeemed, Jew and Gentile alike. From the time of Moses, Israel has been the caretaker of the oracles of God (Rom 3:2). Israel was the line

Graph 25 -- Revelation's Second Chiasm

		CONTENTS	SUBJECT
A.	ch.12	Woman with 12 Stars	Israel
B.	ch.13	Leopard-Lion-Bear Beast	Satanic Kingdom
	ch.14	144,000 & The Gospel	The Saved Within It
C.	ch.15	Song of Moses and Lamb	Victory for Redeemed
C.	ch.16	Bowls of Wrath	Wrath for the Wicked
B.	ch.17	Seven-Headed Beast	Satanic Kingdoms
	ch.18	Babylon	Satanic System
	ch.19	King of Kings	Destruction of Wicked
A.	ch.20	The Thousand Years	The Church

through whom the Savior of the world would come. After Jesus was glorified, Israel and the Church (the spiritual kingdom over which the Lord now reigns, Rev 20:4), would be persecuted but not destroyed. Satan would be bound so as not to deceive the nations during the Christian Era (Rev 20:2, Mat 12:29, Joh 12:31).[1] At the end of the Christian Era, Satan would be released for a little season (Rev 12:12-13 and 20:7). Jesus is the first and only resurrection. There is no other. Blessed, indeed, are those

---

[1] The Greek word used for thousand here is "chilioi" (Strong's 5507). It is the indefinite plural form of the word for thousand,"chiliad." Consequently, though thousand is a correct translation, it cannot be proven that this is only one thousand. Instead, it is an indefinite number of thousands. Scripturally, this time can refer to the Christian Era regardless of length.

who have part in Him as born-again believers. Over them the second death has no power (Rev 20:6). In the culmination of all things on this present Earth, there is Armageddon (Rev 12:17 and 20:7-9). Please notice how the account in Rev 12 parallels Rev 20, and the many parallel verses indicate that they are about the same time and events.

B. *The Beast with Seven Heads, and the Leopard, Bear, Lion: Rev 13, Rev 17*. Straight allegory. Throughout history there will be only seven major empires, and their descendants, who will rule in the Earth. They will be satanically empowered (Rev 17:3) for they are in his domain (Luk 4:6). Out of the Middle East came an empire that is the combination of three ancient ones, Babylon, Medo-Persia, and Greece. That geographic area is Iraq, Iran, and Syria, headquarters of the radical Shiite Moslem world. They are combined by a common religion and have a satanically inspired hatred for the Church and Israel. They will always be at war with the spiritual kingdom of the Lord Jesus (Rev 13:12 and 17:14).

The 144,000, the Eternal Gospel and Babylon: Rev 14-15, Rev 17-19. Straight allegories. All the servants of the Lord are compared with servants of the enemy. After the Cross, the Old Testament saints sing about Jesus.[1] For them it is a new song (Rev 14:3). Then the eternal gospel is preached to the Church (Rev 14:6). The trials of the Christian Era are foretold, followed by the Lord coming in the clouds to reap the Earth of the saints (Rev 14:14-16). In the Grapes of Wrath, more is told about Armageddon (Rev 14:17-19). The battlefront will be 200 miles long, from Jerusalem northward. Knowing that the prophecies in Revelation are parallel makes this a lot easier. The various little pieces at the end of each prophecy, about a great battle, are about the same great battle: Armageddon.

Mighty Babylon falls (Rev 18). She is the haunt for every evil beast and bird and creeping thing. Who is she?

> Rev 18:24 And in her was found the blood of prophets, and of saints, and of all that were slain upon the earth.

---

[1] That the 144,000 are the Old Testament Israelites is provable by comparing their identification as "first-fruits" (Rev 14:4) with Jer 2:3 and other Scriptures.

Since every death on Earth is attributed to her, from the prophets of the Old Testament to the saints of the Church, Babylon is far broader than one single empire or city, no matter how great and long-lasting. Babylon is every unsaved and rebellious person, land, and empire, that has ever existed on Earth. She began when Cain shed the blood of his brother Abel and will continue until the last Christian is impaled or beheaded in some spiritually dark and human-snake infested concrete jungle. Babylon means confusion. Satan is the author of confusion. Babylon is Satan's world. We have been commanded throughout Scripture to separate ourselves from her. We haven't listened very well, so the Lord reminds us here:

> Rev 18:4-5 And I heard another voice from heaven, saying, Come out of her, my people, that ye be not partakers of her sins, and that ye receive not of her plagues. For her sins have reached unto heaven, and God hath remembered her iniquities.

Soon the light of the Word will be heard in her no more, nor the voice of Jesus the bridegroom, nor the witness of the bride (the Church is the bride of Christ), and Babylon will be no more...

> Rev 18:23, 19:1 And the light of a candle shall shine no more at all in thee; and the voice of the bridegroom and of the bride shall be heard no more at all in thee: for thy merchants were the great men of the earth; for by thy sorceries were all nations deceived . . .
>
> And after these things I heard a great voice of much people in heaven, saying, Alleluia; Salvation, and glory, and honor, and power, unto the Lord our God.

C. *The Songs of Moses and the Lamb and the Return of the King: Rev 19.* Straight allegory. In the return of Jesus and in the song of the redeemed, the Lord closes the doors on the great beasts of Revelation. For the world it is all over. As is true in the rest of Revelation, a dual address is made to distinguish between the Old Testament saints and the Church. The song of Moses is sung by Israel, while glory to the Lamb is sung by the Church.

C. *The Seven Bowls: Rev 16.* Straight allegory. The judgment of the bowls is a terrible intensification of the seven trumpets. The plagues are similar. The fifth bowl is directed at only one geographic location, the throne of the beast. Spiritual in nature, this bowl tells us of the spiritual darkness which now engulfs the Middle East and that it will intensify.

Rev 16:13-14 And I saw three unclean spirits like frogs *come* out of the mouth of the dragon, and out of the mouth of the beast, and out of the mouth of the false prophet. For they are the spirits of devils, working miracles, *which* go forth unto the kings of the earth and of the whole world, to gather them to the battle of that great day of God Almighty.

The only other threefold enemy the Lord mentions in Revelation is the Leopard-Bear-Lion, so these three unclean spirits, *like frogs*, are probably the satanic princes who spiritually control those lands, Mohammed being the false prophet. Though these spirits have remained in the Middle East throughout the Christian Era, the malignant poison of Islam is now spreading throughout the world. As is true of the other prophecies which tell us of man's final rebellion, this one, too, ends with Armageddon.

We can now see how the Lord planned the Christian Era. All along, there have been Two Witnesses, the Jews and the Gentile church. The Lord never did forget His chosen people, and through the Gentile church untold numbers of Ephraim have unknowingly returned to the Lord.

Through bifids and chiasms we can now understand that both Daniel and Revelation are repetitive in an organized way. Since the time of the Gentiles was over in 1967AD, Daniel, for the most part, is fulfilled. Using the same bifidic and chiasmic style as Daniel, Revelation continues where Daniel left off. With 12 parallel prophecies in two chiasms, Revelation reviews the Old Testament Era and amplifies what Daniel told us about the time of the Gentiles. Then the Lord expounds on the satanically controlled empires of the world and defines who the final enemies of his Two Witnesses will be. Revelation then closes with a brief description of the glorious eternal kingdom of God.

What you have read here is just the barest of sketches, but it should be apparent that the beasts of Rev 13 and 17 do relate to our own time. How the mark of the beast will eventually show itself is not revealed as yet, and the identity of the final leaders against Israel and the Church are still a mystery, but we can now understand much that was totally unavailable to the Church only a decade ago.

Appendix IV
The Seven Churches of Revelation

There Are Three Interpretations for The Seven Churches. All Three Are Correct:

---

1. The seven churches speak to seven literal churches in Asia Minor during John's time.
2. Throughout the Christian Era every church is like one of these churches. churches like all seven churches have existed somewhere throughout this era..
3. The seven churches represent seven different periods of church history and the general spiritual condition of the Church at a particular time. Church history bears out this "Linear Historic" view, as is detailed below:

32-95AD   **Ephesus..........**_"Lost your first love"_   Rev 2:4, Mar 12:29-30
                 Heresy enters church: Marcionites,
                 Gnostics, Nicolaitans, etc.

95-321AD   **Smyrna...........**_"Persecuted 10 days"_   Rev 2:10
                 Ten major persecutions under ten Roman Emperors:
                      (1) Domitian (2) Trajan (3) Hadrian
                      (4) Antonius Pius (5) Marcus Arelius
                      (6) Septimus Severus (7) Maximin
                      (8) Decius (9) Valerian (10)Diocletian

321-450AD   **Pergamum......**_"Where Satan's throne is"_   Rev 2:13
                 Constantine makes Christianity state religion. church hierarchy
                 begins.

450-950AD   **Thyatira.........**_"That Woman Jezebel"_   Rev 2:20
                 Beginning of Mary worship. Idols brought into the churches.
                 Bishops rise to power.

950-1450AD   **Sardis............**_"But you are dead"_   Rev 3:1
                 Dead Catholic formalism. Bible taken from the people. Persecution of the brethren intensifies.

1450-1948AD   **Philadelphia...**_"You have kept My Word"_   Rev 3:8
                 The Reformation, the Protestant church begins, the Puritan movement, foreign missions founded.

1948AD- ??   **Laodicea........**_"You are neither hot nor cold"_   Rev 3:15
                 Lukewarm church of today. Great church organizations and works, but spiritually cool.

Blow the trumpet in Zion,
Sanctify a fast,
Call a solemn assembly:
Gather the people,
Assemble the elders.
Let the bridegroom go forth of his chamber,
And the bride out of her closet.

FROM JOEL 2:15-16

Index

Scripture Quotes & References

Λ Noτε From Fish House

Fish House is a small group of Christian brethren who have only three concerns:

1. To see Jesus glorified.
2. To prepare the brethren for the troubled times ahead.
3. To awaken us for the glorious return of the Lord Jesus, at the head of His holy ones.

If σώζω, *Survival Guide for a Remnant Church* has been of spiritual benefit to you, please share the truths it contains with others. You, not someone down the street, are the light of the world!

If you are having difficulties getting our publications, please write or call Fish House Publishing, P.O. Box 453, Fort Myers, FL 33902. We usually fill and ship orders on the same day they are received. Our products by this author are:

TITLE	LIST PRICE [1]
σώζω, Survival Guide for a Remnant Church	$12.95
Hidden Beast 2	9.95
HB2 Teaching Outline & Study Guide	30.00
Skolfield on Revelation . . (16 audio cassettes)	45.00
Demons in the Church	8.95

[1] List Price includes postage and handling. Please enclose check or money order *. . made payable to Fish House* with your order. As publishers and wholesalers, we do not have facilities to accept retail credit cards. And besides, after what has been written in this book, we're not sure we are supposed to.